Nineteen Sixty-Eight

The Vietnam Experience

Nineteen Sixty-Eight

by Clark Dougan, Stephen Weiss,
and the editors of Boston Publishing Company

Boston Publishing Company/Boston, MA

Boston Publishing Company

President and Publisher: Robert J. George
Vice President: Richard S. Perkins, Jr.
Editor-in-Chief: Robert Manning
Managing Editor: Paul Dreyfus

Senior Writers:
Clark Dougan, Edward Doyle, Samuel Lips-
man, Terrence Maitland, Stephen Weiss
Senior Picture Editor: Julene Fischer

Staff Writer: Peter McInerney
Researchers:
Kerstin Gorham (Chief), Michael T. Casey,
Susan Freinkel, Scott Kafker, Denis Ken-
nedy, Jane T. Merritt, Carole Rulnick, Glenn
Wallach

Picture Editors: Wendy Johnson, Gail Page,
Lanng Tamura
Assistant Picture Editor: Kathleen A. Reidy
Picture Researchers:
Nancy Katz Colman, Nana Elisabeth Stern,
Shirley L. Green (Washington, D.C.), Kate
Lewin (Paris)
Picture Department Assistant: Kathryn
Steeves

Historical Consultants:
Vincent H. Demma, Lee Ewing, Ernest May
Picture Consultant: Ngo Vinh Long

Production Editor: Patricia Leal Welch
Assistant Editor: Karen E. English
Editorial Production:
Pamela George, Elizabeth Hamilton, Joan
Kenney, Jeffrey L. Seglin, Amy P. Wilson

Design: Designworks, Sally Bindari

Marketing Director: Jeanne C. Gibson
Business Staff: Jane Colpoys, Darlene Keefe

About the editors and authors

Editor-in-Chief *Robert Manning*, a long-time journalist, has previously been editor-in-chief of the *Atlantic Monthly* magazine and its press. He served as assistant secretary of state for public affairs under Presidents John F. Kennedy and Lyndon B. Johnson. He has also been a fellow at the Institute of Politics at the John F. Kennedy School of Government at Harvard University.

Authors: *Clark Dougan*, a former Watson and Danforth fellow, has taught history at Kenyon College. He received his M.A. and M.Phil. at Yale University. *Stephen Weiss*, an American historian, has M.A. and M.Phil. degrees from Yale. Formerly a fellow at the Newberry Library in Chicago, he has coauthored other volumes in *The Vietnam Experience*.

Historical Consultants: *Vincent H. Demma*, an historian with the U.S. Army Center of Military History, is currently working on the center's history of the Vietnam conflict. *Lee Ewing*, editor of *Army Times*, served two years in Vietnam as a combat intelligence officer with the U.S. Military Assistance Command, Vietnam (MACV) and the 101st Airborne Division. *Ernest May* is Charles Warren Professor of History at Harvard University.

Picture Consultant: *Ngo Vinh Long* is a social historian specializing in China and Vietnam. Born in Vietnam, he returned there most recently in 1980. His books include *Before the Revolution: The Vietnamese Peasants Under the French* and *Report From a Vietnamese Village*.

Cover photographs (clockwise, from upper left):

Worn down by the war, President Lyndon Johnson contemplates the text of his historic refusal to run again for president. (UPI)

The Tet offensive: U.S. Marines fire on the enemy during the battle for Hue, February 1968. (UPI)

A shot seen 'round America. The chief of South Vietnam's national police executes a Vietcong officer wearing civilian clothes in Saigon on February 2. (Wide World)

"Peace Now!" An antiwar demonstrator taunts National Guardsmen at the Democratic National Convention in Chicago, August 28. (UPI)

Library of Congress Catalog Card Number: 83-70672

ISBN: 0-939526-06-9

10 9 8 7 6
5 4 3

Contents

"Split the Sky...
Shake the Earth"

0440 Hours January 30, 1968, Pleiku
(II Corps Tactical Zone)

Lieutenant Ray Flynn had been looking forward to this night for a long time. So had his men. Battered at Dak To the preceding November, Flynn's rifle platoon of the U.S. 173d Airborne Brigade had spent several months patrolling the north central highlands. For the most part it had been quiet. But the anxiety, the fatigue, the harsh routine of war had taken their usual toll. Now, on the eve of Tet, the most sacred of Vietnamese holidays, there was time to rest. Beginning at midnight, January 30, there would be a thirty-six-hour cease-fire and stand down. While tens of thousands of Vietnamese rejoined their families, exchanged gifts, and celebrated the advent of the Year of the Monkey, Ray Flynn and his men sprawled out along a rippling stream outside Pleiku and drifted off to sleep.

Several hours later, the calm night of the Lunar New Year exploded in violence. Shocked into consciousness by the sound and glare of 122MM rockets screaming over his head, Flynn determined quickly that the firing site was no more than 800 meters away. "Had to be pre-dug," he thought to himself, "but we missed it." Then, as his men returned fire, a strange realization came over the young lieutenant. "They must know precisely where we are," he thought, "but they're not firing at us. They're firing at the city. They're firing at Pleiku."

0245 Hours January 31, 1968, Saigon
(Capital Military Zone)

As Specialist Fourth Class Charles L. Daniel and Private First Class William E. Sebast stood guard at the night gate of the United States Embassy, a battered taxicab turned the corner onto Thong Nhut Boulevard. Automatic weapons fire belched from its windows. Firing back, Daniel and Sebast quickly backed inside, slammed and locked the large iron gate, and radioed "Signal 300"—code for enemy attack—to Military Police headquarters.

Outside the gate, men of the Vietcong C-10 Sapper Battalion worked swiftly, detonating a plastic explosive charge that blew a three-foot-wide hole in the high wall surrounding the embassy compound. As the enemy troops wriggled in, the two MPs turned and began firing. Daniel seized the radio. "They're coming in! They're coming in!" he shouted. "Help me! Help me!" Then there was silence.

0330 Hours January 31, 1968, Long Binh
(III Corps Tactical Zone)

Lieutenant General Frederick C. Weyand, commander of U.S. field forces in III Corps, was not surprised. A former U.S. Army intelligence officer, he had been troubled by the curious pattern of recent Communist activity. Three weeks before, on January 10, he had shared his suspicions with General William Westmoreland, commander of U.S. forces in Vietnam, and recommended that American units be redeployed from border assignments to the populated areas around Saigon. Westmoreland agreed and ordered fifteen U.S. battalions back to the outskirts of the capital.

Now, as Weyand watched the maps in his tactical operations center light up like "pinball machines," his worst fears were confirmed. The enemy was attacking everywhere. Weyand ordered the necessary moves to counter each attack, deploying more than 5,000 U.S. troops to new

---

Preceding page. Flares and tracer fire from American Cobra gunships illuminate the night sky during the Communist attack on Bien Hoa air base, January 31. Communist efforts to penetrate the base and seize ARVN III Corps headquarters were repulsed by a combined U.S. and South Vietnamese force.

locations within two hours. Then he waited. The enemy, he calculated, had already committed every major unit known to be operating in III Corps. It wouldn't last long. Unless his calculations were wrong.

* * * * *

Thus it began. Under the veil of night and in the midst of a tense holiday truce, Communist forces launched the Tet offensive—a massive, coordinated assault on nearly every population center and major military installation in South Vietnam. Across the length and breadth of the country, from Quang Tri Province in the north to the southernmost tip of the Ca Mau Peninsula, the cities of South Vietnam exploded as if strung together like New Year's firecrackers.

The unprecedented magnitude and ferocity of the attacks stunned the South Vietnamese and their American allies. Never before had the Communists dared to enter the cities in force. Never before had they committed so many troops to a single, costly campaign. Never before had they demonstrated a capacity to synchronize their military planning on a countrywide scale. Now, within forty-eight hours, more than 80,000 soldiers of the People's Liberation Armed Forces (Vietcong), their ranks bolstered by elements of the North Vietnamese People's Army (NVA), suddenly materialized to attack 36 of 44 provincial capitals, 5 of 6 autonomous cities, and 72 of 245 district towns, in addition to countless military headquarters, airfields, and combat bases.

Awakened by the crash of incoming rockets and the crackle of small-arms fire in the streets, city dwellers were shocked to find their neighborhoods transformed into battle zones. As VC soldiers charged toward their designated objectives, regular and irregular forces of the South Vietnamese army scrambled to meet the threat. Everywhere there was confusion, dismay, and disbelief. And everywhere the same question: How had it happened?

Fateful decision

Ambitiously conceived and audaciously executed, the Tet offensive had been meticulously planned. The product of long years of experience in revolutionary warfare and of continual debate among North Vietnamese military strategists, the decision to launch the attacks had been made by the Politburo in Hanoi in July 1967. The leaders recognized that the risks would be considerable, the logistics complex, and the cost in men and material enormous. But they also agreed that the moment was propitious.

For nearly three years they had fought against forces of the greatest military power on earth. They had not been defeated; but neither had they defeated the enemy. They had hoped to make the Americans, as they had made the French, weary of war by pursuing a strategy of "protracted" struggle. Instead, the U.S. had augmented its forces and seemed more confident than ever of its ability

to wear out the North Vietnamese and win the "hearts and minds" of the South Vietnamese people.

Now, the Communists reckoned, all that would change. Relying upon two cardinal principles of the art of war, secrecy and surprise, they would strike when and where the enemy was most vulnerable. Taking the war to the cities, they would shatter the sense of security of the hundreds of thousands of South Vietnamese civilians who had sought refuge from the ravages of war. They would exacerbate the growing strains between the South Vietnamese government and its American allies. And, by raising the ante yet again, they would feed the mounting opposition to the war in the U.S. and around the world. With a single thunderous blow, they would violently announce the advent of the third, and final, stage of the revolutionary struggle—the General Offensive-General Uprising—and alter irrevocably the course of the Vietnam War.

Responsibility for overall military planning of the campaign was placed in the hands of General Vo Nguyen Giap, chief architect of the Vietminh victory at Dien Bien Phu. A long-standing critic of the tactics employed by his arch-rival, General Nguyen Chi Thanh, Giap had repeatedly argued that a commitment to big-unit warfare was inappropriate against an enemy with vastly superior mobility and firepower. With their extended lines of communication and supply, the Americans were far more vulnerable, he argued, to guerrilla warfare. With Thanh's death in July 1967 Giap reemerged as North Vietnam's leading military strategist. But even then the outlines of the offensive bore the marks of a compromise between the advo-

cates of the Main-Force war and the proponents of guerrilla tactics. It was to be a "combined" effort, using both methods to their maximum advantage.

Preparations for the attacks proceeded slowly and methodically. Beginning in August, thousands of tons of Chinese- and Russian-supplied weapons and munitions—AK47 assault rifles, B40 and 122MM rockets, rocket-propelled grenades, and antiaircraft artillery—moved south by bicycle and truck, ox cart and sampan. Communications networks were improved and military districts redrawn to facilitate coordination between units and commands. New cadres and troops were recruited and trained, while veteran soldiers were gathered in reorientation, or *chinh huan*, sessions where they were apprised of their "new situation and mission."

During the fall Giap also initiated a series of major confrontations along the frontiers of South Vietnam—at Con Thien along the DMZ, at Dak To in the central highlands, and at Loc Ninh in the "fishhook" area along the Cambodian border. In retrospect these "border battles" seem to have been designed to serve several purposes: to lure American forces away from populated areas, to screen the infiltration of NVA troops prior to Tet, and in the case of Loc Ninh, to practice coordinating maneuvers between Main-Force and guerrilla units. Each time Giap probed, the Americans responded by sending large numbers of troops to the remote battle zones and concentrating enormous firepower on enemy positions. U.S. intelligence analysts were baffled by the Communist moves, which seemed to invite massive American retaliation to no evident purpose. But Communist losses were so great that MACV was quick to declare the engagements resounding allied victories. Giap in turn taunted the American command with the claim that his border strategy had dealt a blow to allied pacification efforts.

In order to enhance the prospects of military success, the Communists simultaneously made some timely political maneuvers. To reinvigorate and broaden the appeal of the NLF among the South Vietnamese people, "Liberation Radio" launched a campaign in early September that renewed the front's ostensible commitment to freedom of speech and assembly, free elections, and other rights. The same month a high-ranking Vietcong cadre contacted U.S. officials in Saigon, prompting hopes in Washington that the Communists were prepared to negotiate and feeding suspicions among the South Vietnamese that the U.S. might agree to a coalition government. Those fears were heightened when Communist agents began to talk secretly with prominent spokesmen of the GVN's political opposition. The capstone of these efforts was a remark made by North Vietnamese foreign minister Nguyen Duy Trinh on December 30, 1967. Announcing that North Vietnam "will" rather than "could" hold talks if the U.S. halted its bombings unconditionally, a subtle shift in wording that suggested that Hanoi had changed its negotiating position, Trinh provoked a flurry of diplomatic activity—all to no avail—during the first weeks of 1968.

Meanwhile the military chess game moved toward its climax. During the first weeks of the new year, several elite NVA divisions crossed the DMZ and began to surround the U.S. Marine base at Khe Sanh. Further south, Main-Force and guerrilla units moved closer to the cities, using complicated maneuvers to mask their real targets. Commanders left their bases to reconnoiter their assigned areas of operation, while troops disguised as civilians or ARVN soldiers returning home for Tet began to infiltrate the cities. Weapons, explosives, and ammunition were also slipped in, concealed in false-bottomed trucks or flower carts headed for market and then buried in cemeteries, drainage ditches, and garbage dumps.

As D-day approached, middle- and lower-level commanders learned for the first time what their individual missions would be. Gathering their troops together, they distributed arms and a three-day ration of food. Then, on the eve of Tet, came the long-awaited order to attack, broadcast by Radio Hanoi—a poem written by Ho Chi Minh to mark the arrival of the Year of the Monkey.

This Spring far outshines the
previous Springs,

Of victories throughout the land
come happy tidings.

Let North and South emulate each
other in fighting the U.S.
aggressors!

Forward!
Total Victory will be ours.

Troops already infiltrated into the cities test-fired their weapons against the din of holiday firecrackers, while guerrilla units stealthily moved into attacking positions on the outskirts. Many knew they would die. In a display of solidarity with their Vietcong comrades, some North Vietnamese regulars wore armbands with the inscription "Born in the North, Died in the South." All had been told that they were about to inaugurate "the greatest battle in the history of our country"—a flash of lightning that would "split the sky and shake the earth."

Intelligence

Signs of the impending Communist offensive did not go undetected. Throughout the late summer and early fall of 1967, American and South Vietnamese intelligence agencies accumulated a variety of clues indicating a significant shift in enemy strategic planning. Among them was an attack order captured by an element of the U.S. 101st Airborne Division during an operation in Quang Tin Province on November 19. Stating that "Central Headquarters concludes that the time has come for direct revolution and that the opportunity for a general offensive and general uprising is within reach," the attack order spelled out many of the more salient features of the upcoming enemy campaign.

Use very strong military attacks in coordination with the uprisings of the local population to take over towns and cities. Troops should flood the lowlands. They should move toward liberating the capital city, take power, and try to rally enemy brigades and regiments to our side one by one. Propaganda should be broadly disseminated among the population in general, and leaflets should be used to reach enemy officers and enlisted personnel.

Intelligence officers of the U.S. military command regarded the document primarily as a piece of propaganda designed to boost Communist troop morale. When the captured order was subsequently released to the press and published on January 5, twenty-five days before the offensive began, it provoked little comment.

By mid-December, however, mounting evidence convinced prominent officials in Saigon and Washington that something big was underway. On December 18, General Earle G. Wheeler, chairman of the Joint Chiefs of Staff, warned that "it is entirely possible that there may be a Communist thrust similar to the desperate effort of the Germans in the Battle of the Bulge in World War II." On December 20, President Johnson, in Canberra, Australia, to attend memorial services for Prime Minister Harold Holt, confided to the Australian cabinet that he foresaw "kamikaze" attacks by the North Vietnamese in the weeks ahead. The same day General Westmoreland cabled Washington that he expected the enemy "to undertake an intensified countrywide effort, perhaps a maximum effort, over a relatively short period."

During January 1968 more hard evidence fell into allied hands. On January 4, the U.S. 4th Infantry Division captured Operation Order No. 1 calling for an attack against Pleiku prior to Tet. On January 20 the ARVN 23d Infantry Division captured a similar order for an assault on Ban Me Thuot, though no date was specified. Then, on January 28, South Vietnamese Military Security Service agents in Qui Nhon arrested eleven Vietcong cadres who had been meeting inside the city. In their possession were two tapes containing an appeal to the local population to take up arms against the GVN and an announcement that Saigon, Hue, and other South Vietnamese cities had already been "liberated."

There were other signs as well. Beginning in the late months of 1967 and continuing through the first month of 1968, allied intelligence noted a precipitous drop in enemy defections, usually an indication that morale was high. Then, toward the end of January, the government of North Vietnam made a curious announcement. Because of a peculiarly auspicious conjunction between the moon, the earth, and the sun, the Tet holiday would begin not on January 30, as indicated by the lunar calendar, but on January 29. Hanoi, the allies later learned, wanted its people to be able to celebrate Tet before the anticipated American retaliation.

In the South, the change in the North Vietnamese holiday schedule went unnoticed. By the end of January both MACV and the White House were preoccupied by activity near Khe Sanh, where on January 21 an estimated force of 20,000 to 40,000 North Vietnamese regulars had besieged the U.S. Marine base. Convinced that the enemy intended to overrun the base as the first step in an all-out effort to seize the two northernmost provinces of South Vietnam, Quang Tri and Thua Thien, General Westmoreland determined to hold Khe Sanh at all costs. His decision was endorsed by the Joint Chiefs of Staff and a jittery president, who told his field commander that he didn't want "any damn Dien Bien Phu."

To strengthen allied defenses in the north, Westmoreland had ordered the U.S. Army 1st Cavalry Division (Airmobile) to Phu Bai on January 9. As Tet approached, approximately a quarter of a million allied soldiers—including more than half of all U.S. combat maneuver battalions—stood ready to meet the enemy in I Corps. Yet aside from the redeployment of forces to Saigon that General Weyand had suggested, little was done to reinforce South Vietnam's cities. It was a calculated risk, but one that General Westmoreland was willing to take.

Thus, despite a surfeit of intelligence data concerning enemy plans, the details of the offensive were never deciphered. But this was only part of the problem. According

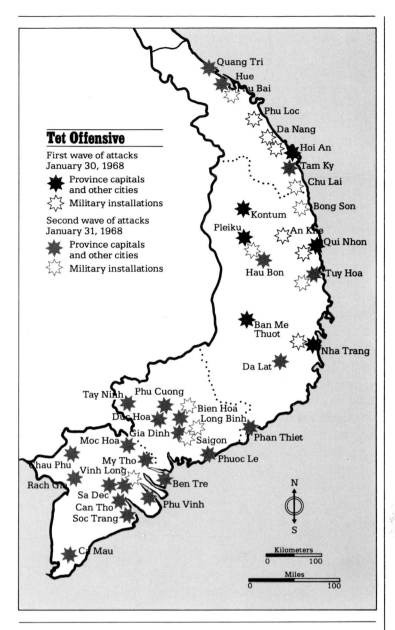

Tet Offensive

First wave of attacks
January 30, 1968

★ Province capitals and other cities

☆ Military installations

Second wave of attacks
January 31, 1968

✶ Province capitals and other cities

✷ Military installations

to the report of a special intelligence review board established by President Johnson in the wake of Tet, American estimates of attrition, infiltration, local recruitment, and morale had "degraded our image of the enemy." Throughout the fall of 1967, in fact, MACV had reduced its estimates of enemy combat strength and, in light of these new figures, concluded that the allies were winning (see sidebar, page 22).

As one U.S. Army intelligence officer later noted, "If we'd gotten the whole battle plan, it wouldn't have been believed. It wouldn't have been credible to us." MACV simply did not believe the Communists capable of synchronizing major attacks throughout South Vietnam. Even if they could, such a campaign would be "suicidal," according to General Westmoreland. By dispersing their forces they would multiply their points of vulnerability and deprive themselves of sufficient concentrated force to achieve any single objective.

By mid-January Westmoreland was convinced that the

enemy's predicted "maximum effort" would come just before or after the Tet holiday. He discounted the possibility
that they would hit at Tet itself and profane the sacred national rite. Ironically, Westmoreland had placed in his
Saigon villa a statuette of the Vietnamese hero Quang
Trung. Trung was responsible for one of the legendary
feats in Vietnam's history—a surprise attack on the Chinese garrison in Hanoi during Tet 1789.

Attack!

Whether by accident or design, the Communist command
launched an initial wave of attacks, centered in the II
Corps area, one day in advance of the others. Nha Trang,
headquarters of the U.S. I Field Force, was the first to be
hit, shortly after midnight on January 30. Attacks on other
major cities soon followed. At 1:35 A.M., a barrage of mortar and rocket fire slammed into Ban Me Thuot, followed
by a ground assault by more than 2,000 enemy troops. At
2:00 A.M., Kontum was struck by five enemy battalions. At
2:55 A.M., Hoi An came under attack; at 3:30, the city and
air base at Da Nang; at 4:10, Qui Nhon; at 4:40, Pleiku.

At Military Assistance Command headquarters at Tan
Son Nhut air base outside Saigon, Brigadier General Phillip B. Davidson, chief of MACV intelligence, scrutinized
the reports coming in from the north. "This is going to happen in the rest of the country tonight or tomorrow morning," he told General Westmoreland. Westmoreland
agreed, but with half of his combat forces concentrated in
I Corps and the other half already stretched thin, he was
not in a position to make any rapid redeployments. He
was also unwilling to do so, since he regarded the city attacks as secondary to the enemy's main effort. Instead he
immediately dispatched an order placing all U.S. troops
on maximum alert.

Aside from the purely military realities, Westmoreland
had to take into account a number of delicate political
considerations. He had repeatedly urged South Vietnamese President Nguyen Van Thieu to cancel the Tet
cease-fire altogether, but Thieu had demurred, claiming
that it would damage ARVN morale and only benefit
enemy propagandists. Thieu did agree to reduce the official cease-fire to thirty-six hours, but he also authorized
holiday leaves for half of all ARVN troops. As a gesture of
American confidence and at the insistence of the GVN,
protection of the cities, including Saigon, had been entrusted to South Vietnamese forces. If, as Westmoreland
expected, the attacks of January 30 were repeated elsewhere the following night, those understrength forces
would bear the brunt of the fighting. The American commander could only wait and hope that the South Vietnamese would prove equal to the task.

The forewarning provided by the first attacks thus went
largely unheeded. The GVN canceled the rest of the
cease-fire but President Thieu himself did not return to

Saigon, preferring to remain with his wife's family in My
Tho. While some ARVN commanders responded to the
cancellation with precautionary measures—confining
troops to barracks, tightening security, limiting access
routes into the towns—others greeted the news with casual
disregard. Many thought it simply incredible that the
enemy could be so bold, or foolish, as to attempt to seize
the cities.

As a result, the second, and much larger, wave of attacks that swept across South Vietnam during the early
morning of January 31 once again found allied forces unprepared. "The surprise," ARVN Colonel Hoang Ngoc
Lung recalled, "was total." In I Corps Communist troops
penetrated in strength into Quang Tri City, Tam Ky, and
Hue, in addition to attacking the U.S. military installations
at Phu Bai and Chu Lai. In II Corps they followed up the
previous night's attacks with assaults on Tuy Hoa, Phan
Thiet, and the American bases at Bong Son and An Khe.
In III Corps the principal targets lay within the Capital
Military Zone of Saigon and outlying Gia Dinh Province,
although major attacks were also directed against ARVN
Corps headquarters at Bien Hoa and U.S. II Field Force
headquarters at Long Binh. In IV Corps, where U.S. forces
served largely in an advisory capacity to the South Vietnamese, fighting was particularly fierce as the VC struck
Vinh Long, My Tho, Can Tho, and Ben Tre, as well as virtually every other provincial and district capital in the Mekong Delta.

Although the size of the attacking forces varied, everywhere the pattern was similar. Behind a shield of mortar
and rocket fire, highly trained VC sappers spearheaded
the assaults. Once inside the cities the commandos linked
up with troops that had previously infiltrated and with local sympathizers, who often acted as guides. As they
moved toward predetermined objectives—the local radio
station, the prison or POW camp, the local ARVN and provincial headquarters—Main-Force reinforcements followed. Other units stayed behind to interdict LOCs or pin
down allied reaction forces. Frequently the soldiers were
accompanied by political cadres who exhorted the populace by bullhorn to join in the "uprising" against the "dic-
tatorial Thieu-Ky regime," staged demonstrations of support for the NLF, and in some instances combed the streets
for suspected "enemies of the people."

Overall the Communist offensive was, in the words of
Brigadier General John Chaisson, "surprisingly well-
coordinated, surprisingly intensive, and launched with a
surprising amount of audacity." Yet for all their boldness
and intensity, the attacks were in many places poorly executed, inadequately supported, and extraordinarily costly.
At Nha Trang the opening volley of mortar rounds missed
the target, the Vietnamese Naval Training Center, and the
follow-up ground assault was delayed for an hour and a
half. After fourteen hours government forces declared the
city clear and reported 377 enemy killed, 77 captured, and

Shielding his ears from the sounds of war, a child runs for cover during the Communist attack on Da Nang, one of the first cities to be struck during the Tet offensive.

1 surrendered. At Pleiku the VC H-15 Local Force Battalion was ordered to proceed alone when the NVA 95B Regiment failed to arrive at a rendezvous point, and the battalion suffered heavy casualties at the hands of an ARVN armored unit. By February 3, when the battle of Pleiku officially ended, Communist losses included 632 killed, 182 captured, and 189 weapons forfeited to the allies.

Nor were these the only problems. Because they were often unfamiliar with the cities they invaded, some Communist troops became disoriented and failed to fulfill their missions. In Saigon several Vietcong suspects were apprehended after asking for directions to their assigned targets; another young recruit, separated from his unit, was found sitting on a curbstone, weeping. Other units, upon attaining their objectives, became immobilized or were forced to retreat for lack of follow-up orders.

Perhaps the most crucial determinant of the relative success or failure of Communist efforts, however, was the performance of the Armed Forces of the Republic of Vietnam. While some units responded courageously to the assaults, exceeding American expectations, others were

tentative and disorganized. There was no concerted resistance whatsoever to the attack at Chau Doc, and at Vinh Long elements of an ARVN armored cavalry detachment became involved in a ferocious firefight with their own River Assault Group boats stationed in the Vinh Long River. Contrary to the Communist boasts, there were few ARVN defections to the enemy side, although in several cities there were reports of South Vietnamese soldiers removing their uniforms when the fighting broke out. A more common problem was their frequent unwillingness to counterattack the enemy aggressively. Time and again, artillery, armor, and air strikes had to be called in to dislodge small enemy contingents from entrenched positions.

Since the forces initially reacting to the raids were often ad hoc collections of Regional Force and Popular Force companies, headquarters companies, and other units that happened to be stationed in the vicinity, leadership was a decisive factor. In Da Lat, site of the ARVN military academy, the deputy province chief defended the town for several days with two undermanned RF companies, a company of freshman cadets, and several unidentified American soldiers who were visiting a local brothel when

13

the fighting broke out. At Can Tho, on the other hand, IV Corps commander Major General Nguyen Van Manh barricaded himself inside his heavily fortified mansion for several days while his American military advisers took over.

By the end of the first week of fighting most towns were once again secure, though Communist forces continued to hold on in at least a dozen places, including Saigon. There enemy forces made a determined stand, tenaciously clinging to sections of the city against an increasingly strong allied counterattack.

War comes to Saigon

A teeming metropolis of more than 2 million people on the eve of Tet 1968, Saigon was a city shaped by the pressures of war. The effects were everywhere evident: in the sprawling tenements of Cholon and other impoverished districts swollen by hundreds of thousands of refugees from the countryside; in the profusion of concrete and steel structures built by the Americans; in the hotels jammed with foreign correspondents; in the streets bustling with French and American cars, American soldiers on leave, and government officials at work; and in the rickety South Vietnamese economy, so grossly inflated that shoe-shine boys could earn as much as ARVN officers, and black-market profiteers could live like feudal barons.

If it was a city nourished by war, it was also a city relatively insulated from the bloodshed that had consumed the surrounding countryside. Aside from occasional incidents of small-scale terrorism during more than twenty years of

civil strife, the Communists had done little to disturb the sense of security enjoyed by most Saigonese. Defended by some ten ARVN battalions as well as 17,000 members of the National Police, and encircled by a series of major American command centers, airfields, and combat bases, the capital seemed invulnerable to serious attack. Even the news of the city attacks on Tet eve did not cause much concern. On January 31, 1968, most people in Saigon went about their traditional holiday business, visiting relatives and friends and feasting on squid, sugar cane, and rice wine.

Not surprisingly, the Communists made a major commitment to the assault on Saigon and its densely populated environs. Attacking from the north, the west, and the south, North Vietnamese General Tran Do, one of the highest-ranking officials in COSVN, hurled thirty-five battalions into battle. Leading the attacks were 250 men and women of the elite Vietcong C-10 Sapper Battalion, all native Saigonese, whose mission was to take and hold the presidential palace, the United States Embassy, the National Radio Station, and other principal targets. Behind them stood some four to five thousand local force troops, most of whom had infiltrated the city in the days just prior to Tet. Outside the city the Communists created a ring of fire: the Vietcong 5th Division hit the giant U.S. and Vietnamese bases at Long Binh and Bien Hoa; the NVA 7th Division attacked the U.S. 1st Infantry Division at Lai Khe and ARVN 5th Division headquarters; the Vietcong 9th Division struck the headquarters of the U.S. 25th Infantry Division at Cu Chi. The plan was simple. As forces inside the city seized key military and government installations, paralyzing the capacity of the allies to react effectively, forces outside the city would disrupt LOCs and neutralize potential allied reinforcements. Success, however, required the efficient coordination of an intricate series of independent operations, beginning with raids by the commandos of the redoubtable C-10 (see map, below).

It was 1:30 A.M. when thirteen men and one woman of the C-10 arrived at the staff entrance of the presidential palace on Nguyen Du Street. Shouting "Open the palace gates! We are the Liberation Army!" the sappers blasted the gate with B40 rockets and attempted to crash through. Met immediately by automatic-weapons fire from palace security, they retreated to an unfinished apartment building across the street, killing two American MPs who had rushed to the scene and seizing their M60 machine gun. During the next two days a running gun battle ensued, as ARVN troops, U.S. MPs, and the National Police attempted to root out the enemy while American TV cameras recorded the action. In the end, all of the commandos were either killed or captured.

An hour later and three blocks away, another platoon of the C-10 Battalion struck the United States Embassy. Like the presidential palace, the embassy had been selected as a target primarily because of its symbolic significance. First opened in September 1967, the $2.6 million six-story chancery building loomed over much of central Saigon as a constant reminder of American presence, prestige, and power. As protection against attack, the chancery had been encased in a concrete rocket shield that overlapped shatterproof Plexiglas windows, and the entire embassy compound had been surrounded by an eight-foot-high wall.

With all its fortifications, the embassy was minimally defended. Besides the two army MPs at the main gate, SP4 Daniel and PFC Sebast, only three marine security guards were assigned to the compound on the night of the attack—one more than usual because of the heightened state of alert. As the Vietcong commandos breached the wall and gunned down the MPs, two of the marine guards, Sergeant Ronald W. Harper and Corporal George B. Zahuranic, rushed across the central lobby of the chancery building and heaved shut its huge teak doors. Moments later an antitank rocket tore through the lobby and exploded, seriously wounding Zahuranic and knocking Harper to the floor. Two more rockets followed. Certain that the enemy would penetrate the building momentarily, Harper grabbed his .38, a twelve-gauge shotgun, and a Beretta submachine gun and stared at the doors, waiting, he thought, to die.

At his post on the roof of the chancery, the third marine guard, Sergeant Rudy A. Soto, Jr., entertained similarly grim thoughts. His shotgun had jammed when the sappers first entered the compound, and he soon expended all six shots from his .38. Now defenseless, he radioed Harper and Zahuranic. There was no response. Assuming that they had been killed and that he would be next, Soto radioed security headquarters that the VC were probably in the building.

Soto was wrong. Perhaps because Daniel and Sebast killed the leaders of the enemy unit during the initial exchange of fire, the VC never penetrated the chancery building. Instead the sappers wandered aimlessly about the embassy grounds, eventually taking cover as additional American forces arrived on the scene. By morning, when a thirty-six-man detachment of the U.S. 101st Airborne Division landed on the rooftop helipad of the chancery, all nineteen commandos had been killed or captured. At 9:15 A.M., six-and-a-half hours after the assault began, the embassy was declared secure.

Better organized, and of more immediate tactical significance, was the attack directed against the National Radio Station. Shortly before 3:00 A.M. on February 1, a convoy of jeeps and Toyota sedans pulled up in front of the station and discharged twenty VC sappers, all of them disguised as South Vietnamese riot police. Their mission was to seize the station and, with the aid of a North Vietnamese radio specialist, to broadcast tapes announcing the General Uprising and proclaiming the liberation of Saigon. Although they succeeded in blasting their way into the compound, their plans were thwarted when a government technician signaled the night crew at the transmitter site fourteen miles away to shut down the lines to the downtown studio. Upon realizing what had happened, the sappers rampaged through the main control room and destroyed its sophisticated equipment. Several hours later a company of ARVN paratroopers arrived and, after setting the station on fire, shot the invaders as they attempted to flee.

Just north of the city, around 3:00 A.M., a heavy barrage of rocket and mortar fire thundered into Tan Son Nhut air base, site of MACV headquarters and the U.S. 7th Air Force, initiating the most massive attack of the night. As clouds of black smoke billowed hundreds of feet into the

Battle of Saigon

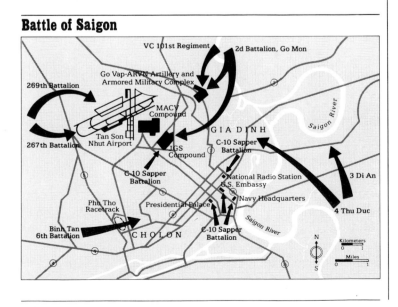

Battle of Saigon

Above. Crouching behind a makeshift street barricade, South Vietnamese troops fire on Communist positions in Cholon on February 7.

Firemen fight a blaze set by ARVN troops to rout the enemy from the National Radio Station on January 31. Members of the elite VC C–10 Sapper Battalion lie dead outside the building.

Right. Saigon in flames. Parachute illumination flares descend over a gutted section of the capital.

American MPs close in on the last enemy sappers trapped inside the U.S. Embassy compound during the VC raid on January 31. Beside them lie two American soldiers killed earlier in the fighting.

One of the few survivors of the attack on the embassy, a VC guerrilla is led away for interrogation.

air, three enemy battalions simultaneously assaulted the perimeter from the west, north, and east. Approaching from the west across a mined field, one Communist contingent overran an ARVN outpost and advanced 200 meters inside the fence before meeting stiff resistance from two companies of the ARVN 8th Airborne Battalion. Dressed in full battle gear, the ARVN troops had been waiting in the terminal for transport to I Corps when the fighting unexpectedly broke out. Their flight had been delayed.

Meanwhile, the 3d Armored Squadron of the U.S. 25th Infantry Division raced from its base at Cu Chi toward the beleaguered airfield, flares dropped from the commander's control helicopter lighting the way. Arriving at 6:00 A.M., the squadron's tanks attacked from the rear, compelling enemy forces to retreat to the nearby Vinatexco textile mill, which served as the Communist command post for the attack on Tan Son Nhut. Several hours later, allied jets and helicopter gunships, dodging flak from antiaircraft guns mounted on the roof, swooped in and pummeled the factory. One hundred sixty-two bodies were later found inside.

Other major targets hit during the night included the South Vietnamese Joint General Staff headquarters, Navy headquarters, Armored Command headquarters, and Artillery Command headquarters. In each case the attacks failed. At the JGS compound, one Vietcong unit arrived five hours late for what was to have been a coordinated attack and then seized the wrong building. At Navy headquarters, Communist reinforcements were stranded on the far side of the river when an initial assault force failed to capture several boats docked along a nearby quay. At Armored Command and Artillery Command headquarters on the northern edge of the city, plans to commandeer South Vietnamese tanks and howitzers evaporated when the enemy discovered that the tanks had been moved to another base and that the breech locks had been removed from the artillery.

In other parts of the city, small VC squads fanned out and attacked numerous officers' and enlisted men's billets, the homes of ARVN officers, and district police stations. Other units pursued more political assignments. Carrying "blacklists" bearing the names of ARVN officers, civil servants, and others connected to the GVN, armed cadres conducted house-to-house searches through residential quarters of the city. As one civilian witness recalled:

They guarded the street, checked houses and ID cards, and forbade us to leave. Soldiers on leave were arrested and shot on the spot.... Ordinary people weren't arrested, but weren't allowed to leave the area.

To demonstrate their power, the Vietcong herded people into the streets for group criticism sessions to discuss past "crimes" against the NLF, conducted ritual burnings of the GVN flag, and held "people's courts" to decide the fate of suspected "traitors." Repeatedly, they proclaimed their ability and intention to attack Saigon again and again until the city was "liberated."

"Liberation" was the last thing Westmoreland was worried about. As he evaluated the telephone reports that flowed into his villa on Tran Quy Cap Street throughout the long night, the American commander soon concluded that the battle of Saigon would be short-lived. By morning, as much of the major fighting subsided, his confidence grew proportionally. Arriving at the U.S. Embassy compound five minutes after it had been pronounced secure, he strode through a crowd of reporters and inspected the damaged buildings and grounds. Minutes later he returned and told a startled press corps that "the enemy's well-laid plans went afoul."

At a press briefing later that day, Westmoreland elaborated. The attacks on the cities, he asserted, had been launched as a "diversion" for the "main effort" soon to come in I Corps. The following day, February 1, he modified his position, stating, first, that the Tet offensive represented only the second phase of a three-phase campaign that had begun with the border battles of the previous fall and would culminate in a major drive in Quang Tri and Thua Thien provinces, and second, that each successive phase was diversionary for the one that followed. Characterizing the current phase as an "all-or-nothing" proposition and noting that the Communists had already lost 5,800 killed, Westmoreland concluded that the enemy offensive "is about to run out of steam."

Early assessments

Back in Washington, Westmoreland's sanguine appraisal proved reassuring to his troubled and weary commander in chief. Already haunted by the possibility of a major U.S. defeat at Khe Sanh and further shaken by North Korea's seizure on January 23 of the U.S. intelligence ship *Pueblo*, Lyndon Baines Johnson didn't need any more bad news. Neither did the American people. At a White House press conference on February 2, President Johnson announced that the Tet offensive was a "complete failure." "We have known for some time that this offensive was planned by the enemy," he asserted. "The ability to do what they have done has been anticipated, prepared for, and met." Not only had Communist forces suffered staggering losses, now estimated at more than 10,000 killed, but the vaunted General Uprising had not taken place. He also sounded a note of caution. "The situation is a fluid one," and all of the "facts" were not yet in. The third phase of the Communist campaign—"a massive attack" across the demilitarized zone in the area of Khe Sanh—was "imminent." "I don't want to prophesy on what is going to happen, or why," President Johnson said. "We feel reasonably sure of our strength."

The president had good reason to temper his optimism. Reports from the war zone painted an incomplete, and at times confusing, picture of the situation. By all accounts the pacification program had suffered a grievous setback, as Revolutionary Development teams evacuated the countryside with the onset of the attacks. It would probably take six months, the president was informed, to regain the ground that had been lost. As for the GVN, the prompt declaration of martial law by President Thieu had helped to restore order, but many American officials doubted the government's ability to sustain its efforts and rally the nation behind it. Assessments of the performance of the South Vietnamese armed forces were similarly mixed. The American command was clearly encouraged by the fact that the South Vietnamese, in most cases operating at half-strength, had not collapsed. But there were also numerous reports of deficient leadership, poor troop discipline, and above all, excessive reliance on American firepower.

The damage to civilian property in some towns was enormous. An estimated 50 percent of the provincial capital of Pleiku was destroyed during the fighting; 45 percent of the town of Ben Tre; 25 percent of Vinh Long and Ban Me Thuot; and 20 percent of Da Lat. While the total cost of the devastation is impossible to determine, estimates run into the hundreds of millions of dollars.

Equally difficult to gauge, and far more crucial in the long run, was the impact on the South Vietnamese civilian population. All told, the battles of Tet generated more than half a million new refugees, in addition to an estimated 36,000 to 38,000 civilian casualties (14,000 killed, 20–22,000 wounded). Everywhere there were shortages of food and water, medicine and hospital beds, building materials and coffins. While many urban dwellers blamed the Communists and accepted the necessity of the allied bombings and shellings, others did not. Angry that the allies had not provided adequate protection against the invaders in the first place, they bitterly criticized the government for the destruction of their homes. Looting by South Vietnamese soldiers in the aftermath of some battles only compounded their distress.

Nowhere was the ordeal of the cities more painfully visible than in the continuing battle of Saigon. In the wake of the night attacks of January 31, some 10,000 South Vietnamese soldiers and National Police began to move against "pockets of enemy resistance" in what were officially described as "mopping up operations." In a number of districts, however, Communist forces proved far more resilient than anticipated. Striking at night and mingling with the civilian population by day, they managed to frustrate all efforts to dislodge them until, on February 4, the allies unleashed the full fury of their firepower on enemy strongholds. In the days that followed, American F-100 jets and South Vietnamese A-1 Skyraiders pounded some of the more heavily populated sections of Saigon after the government told the residents to flee their homes or risk death. Particularly hard hit was the Chinese district of Cholon, where the Communists had set up a central command post and field hospital at the Phu Tho racetrack. Day after day, the methodical destruction of Cholon continued, adding to the toll of refugees and civilian casualties, and horrifying a worldwide audience that watched it on television. Eventually the enemy was eliminated from Saigon, but not before the U.S. Army 199th Light Infantry Brigade was called in on February 10 to secure, once and for all, the Phu Tho racetrack.

By the time the bloody battle of Saigon came to a close, President Johnson was in a truculent mood. Outraged by the Communists' "deception" and "lack of concern for the basic elements that appeal to human beings," and equally angered by mounting criticism of U.S. war policy in the press, he had made it clear that he did not intend to yield. He told his senior advisers that "all options" should be considered, including an extension of enlistments, a call-up of the reserves, a troop increase in Vietnam, and even a declaration of war.

Yet for all his bravado, the president seemed reluctant to commit himself to any specific course of action until all of the facts were clear. There were many questions yet to be answered, including the all-important question of enemy intentions. On February 4 the ambassador to South Vietnam, Ellsworth Bunker, had reported to the president that there were two possible interpretations of "the motives and purposes of Hanoi and the Front" in staging the Tet offensive. "Were they prepared to suffer these tremendous casualties in order to gain a psychological and propaganda victory" in South Vietnam by demonstrating the weakness of the GVN and thus strengthening their position in future negotiations for a coalition government? "Or is this part of a longer Winter-Spring offensive" designed "to score some major victory" that "might create adverse psychological reactions in the United States and thus a change in policy?" Bunker told Johnson that he was personally "inclined to the former theory" and "Thieu expressed similar views."

The president, however, was clearly inclined to the latter view. Relying on the judgment of his field commander, he fully expected the Communists to launch the "third phase" of their campaign at any moment, in the hope of achieving a "major victory" that would sap America's will to fight. By the second week of February 1968, as fighting sputtered out in the south, the attention of the president and of the American people shifted north to I Corps, where 6,000 U.S. Marines at Khe Sanh shuddered under the impact of incessant North Vietnamese shelling, steeling themselves for the onset of what they were told could be the most decisive battle of the war; where other marines fought house-to-house and street-by-street in an effort to bring down the fledgling "revolutionary people's government" of the city of Hue; and where the outcome of the Tet offensive seemed to hang in the balance.

Ben Tre, February 1968. "It became necessary to destroy the town in order to save it," a U.S. Army major told the American journalist Peter Arnett.

Order of Battle

In the fall of 1967, one simple question reverberated in corridors from Washington to Saigon's Pentagon East: Who is winning the war? In a conflict without clear territorial objectives, President Johnson, Congress, and the public pressured General Westmoreland for statistical evidence that America and its allies were killing more of the enemy than could be thrown into battle. As more American troops prepared to join the 450,000 already in Vietnam, final meetings were scheduled in Saigon in September to hammer out an official intelligence estimate, one that would inevitably be used to gauge the effectiveness of the American strategy of attrition.

Who is winning? Seemingly a simple question, a matter of adding up enemy forces, subtracting the number killed, and determining the "cross-over point" when allied forces would finally kill more Vietcong and North Vietnamese than were being replenished through recruitment and conscription. But that tabulation procedure, beginning with the breakdown of Communist forces known as the enemy "order of battle" (OB), was fraught with the inherent ambiguities of separating soldiers from citizens in a "people's war." Should a twelve-year-old peasant boy who plants land mines and acts as a scout for local VC troops be counted as part of the enemy's "combat potential"? What about this boy's sixty-year-old grandmother: For sheltering and feeding guerrillas should she be counted among "support troops" equivalent to American cooks and maintenance men at Cam Ranh Bay? Strong differences of opinion over the number and importance of political cadres and part-time guerrillas existed among the military and civilian analysts charged with enemy strength estimation.

In 1967, MACV and the CIA argued bitterly over the new Special National Intelligence Estimate that would measure in relatively "hard" numbers allied progress in the destruction of the Vietcong military and political apparatus. Operations Cedar Falls and Junction City set the stage for the statistical showdown that would come during September's interagency meeting in Saigon. During these huge search and destroy operations, over a million pages of captured documents were sent on their way to intelligence authorities. Order of battle experts at CIA headquarters in Langley, who suspected that VC "irregulars" had been underestimated in the past by their counterparts at MACV, found their higher figures confirmed by the document windfall. In a May 1967 memo to Secretary of Defense McNamara, the CIA estimated that overall Communist strength, including "irregulars," might lie in the neighborhood of 500,000—nearly double earlier estimates.

Officers at the order of battle section of MACV's intelligence arm, who had previously estimated total enemy strength at well below 300,000, were also shocked by the new evidence. In a briefing for General Westmoreland in May, OB expert Colonel Gains Hawkins suggested that as many as 200,000 guerrillas, irregulars, and political cadres had been overlooked in the past. The CIA figure was, in effect, seconded by experts at MACV.

General Westmoreland was gravely concerned about the public impact of the new estimate. "What am I going to tell the press?" he asked Hawkins, "What am I going to tell the Congress? What am I going to tell the President?" Major General Joseph McChristian, then chief of military intelligence, Vietnam, and Hawkins's superior, recalled, "I had the definite impression that if he sent those figures back to Washington, it would create a political bombshell."

According to Hawkins, General Westmoreland ordered him to "take another look" at the new figures. Hawkins understood the order to mean that a bottom-line number measuring total Communist strength in South Vietnam should not greatly exceed the previous MACV estimate: MACV should not appear, in other words, to be losing the war of attrition. In McChristian's view, the new figures showed exactly that. "The North Vietnamese and the Vietcong had the capability and the will to continue a protracted war of attrition," he said.

Colonel Hawkins returned to the sprawling Combined Intelligence Center at Tan Son Nhut and, in his own words, "arbitrarily reduced the damn figures." As rosters of VC strength in the MACV estimate were cut, Hawkins recalled, analysts below him were "looking a little askance at me." Because of what Hawkins describes as the "acute consciousness of a ceiling," cynicism pervaded the estimates shop at Tan Son Nhut.

Before MACV and the CIA met in Saigon in September to discuss a compromise position between their now radically different estimates, Brigadier General Phillip Davidson had replaced General McChristian as senior MACV intelligence officer and immediately gave Hawkins's new estimate a rationale. According to Davidson, the increase in the OB suggested by Hawkins and the CIA had been based on an exaggerated appraisal of the military significance of VC supporters organized into "self-defense" militia. These male and female VC sympathizers, many unarmed and poorly trained, took up duties of fortification building, village defense, and observation of allied force movements. Since self-defense cadres did not leave their home areas, worked only part-time, and were unavailable for mobile operations, MACV reasoned, they could not be considered a combat force. The paradox that their death in combat was incorporated into the body count was ignored.

The CIA's George Allen, deputy assistant director for Vietnamese affairs, disagreed with the MACV approach to the militia. "They were the ones that ambushed our forces when they would enter VC-controlled areas. They were the ones who booby trapped." Pointing out that the militia helped the populace build punji-stakes and other incapacitating devices, which accounted for over half of American casualties in the Da Nang area alone, Allen concluded that, nationwide, "the self-defense militia were responsible for a large portion of our casualties" and should be included in the official order of battle.

MACV analysts challenged this view, and a MACV spokesman gave a briefing to the press in which he characterized the militia as "essentially low level fifth columnists, used for information collection. Although they cause some casualties and some damage, they do not form a valid part of the enemy's military force." The briefing incensed the CIA officers present, who felt it to be a conscious effort on the part of the MACV to understate the difficulties faced by troops in the field. The CINCPAC representative to the September meeting in Saigon expressed the view of many participants when he complained about the elimination of "cat and dog units." It "sent me into shock when I saw these units being crossed off. You can't on the one hand say these people

who put in the punji-stakes and who planted the bombs and so on weren't actually part of a military force and turn around in the next breath and say, 'We can't go around shooting civilians.'"

With the embattled MACV delegates standing firm on the deletion of support personnel, and with CIA representatives, especially intelligence specialist Samuel Adams, crying foul play, the conference was sorely in need of high-level mediation. Enter George Carver, CIA deputy director for Vietnamese affairs. After consultation with CIA Director Richard Helms and Ambassador Bunker, Carver arranged a private meeting with Westmoreland. On the third day of the conference, the two men examined the nature of the controversy, which included disagreements over the counting of administrative service units, guerrillas, and political cadres. It was Carver who devised the final compromise: The CIA would drop its insistence on including these units in the final quantification of the order of battle if the drafters of the final document would "describe in prose what we're talking about and what order of magnitude we're thinking of."

When Carver returned to the conference table on the same day of his morning meeting with Westmoreland, he presented the compromise to the assembled delegates. "At that point six colonels jumped up," Carver recollected, "and said, 'No, no, absolutely impossible. General Westmoreland would never accept that.' And I said, 'Well, that's interesting, because he just did—five minutes ago.'" If the MACV analysts were taken aback, CIA delegates favoring the higher number for total enemy strength were appalled. While Carver claimed that technical problems associated with producing a bottom-line number would be judiciously addressed by means of a prose insert in the final report, others claimed that the essential problem with the disputed higher figure was not so much technical as political. George Allen laid

the responsibility for the CIA's apparent capitulation to MACV at the feet of the director. Allen says, "The feeling was, naturally, that it was a political problem, that he [Helms] didn't want the agency ... to be perceived as persisting in a line which was contravening the policy interest of the administration."

In late September, an "eyes-only" cable from Westmoreland, Bunker, and Bunker's assistant for pacification, Robert Komer, to presidential aide Walt Rostow underscored the political sensitivity of the estimate. "We have been projecting an image of success over the recent months. The self-defense militia must be removed [from the OB], or the newsmen will immediately seize on the point that the enemy force has increased." Westmoreland was concerned, on the basis of experience, that the abstruse controversy over intelligence methods would be lost on the press. They would report a large increase in enemy forces inconsistent with the relative decline in guerrilla activity in the early fall. In another cable, however, Ambassador Bunker reemphasized the media issue. "Given the overriding need to demonstrate our progress in grinding down the enemy," Bunker wrote, "it is essential that we not drag too many red herrings across the trail. ... The credibility gap is such that we don't want to end up conveying the opposite of what we intend."

When the Special National Intelligence Estimate was issued on November 13, 1967, the Carver compromise stuck. Militia units were listed as "not quantified," and the CIA appended its views on their importance to the Communist war effort. But the bottom-line figure did not contradict Westmoreland's pronouncement in the fall of 1967 that "whereas in 1965 the enemy was winning, today he is certainly losing."

The Agony of Hue

In an informal meeting with General Westmoreland during the Honolulu conference of February 1966, President Johnson asked his field
commander what he would do next if he were
the enemy. His response was immediate and
succinct: "Capture Hue."

"To come to that conclusion," the general later
remarked, "required little perspicacity." The former imperial capital of a united Vietnam and the
current capital of Thua Thien Province, for more
than a century the center of Vietnamese religious
and cultural life, Hue was a city rich in historical,
symbolic, and strategic significance. "Taking it,"
Westmoreland pointed out, "would have a profound psychological impact on the Vietnamese in
both the North and the South, and in the process
the North Vietnamese might seize the two northern provinces as bargaining points in any negotiations." Cut off from the rest of South Vietnam
by the Annamese Mountains, bordered by the
DMZ to the north and Laos to the west, and lack-

ing any major harbors or ports, Quang Tri and Thua Thien provinces posed "serious defensive problems" for allied forces. Losing them, the American commander feared, might well mean losing the war.

That the Communists attached equal importance to the two northern provinces was demonstrated by their establishment of a "Tri-Thien Front" controlled directly from North Vietnam, rather than indirectly through the Central Office of South Vietnam (COSVN). Proximity to North Vietnam meant shorter lines of communication, supply, and infiltration, making it possible for NVA forces to put unrelenting pressure on allied defenses. Beginning in mid-1966, when NVA troops first began to infiltrate across the DMZ in battalion and even division strength, the Quang Tri-Thua Thien area became the site of a series of major yet inconclusive confrontations between American and North Vietnamese forces. Until 1968, however, the Communists had made little headway in their effort to gain control of the region or to capture the prize that General Westmoreland sought to deny them, the city of Hue.

Dominated by the massive Imperial Citadel of the Nguyen emperors, renowned for its elegant boulevards and pagodas, and inhabited by a cultured and cosmopolitan population, Hue was the most exotic city in Vietnam. It was also considered to be among the most secure. Although in recent years Hue had become a cradle of popular discontent with the Saigon government, GVN officials and ARVN officers continued to offer substantial bribes for assignment there. An island of peace in a nation wracked by war, Hue, on the eve of Tet 1968, was supremely unprepared for the tragedy that was about to engulf it.

Red flag over the Citadel

Toward the end of January several allied intelligence agencies uncovered evidence of a possible Communist assault on the city. On January 22, General Westmoreland had cabled Washington that the enemy might be preparing to launch a multibattalion attack, but for some reason the alert never reached military authorities in Hue itself. A second warning came on January 28, when an American military adviser assigned just east of the city reported that three Communist battalions had apparently left their mountain base camps and moved into his lowland area. Because the adviser was reputed to be an excessive worrier, however, intelligence analysts in Hue discounted the uncorroborated report. On January 30, the eve of Tet, the U.S. radio intercept station at Phu Bai picked up a flurry of Communist radio signals, a clear indication of increased enemy activity in the area. The information was then sent to Da Nang regional headquarters for posting

and analysis. By the time the word reached Hue, it was already too late.

A thick, low fog blanketed the city when the barrage began at 3:40 A.M. on January 31, signaling the moment of attack for the Communist troops who had been impatiently waiting in the chill night air. As 122MM rockets shrieked into the Imperial Citadel on the north bank of the River of Perfumes, soldiers of the 800th and 802d battalions of the NVA 6th Regiment charged across lightly defended bridges and through the western gates of the huge ramparts surrounding the fortress (see map, page 34). Moving swiftly but separately toward the headquarters of the ARVN 1st Division inside the Citadel, the two battalions encountered little resistance until the 800th ran into the ARVN Black Panther Company at Tay Loc airfield. Alerted by the attacks in II Corps and Da Nang the previous night, ARVN 1st Division commander Brigadier General Ngo Quang Truong had called upon the elite company to reinforce the headquarters compound and strategically positioned them at the eastern end of the runway. Lacking cover, men of the NVA 800th were unable to traverse the airfield and moved south into the residential quarters of the Citadel. The 802d was initially more successful, briefly penetrating the ARVN compound before it, too, was hurled back by the Black Panthers.

On the south bank of the river the Communists launched a simultaneous attack on the Hue headquarters of the U.S. Military Assistance Command, Vietnam—a converted three-story hotel surrounded by a high, brick wall. Striking from a rice field several blocks away, elements of the NVA 4th Regiment directed a continuous stream of rocket, mortar, and machine-gun fire against the compound but failed to breach its walls. Inside, a makeshift force of approximately 200 Americans struggled to repel the attackers, some of whom were so close that the defenders could hear the clink of mortar rounds dropping into tubes.

Other Communist units swept through the streets of the city on both sides of the river, carrying out systematic assaults on more than 200 specific targets, including Thua Thien Province headquarters, police stations, and houses occupied by American and GVN personnel. Outside the city two additional NVA battalions established blocking positions along Highway 1.

As daylight broke and the fog began to lift, the gold-starred, blue-and-red flag of the NLF could be seen flying high over the Citadel, brashly proclaiming that the Communists controlled the city. The only pockets of allied resistance still remaining were the embattled MACV and ARVN 1st headquarters compounds, and their defenders could do little more than watch the enemy dig in and wait for reinforcements.

Ironically, when news of the attack reached the U.S. Marine base at Phu Bai, eight miles southeast of Hue, it caused no great alarm. Believing that only a small enemy

Posing for a western photographer, a young North Vietnamese aims a captured M79 grenade launcher from the garden of a captured villa on the south bank of the Perfume River.

force had penetrated the city, the marine command sent a single company to relieve the besieged American advisers. Along the way Company A, 1st Battalion, 1st Marines, chanced upon four U.S. tanks scheduled to move up to the DMZ and added them to their reaction force. Pinned down by intense automatic-weapons fire as it neared the city, the column soon had to call for help. A second marine company, equipped with two self-propelled 40MM guns, was immediately dispatched from Phu Bai. This combined force fought its way into the city and reached the MACV compound six hours after Company A had left Phu Bai. The cost, however, had been high: 10 marines killed, another 30 wounded. They would need reinforcements. During the next three days, three more marine companies, three marine command groups, and a tank platoon—about 1,000 men in all—arrived at the advisory headquarters.

At his command post inside the Citadel, General Truong had no illusions about the size and strength of the enemy force that now ruled Hue. Desperately in need of reinforcement, he immediately ordered outlying units of the ARVN 1st Division to fall back toward the Citadel. Like the Americans, the South Vietnamese encountered strong resistance from NVA blocking units as they approached the city and suffered heavy casualties. Within twenty-four hours, however, Truong had the troops he needed to hold his position.

In the meantime the Communists consolidated their own positions. On the south bank, where only days before university students had strolled leisurely along Le Loi Street and white-clad tennis players met over aperitifs at the Cercle Sportif, the invaders seized key civil and military installations, sealed off residential streets with captured tanks, and freed more than 2,000 inmates from the municipal prison. The central hospital was converted into a command post, while the illustrious Quoc Hoc High School—alma mater of Ngo Dinh Diem, Ho Chi Minh, and Vo Nguyen Giap—became an armory and barracks.

On the north bank Communist forces had the Citadel for protection. Built by Emperor Gia Long in 1802, this gigantic fortress was intended to be as impregnable as it was imposing. The Citadel was surrounded by a zigzag moat, an outer wall of earth and stone thirty feet high and twenty feet thick, and an inner wall made of brick. The interior, measuring more than two square miles, formed three concentric interior cities and a labyrinth of readily defensible positions. In addition to the well-fortified Imperial Palace, where the North Vietnamese established their central command post, the long, straight streets and walled gardens of the residential quarters offered ideal cover and clear fields of fire for snipers. As one American adviser commented: "It would take the battleship *New Jersey* to get them out of those walls."

The Americans didn't have the *New Jersey*, but they did have a vast arsenal of heavy weaponry for their counterattack: 105MM, 155MM, and eight-inch howitzers; self-propelled 40MM guns, Ontos vehicles mounted with 106MM recoilless rifles, and tanks; helicopter gunships, fighter-bombers carrying 500- and 750-pound bombs and, just off the coast, cruisers and destroyers equipped with five-inch, six-inch, and eight-inch guns. Rapidly deteriorating weather conditions, as well as a wish to minimize property damage and civilian casualties, initially inhibited the use of allied firepower. But after a few days of bitter fighting, the allied command realized that much greater force would be required to expel the enemy from Hue. At times fixing coordinates by sound rather than sight, American commanders began to call in artillery strikes while helicopter gunships and tactical aircraft strafed and napalmed the enemy.

Meanwhile both sides continued to augment their ranks. Their hold on the west wall still secure, the Communists funneled fresh troops and supplies into the Citadel by night, eventually committing ten battalions—more than a full division—to the struggle. The allies countered by calling in three understrength Marine Corps battalions, six U.S. Army battalions, and eleven South Vietnamese battalions.

House to house, street by street

After an early attempt by U.S. Marines to cross the river failed, the allies divided the city into two tactical areas of operation, the Americans responsible for clearing the south bank, the South Vietnamese concentrating on the Citadel. On both sides the fighting proved to be brutal, bloody, and frustrating—house to house and street by street in a misty drizzle that occasionally turned into cold, drenching rain. The initial marine detachment required six days to fight its way from the MACV compound to the provincial hospital four blocks away, at a cost of more than 150 casualties. "Seoul was tough," said one marine commander recalling the corps' last major city battle, "but this—well, it's something else." Accustomed to fighting in the sparsely populated countryside of I Corps, the young marines who had not been in Korea had to learn the tactics of urban fighting on the spot. Supported by mortars, recoilless rifles, machine guns, and tanks, ten- or eleven-man fire teams spearheaded the assaults. "Four men cover the exits of a building, two men rush the building with grenades, while two men cover them with rifle fire," explained Lieutenant Colonel Earnest C. Cheatham, commander of the 2d Battalion, 5th Marines.

We hope to kill them inside or flush them out for the four men watching the exits. Then, taking the next building, two other men rush the front. It sounds simple, but the timing has to be just as good as a football play.

Frequently the Americans found it much easier, and far less costly, simply to destroy the buildings. "Some South

Bayonets fixed, a marine fire team searches for enemy units on February 16 in a district of Hue already shattered by more than two weeks of fighting.

His squad pinned down in the rubble, a marine hurls a grenade toward an enemy position. Moments later another grenade exploded in his hand.

Vietnamese are complaining about the damage to their buildings, but I have no sympathy," declared one commander. "If you can save a marine by destroying a house to get to Charlie, then I say destroy the house." Even so, by the end of the first week of fighting the marines had managed to secure less than half of the south bank while suffering some 250 casualties.

On the outskirts of the city the soldiers of the U.S. Army found the going equally tough. Assigned the mission of severing the main enemy infiltration and supply routes, the 3d Brigade, 1st Air Cavalry Division, air assaulted into a landing zone six miles northwest of Hue on February 2. Three days later, following a grueling night march through ankle-deep water, weary men of the 2d Battalion, 12th Cavalry, of the 3d Brigade, stormed a hill four miles west of the city and immediately began shelling Communist positions in the valley below. Sweeping in from the west, the 5th Battalion, 7th Cavalry, 3d Brigade, tried to link up with the 2d Battalion but was halted by NVA units that had slipped in behind the first wave of Americans. Forced to abandon their high ground, the 2d Battalion attacked northward toward their sister battalion on February 9 and, after a day-long fight in the village of Thong Bon Tri, drove the NVA out of the area.

It had become clear that enemy blocking forces were stronger than anticipated and that reinforcements would be needed. After conferring with marine commander General Robert E. Cushman and MACV deputy commander Creighton W. Abrams, General Westmoreland ordered two battalions of the 101st Airborne Division to join the battle for Hue. In the weeks that followed, the 101st attacked from the south while the 3d Brigade of the 1st Air Cav—reinforced to a strength of four battalions—fought its way from the north and west, gradually tightening the vise of the allied counterattack.

On February 10 the south bank of the city was finally declared secure, but it was a fragile security. Communist rockets and mortar rounds continued to flash across the river, while isolated snipers harassed marine patrols. Adding to the tension and confusion were thousands of refugees, many of whom now crowded into a few unscathed buildings that served as temporary relief centers. Others roamed the streets searching for missing family members and friends or sorted through the broken pieces of their homes and possessions. Brutalized into indifference, few expressed any interest in the outcome of the battle. They just wanted the war to go away. As one student bitterly explained: "We here and now don't care about anything except rice. We know well the VC. We know well the Americans. We want to go to our homes and not be afraid of being killed by either side."

From the start both the Americans and the South Vietnamese tried to minimize the significance of the Communist occupation of Hue. On February 1, General Wheeler

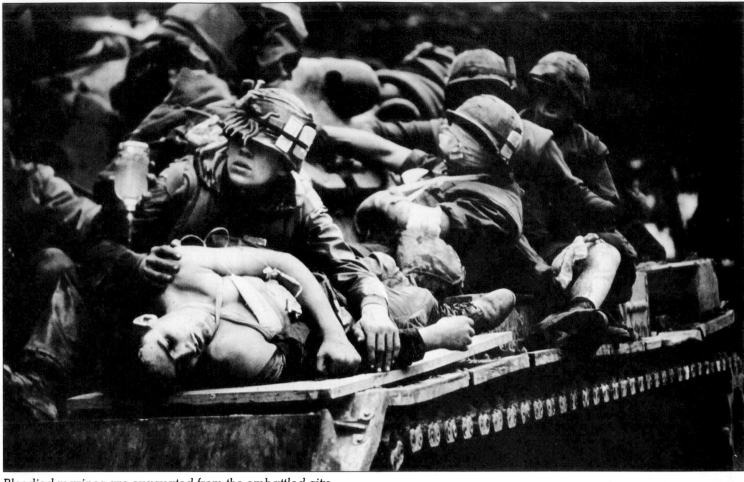

Bloodied marines are evacuated from the embattled city.

told the Senate Armed Services Committee that the enemy had only "a remnant of a battalion" on the south bank and "some troops" in the Citadel, and throughout the first week military officials referred to the battle as a "mopping up operation." Now, with the battle more than ten days old and the Communists still in control of most of the north bank, the allies intensified their counterattack.

Fanning out from the 1st Division headquarters compound, ARVN forces had already regained considerable ground in the northern half of the Citadel, including the airfield. But they had been unable to penetrate the main enemy strong points in the southern half. Sixty percent of the fortress still lay in Communist hands, and despite steady reinforcement and the use of armor, every attempt to breach the Communist defenses had been repulsed. To expel the enemy the allies would have to widen the arc of their attack and open up the walls of the Citadel brick by brick.

As darkness fell on February 11, the 1/5 Marines, escorted by a platoon of tanks and several Ontos vehicles, crossed the river and joined the fight for the north bank. The following day, after conferring with President Thieu, South Vietnamese I Corps commander Lieutenant General Hoang Xuan Lam authorized allied forces to use whatever weapons were necessary to dislodge the enemy

from Hue. Only the Imperial Palace remained off limits.

In the days that followed, shells from American tanks, howitzers, and navy ships relentlessly pounded the walls of the Citadel, while South Vietnamese A-1 Skyraiders and U.S. F-4 Phantoms dropped napalm canisters and 500-pound bombs on Communist emplacements. Entrenched along the jagged ramparts of the Citadel's six-mile wall, behind the foundations of collapsed buildings, or inside darkened homes, the enemy retaliated with machine guns, antitank rockets, mortars, and fire from captured tanks. The fighting proved even more savage than the battle for the south bank. In their first assault on the south wall, the 1/5 Marines lost fifteen killed and forty wounded; by the end of the week they had suffered approximately one casualty for every yard gained. Constantly under fire, sleeping in three- to four-hour snatches, and unrelieved by fresh troops, many of the men grew numb with fatigue. "On the worst days, no one expected to get through it alive," wrote Michael Herr.

A despair set in among members of the battalion that the older ones, veterans of two other wars, had never seen before. Once or twice, when the men from Graves Registration took the personal effects from the packs and pockets of dead marines, they found letters from home that had been delivered days before still unopened.

"Most of the battalion were killed or wounded," recalled photographer Don McCullin about this marine's unit. *"There were only about a half dozen men in one company. I think what happens is that one goes over the edge—you become slightly mad."*

Casualties backlogged so quickly that doctors simply set aside the worst cases, but even then they could not keep up with the steady flow of wounded. "I've seen too much of this," said one anguished marine. "We've got to get some help. They're going to annihilate 1/5."

By the end of the second week of fighting, large sections of Hue had been reduced to rubble—a ghastly mosaic of shattered buildings, bullet-riddled walls, and rotting corpses. "A woman knelt in death by a wall in the corner of her garden," wrote one correspondent. "A child lay on stairs crushed by a fallen roof. Many of the bodies had turned black and begun to decompose, and rats gnawed at the exposed flesh."

Yet for all the devastation that it wrought, the ferocious battle between the Communist and allied armies formed only a part of the tragic story of Hue. The other part took place behind enemy lines, where a "revolutionary government" had begun to mete out "revolutionary justice."

Liberation and death

According to Vietnamese custom, the fortunes of an individual for each new year are foreshadowed by the first visitor to call at Tet. It was therefore with some interest, and perhaps a little trepidation, that Mr. Vinh, a resident of the southern part of the Citadel, answered the rattle at his gate during the dark morning hours of January 31. The caller was an old acquaintance he had not seen for years, a veteran of the war against the French and a current member of the Vietcong. He told Mr. Vinh that victory was near, and then he left.

Like many residents of Hue, Mr. Vinh had heard rumors in recent weeks of an imminent Communist attack. As in the past, he had dismissed them as empty boasts. But now, as dawn broke, he could scarcely doubt his old friend's claim that the Communists controlled the "liberated" city of Hue. Up and down the streets of his neighborhood VC cadres and NVA soldiers moved freely on foot and bicycles, on Hondas and Suzukis, or in cars and captured jeeps. Some were clearly city boys, identifiable by their long hair and American-style blue jeans. Others were local country girls clad in black pajamas and wearing their hair in stiffly drawn buns. All were engaged in feverish activity—carrying mortar tubes and rockets, setting up machine-gun emplacements, and enlisting the population against the "puppet" Saigon government and the American "imperialists."

Preparations for the Communist occupation of Hue had been made long in advance. Beginning in September 1967, when local Communist leaders first learned of plans for the General Offensive-General Uprising, Vietcong agents worked assiduously to insure the triumph of the fu-

As black smoke billows from a napalm strike inside the Citadel, a squad of U.S. Marines finds cover near the ruins of the East Gate.

Burrowed into the ruins of a temple inside the Citadel, ARVN soldiers return Communist fire. Entire sections of the city were destroyed in the effort to drive the enemy from Hue.

ture "new order"; they organized political cells among small businessmen and youths, drew up blueprints of allied defenses and schedules of military and police patrols, and provided names and addresses of suspected "counterrevolutionaries" throughout the city. As soon as the city was firmly under Communist control, the political cadres of the NLF announced the formation of the Alliance of National, Democratic and Peace Forces of Hue City, headed by a Hue University professor and the former principal of a local girls' high school. A former chief of the city's National Police became the new mayor. Everyone was ordered to rip down all South Vietnamese flags and urged to join newly formed patriotic organizations in support of the revolutionary government; and everywhere there were rallies and political meetings. At the end of one local meeting, a group of young men and women was handed weapons and acclaimed as the uprising troops for their area. In another instance a cultural drama troupe from North Vietnam commemorated the election of a student group leader by staging an anti-American, anti-government show.

Amid the exhilarating atmosphere of revolutionary change, however, there was cause for apprehension. On the second day of the occupation, bullhorns in the streets began to summon all civil servants, military personnel, and "whoever works for the Americans" to report immediately to Communist officials. Although assured that nothing would happen if they did as they were told, many functionaries elected to flee or hide inside their homes, hoping that allied forces would momentarily come to their rescue. But as the days passed and the fighting persisted, their hopes dimmed, while the announcements became more strident. Houses would be searched, the Communists declared, and anyone found hiding would be summarily executed.

The searches had in fact begun at the very outset of the occupation. Using target lists furnished by local intelligence agents, small bands moved up and down the streets like grim census takers, looking for those who had been designated as "cruel tyrants and reactionary elements": government officials, ARVN officers, political figures, and foreigners other than the French. Once identi-

33

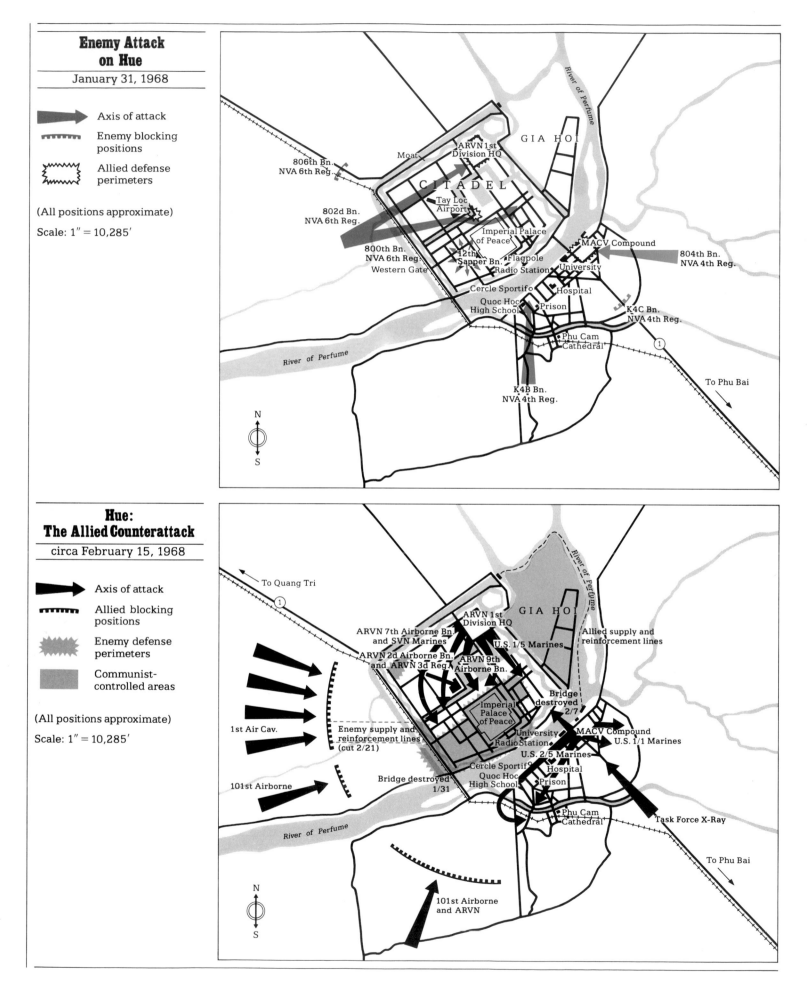

Enemy Attack on Hue

January 31, 1968

Axis of attack

Enemy blocking positions

Allied defense perimeters

(All positions approximate)

Scale: 1" = 10,285'

806th Bn. NVA 6th Reg.

Moat

ARVN 1st Division HQ

GIA HOI

802d Bn. NVA 6th Reg.

CITADEL

Tay Loc Airport

800th Bn. NVA 6th Reg.

Imperial Palace of Peace

MACV Compound

804th Bn. NVA 4th Reg.

12th Sapper Bn.

Flagpole

Radio Station

University

Western Gate

Cercle Sportif

Hospital

Quoc Hoc High School

Prison

K4C Bn. NVA 4th Reg.

Phu Cam Cathedral

River of Perfume

To Phu Bai

K4B Bn. NVA 4th Reg.

N S

Hue: The Allied Counterattack

circa February 15, 1968

Axis of attack

Allied blocking positions

Enemy defense perimeters

Communist-controlled areas

(All positions approximate)

Scale: 1" = 10,285'

To Quang Tri

ARVN 1st Division HQ

GIA HOI

ARVN 7th Airborne Bn. and SVN Marines

U.S. 1/5 Marines

Allied supply and reinforcement lines

ARVN 2d Airborne Bn. and ARVN 3d Reg.

ARVN 9th Airborne Bn.

1st Air Cav.

Bridge destroyed 2/7

Imperial Palace of Peace

Enemy supply and reinforcement lines (cut 2/21)

University

Radio Station

MACV Compound

U.S. 1/1 Marines

U.S. 2/5 Marines

101st Airborne

Cercle Sportif

Hospital

Quoc Hoc High School

Prison

Bridge destroyed 1/31

Phu Cam Cathedral

Task Force X-Ray

River of Perfume

To Phu Bai

101st Airborne and ARVN

N S

fied, most of the suspects were marched to prisoner collection points, their hands tied behind their backs.

On the third day of the occupation, a group of VC called at a house on the south bank that was occupied by a U.S. Army communications team. When one of the Americans opened fire on the visitors they withdrew, only to return two days later with reinforcements. Some of the Americans managed to escape but others, finding themselves trapped, were forced to surrender. They were never heard from again.

On the fifth day, Communist troops on the south bank entered Phu Cam Cathedral and arrested several hundred Vietnamese Roman Catholics, all of them men or boys of military age. As they were led away, a Vietcong leader told everyone not to worry: They were only being taken to a nearby pagoda for political reorientation sessions. Two days later, the soldiers returned and told the women still living in the sanctuary to prepare provisions for their loved ones. None of the men of Phu Cam ever returned.

The savage intensity of the fighting curtailed Vietcong political activity inside the Citadel, but in Gia Hoi, a densely populated district just east of the fortress, the roundups continued unabated to the end. Since no major government or military installations were located in the area, the allied command had decided to ignore Gia Hoi until they had recaptured the Citadel. For twenty-six days it was the seat of a working "revolutionary" government, ruled by a Communist mayor in conjunction with local "revolutionary councils" and policed by Vietcong and North Vietnamese soldiers. To insure the security of the new regime, all citizens were required to fill out questionnaires describing their life, work, and political attitudes. Those who expressed acceptable political ideas were then assigned tasks: disseminating propaganda, organizing political cells, and setting up local defense groups. Those with unacceptable or "erroneous" views were called in for further interrogation. Some were then visited by propaganda teams, or sent to reeducation classes where they received instruction in the history, logic, and goals of the revolutionary struggle. Others were dealt with more harshly.

Le Van Rot, a government block leader, was working in his Chinese soup shop when four armed soldiers walked in, sat down, and placed an order. The same men had come by earlier in the day, taken Rot away for questioning, and then released him. They had also interrogated some of his neighbors and discovered a cache of weapons in his house. Now, as the soldiers finished their soup, one of them turned to him and said: "We found out you sold soup here as a cover for spying." After binding Rot's hands behind his back with wire, they pulled him toward the door. When he resisted, he was shot on the spot.

Pham Van Tuong, a worker at the government information office, was hiding with his family inside a bunker when a group of men in black pajamas came to the door. "Mr. Pham, Mr. Pham, the information cadre, come here!" they called. Pham and four members of his family quickly emerged, only to be gunned down before they had a chance to explain that he was only a part-time janitor.

During the weeks and months following the battle, South Vietnamese authorities and American soldiers discovered a series of shallow mass graves in and around the city of Hue containing the remains of some 2,800 people. Their arms bound behind their backs by coarse wire, many of the victims had been shot in the head or bludgeoned to death. Others had apparently been buried alive. Among the dead were numerous government officials and civil servants; RVNAF officers and enlisted men; local leaders; policemen and members of the local militia; priests and religious leaders; Germans, Filipinos, Koreans, and Americans; and some ordinary citizens who had no tie to either side in the struggle.

"Blood bath"

The South Vietnamese and American governments later asserted that all had been ruthlessly murdered by the Communists, and in November 1969 President Nixon cited the "atrocities at Hue" as "a prelude of what would happen in South Vietnam" if the Communists ever gained power.

Further elaboration on the "blood bath" theory was provided by United States Information Agency officer Douglas Pike, an acknowledged authority on the NLF, in his 1970 study, *The Viet-Cong Strategy of Terror.* Basing his conclusions on official GVN reports, captured enemy documents, the testimony of enemy prisoners and defectors, eyewitness accounts, and "the internal logic of the Communist situation," Pike contended that the killings at Hue differed "not only in degree but in kind" from previous Communist acts of terrorism. According to Pike, the Communists' ultimate aim in Hue was not simply to weaken the GVN administrative apparatus or to terrorize the local population into compliance, but to purge entire classes of people—intellectuals, prominent religious and political leaders, and others deemed "social negatives" from an ideological point of view. In support of what was admittedly a "hypothesis," he called attention to "three facts" about the killings "which constantly reassert themselves": that they were not random; that "virtually all were done by local Communist cadres" rather than NVA soldiers; and that most were carried out in secrecy "with extraordinary effort made to hide the bodies." Secrecy alone, Pike noted, represented a significant deviation from prior practice, where the objective was to demonstrate publicly the "omnipotence" of the VC. So much care was taken to conceal the bodies that Pike speculated that as many as 5,700 people may have been assassinated in Hue during the period of Communist occupation.

Other scholars, however, raised serious questions not only about Pike's interpretation of the facts but also about the facts themselves. "[T]he story conveyed to the American public," wrote D. Gareth Porter, a former fellow of the International Relations of East Asia Project at Cornell University, "bore little resemblance to the truth, but was, on the contrary, the result of a political warfare campaign by the Saigon government, embellished by the U.S. government, and accepted uncritically by the U.S. press." Although many of the corpses were initially unearthed by local citizens and U.S. soldiers, Porter noted, the agency responsible for collecting and publicizing data on the alleged massacre was the ARVN 10th Political Warfare Battalion, a unit "whose specific mission was to discredit the National Liberation Front." Journalists and other independent observers were never allowed to inspect the graves and consequently, in Porter's view, "neither the number of bodies found nor the causes of death were ever confirmed."

The full story of what happened in Hue between January 31 and February 25, 1968, may never be known. But the preponderance of evidence, including the testimony of many survivors, indicates that Communist forces did in fact carry out systematic assassinations. The most persuasive case is that made by reporter Don Oberdorfer of the *Washington Post* in his authoritative work, *Tet!* Following up rumors of large-scale executions behind enemy lines, Oberdorfer made three visits to Hue—one during the battle, another just after, and a third in December 1969 "to reconstruct the experiences of the Hue people." Their pseudonymous accounts of the fates of relatives, neighbors, and friends—some of which have been recounted in this chapter—left no doubt in Oberdorfer's mind that mass executions had been carried out by the Communists. He also found evidence, however, that some of the victims may have been killed by South Vietnamese troops. One U.S. Army intelligence officer told Oberdorfer that during the final stages of the battle, a South Vietnamese intelligence unit sent its own "black teams" of assassins into Hue to eliminate those who had aided the enemy.

Precisely how many died at the hands of the Communists, no one can be sure. As Oberdorfer later noted, the victims of the slayings "did not pass through turnstiles." Nor is the rationale for the executions altogether evident. But since most of the victims were connected, however tenuously, with either the South Vietnamese government and military or the Americans, it would seem that the primary motivation was political and thus in keeping with past Communist practice. Whenever Communist forces took over a country village or hamlet, they commonly liquidated key government personnel in order to undermine the authority of the GVN and remind the local populace of the price of "collaboration." What distinguished the Hue assassinations from other acts of terrorism was neither the end sought nor the means employed: It was the sheer enormity of the killing.

The bodies of victims of the Hue massacre, discovered and exhumed more than a year after the executions took place, are given proper burial in September 1969.

ARVN soldiers cheer as the South Vietnamese flag once again flies over the Citadel on February 24.

A legacy of despair

For most of the people of Hue who, like Mr. Vinh, had ties to both sides, or who were simply indifferent about the outcome of the struggle for South Vietnam, the chief source of terror was not VC death squads but the seemingly endless trauma of war itself. Holed up inside the family bunker, a closet, or any other alcove that offered the most protection, they listened to the battle raging all around, preoccupied with survival. At the home of Mr. Vinh, Oberdorfer later learned, the family could hear the jets screaming into their dives overhead, and moments later they would shudder under the impact of exploding bombs. In the distance they heard the thunder of artillery shells and sporadic bursts of automatic-weapons fire. The sounds edged ever closer. A mortar round blew a hole in the side of the house; shrapnel penetrated the front door and roof; rockets slammed into another part of the house; a helicopter gunship strafed the neighborhood. A government plane with a loud-speaker circled their area, assuring them that allied forces would soon arrive and destroy the invaders. Minutes later Liberation Radio informed them that the entire city was still in Communist hands. Another government loud-speaker urged all VC to surrender; each soldier was promised two cans of dried food and a traditional Tet rice cake. Megaphones in the street continued their appeals

for all government and military personnel to report at once. A nervous aunt who lived with the Vinhs tried to cope by talking a lot, prompting occasional laughter. A cousin was killed by a mortar shell while praying at an altar outside. And still the fighting continued.

On February 16 the allies received encouraging news. An intercepted radio transmission revealed that the commander of NVA forces inside the Citadel had been killed. His successor had requested permission to withdraw. Although the request was denied, it clearly suggested that Communist morale was weakening, and the allied counterattack was immediately intensified. The ARVN command dispatched another battalion to the Citadel, while the U.S. 1st Air Cav pressed in from the west and south, severing the sole remaining enemy supply route on February 21.

The end itself proved anticlimactic. In the predawn hours of February 24, the 2d Battalion of the 3d Regiment, ARVN 1st Division, overran defenders along the south wall of the Citadel and secured the main flagpole at the Midday Gate of the Imperial Palace. At 5:00 A.M. they tore down the NLF flag and replaced it with the yellow-and-red banner of the Republic of Vietnam. The next day ARVN soldiers swept triumphantly into the Imperial Palace, only to find that the enemy had fled during the night.

The agony of Hue did not end with the expulsion of the

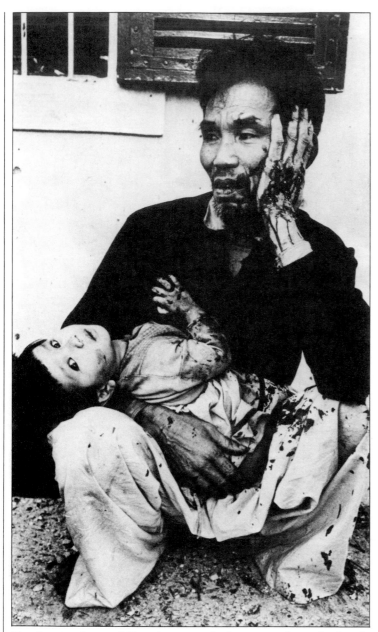

For the residents of Hue there was little escape from the battle that raged around them. This father and daughter were injured by American hand grenades thrown into a bunker in which they were hiding.

Communists from the Citadel. After the battle the citizens of Hue watched helplessly as South Vietnamese soldiers, and some American troops, ransacked their homes and took their few remaining possessions. Then came revelations concerning some of the city's authorities: the mayor of Hue who had known in advance about the attack but had done nothing except find himself a hiding place until he could safely reappear in time to steal emergency rice shipments; ARVN soldiers, even full colonels, who had taken off their uniforms and pretended to be refugees; the doctors of Hue who had withdrawn into a room at the university while their city slowly bled to death. And finally, there were the mass graves—the terrible last testament to the longest and bloodiest battle of the Tet offensive.

As in so many battles in the Vietnam War, both sides claimed victory at Hue. Ordered to seize and hold the city for seven days, Communist forces had defended the incipient revolutionary government in the old imperial capital for more than three weeks, earning a commendation from General Giap for their "unprecedented victory of scientific quality." "We won an overall success, militarily and politically," concluded one Communist after-action report; "Hue was the place where reactionary spirit had existed for over ten years. However, it took us only a short time to drain it to its roots."

Despite the duration, difficulty, and destructiveness of the battle, the allies pointed to the relative cost to each side as the principal index of their success. Whereas Communist losses were estimated at more than 5,000 killed and 89 captured, allied casualties were reported as 142 U.S. Marines killed in action and 857 seriously wounded; 74 American soldiers killed and 507 seriously wounded; 384 South Vietnamese troops killed and 1,830 wounded. The U.S. 1st Marines earned a presidential unit citation for having "soundly defeated a numerically superior enemy force . . . by their effective teamwork, aggressive fighting spirit and individual acts of heroism and daring," and Hue was added to the battle streamers of the Marine Corps.

Whoever may have won the battle, the sure losers were the city and citizens of Hue. It was officially estimated that more than 50 percent of the city had been damaged or destroyed, leaving 116,000 civilians homeless out of a population of approximately 140,000. Another 5,800 were listed as dead or missing. Eventually the corpses would all be buried, the wounds would be treated and begin to heal, and the houses and monuments would be patched or restored, but the city of Hue would never again be the same. Once synonymous with the grandeur of the Nguyen dynasty and the vitality of Vietnamese culture, in the future the city's name would evoke memories of destruction and death.

The battle of Hue proved a sobering experience for the allied command. Despite the strategic importance of the city, despite Westmoreland's prediction that the Communists would attempt to seize it, and despite forewarning of a possible multibattalion attack at Tet, American and South Vietnamese forces had been taken by surprise. Even more disturbing was the discovery made by the 3d Brigade of the U.S. 1st Cavalry Division after the battle had begun. Fighting their way eastward toward the Citadel, the brigade ran into unexpectedly intense resistance from elements of three NVA regiments: the 24th Regiment, 304th Division; the 29th Regiment, 325C Division; and the 99th Regiment, 324B Division. According to allied intelligence, they weren't supposed to be there. They were supposed to be at Khe Sanh.

A dead NVA soldier lies half buried in a shell crater inside the Citadel.

The Riddle of Khe Sanh

On the morning of January 31, as the Tet offensive raged across South Vietnam, 6,000 allied
troops at Khe Sanh combat base sat in their
bunkers and trenches, peered into the opaque
sheet of fog that surrounded their tiny mountain
plateau, and waited. For ten days they had been
living in a tense state of siege, encircled by two to
four divisions of seasoned NVA regulars, steadily
pounded by incoming rockets and shells, isolated
from all the world save for a narrow airstrip of
crushed rock and pierced steel. Their commander, U.S. Marine Corps Colonel David E.
Lownds, had told them that they were "going to
be remembered in American history books."
Their mission had been ordered by the highest
authority. They were to hold Khe Sanh, and hold
it "at all costs."

As early as 1964, when Khe Sanh was simply
the northernmost of a string of small Special
Forces camps along the western border of South
Vietnam, General Westmoreland had been

struck by the strategic location of the site. Tucked away in a remote corner of Quang Tri Province eighteen miles south of the DMZ and eight miles east of the Laotian border, Khe Sanh seemed to be ideally positioned for "blocking enemy infiltration" eastward along Route 9. It could also serve as a base for clandestine operations into Laos, as an airfield for reconnaissance flights over the Ho Chi Minh Trail, and potentially as a jumping-off point for a three-division drive into Laos to cut off the main enemy infiltration and supply routes. "Relinquish Khe Sanh," Westmoreland argued, "and you gave up all those advantages, while accepting the inevitability of carrying the fight into the populated coastal strip of Quang Tri Province and affording the enemy an avenue of advance along the coast leading south." Khe Sanh was the gateway to South Vietnam. Westmoreland was not about to give away the key.

When the North Vietnamese began to step up infiltration in mid-1966, Westmoreland promptly reinforced the Special Forces team, dispatched a navy Seabee unit to improve and extend the runway, and recommended that the marines deploy a battalion to Khe Sanh. The marines resisted, arguing that the base was too isolated to be adequately supported. "When you're at Khe Sanh, you're not really anywhere," asserted Brigadier General Lowell English, assistant commander of the 3d Marine Division. "You could lose it, and you really haven't lost a damn thing." But Westmoreland stood firm, and the marines obeyed. In early October 1966, the 1st Battalion, 3d Marines, arrived at Khe Sanh, and the Special Forces CIDG camp was relocated to Lang Vei, seven miles away.

In the spring of 1967, following a series of savage battles between the 3d Marines and the NVA 325C Division on the hills near Khe Sanh, the base was turned over to the 1st Battalion of the 26th Marines. By the end of the summer, Khe Sanh had become the "western anchor" of a chain of strong points designed to thwart an anticipated North Vietnamese invasion across the DMZ. In November, reconnaissance patrols from the 1/26 began to stumble upon fresh trails, while air force sightings of trucks moving down the Ho Chi Minh Trail jumped from a monthly average of 480 during the first nine months of the year to 1,116 in October; 3,823 in November; and 6,315 in December. The enemy was moving into northern I Corps in regiment—perhaps division—strength, and they seemed to be heading for Khe Sanh.

On December 13, Lieutenant General Robert E. Cushman, commander of the III Marine Amphibious Force, ordered the 3d Battalion, 26th Marines, to move to the combat base. Three weeks later, on January 2, 1968, six men in marine uniforms were spotted outside the western perimeter of the base. When they failed to respond to a challenge from a security guard, five of the six were gunned down. All were later identified as high-ranking officers of a North Vietnamese Army regiment. It was the hardest piece of evidence to date of the enemy's intentions. Only the highest priority target would require the personal reconnaissance of key commanders. The news flashed up the chain of command, straight to the headquarters of COMUSMACV.

General Westmoreland was pleased. Frustrated by years of chasing an elusive enemy back and forth across South Vietnam, frustrated further by the constraints that Washington had imposed upon his military operations, he had long yearned for a set-piece battle in which the Communists would be forced to stand and fight. Now he didn't need to go after the enemy; the enemy was coming to him. A major battle in the barren, unpopulated reaches of northern I Corps afforded an opportunity to score a victory of unprecedented proportions—the crowning achievement of Westmoreland's years of service as COMUSMACV.

During the first week of January 1968, Westmoreland began to put his plan for Khe Sanh into operation. Code-named Niagara "to evoke an image of cascading bombs and shells," the operation was conceived in two parts: Niagara I, a comprehensive intelligence effort, would find the enemy; Niagara II, the most concentrated application of aerial firepower in the history of warfare, would destroy him. Circling the skies above Khe Sanh for thirty miles in every direction, aircraft took high-resolution photographs, scanned the ground with radar for evidence of enemy movement, and recorded the findings of an array of complex, highly classified gadgets designed to locate enemy positions and movements: acoustic sensors that picked up voices; seismic sensors that registered vibrations from marching soldiers, trucks, and armored vehicles; infrared heat sensors that could identify cooking fires; and electrochemical analyzers that could detect high concentrations of human urine. Technicians in an airborne electronic laboratory read, collated, and interpreted the data and passed it to MACV headquarters in Saigon.

For Niagara II, Westmoreland assembled an awesome armada of more than 2,000 strategic and tactical aircraft, from giant B-52 Stratofortresses down to prop-driven South Vietnamese A-1 Skyraiders, in addition to some 3,000 helicopters. To orchestrate the round-the-clock bombardment that he envisioned, Westmoreland installed—over the objections of the marines—a "single manager for air," based at Tan Son Nhut and invested with final authority over all U.S. air power throughout South Vietnam. He also ordered into the air a "Sky Spot" airborne computer control center to coordinate the altitudes and speeds of as many as 800 aircraft at one time. Niagara was to be a controlled deluge of firepower, one that the commander could turn on and off at will.

In the meantime the intelligence analysts refined their

Digging deeper. By early March the main base had become a warren of trenches and sandbagged fortifications like these surrounding the headquarters command post.

estimates of the enemy order of battle. The NVA 325C Division was said to be northwest of the base; the 304th, an elite home-guard division from Hanoi, to the southwest. In addition, one regiment of the NVA 324th Division had been located inside the DMZ ten to fifteen miles north of Khe Sanh, while the NVA 320th Division was believed to be north of the Rockpile within easy reinforcing distance of the other enemy units. There seemed to be little doubt about the enemy's intentions. The question was not whether the enemy would strike, but when.

As the pressure mounted, the marines fortified their positions. They dug trenches, built bunkers, and reinforced the perimeter with claymore mines, triple coils of barbed wire, German razor tape, and trip flares. Similar preparations were made on the tactically crucial hills surrounding the base, where Colonel Lownds had positioned several detachments of the 3/26: Company I, with about 200 men, entrenched itself atop Hill 881 South; Company K, reinforced to a strength of about 300 marines, on Hill 861; and the 2d Platoon, Company A, on Hill 950, the site of a radio relay station. Additional hill deployments were ordered following the arrival of the 2/26 Marines on January 16, a move that brought the regiment's three battalions together

for the first time since Iwo Jima. To support the infantrymen and supplement the firepower of Niagara, the base had eighteen 105MM and six 155MM howitzers, six 4.2MM mortars, six tanks, and ninety-two single- or Ontos-mounted 106MM recoilless rifles, in addition to the behemoth 175MM guns at the Rockpile and Camp Carroll seventeen miles to the east. The marines were ready.

The siege begins

On the morning of January 20, Company I set out from its base camp on Hill 881 South to investigate the site of an ambush the day before. Moving slowly and cautiously through a thick blanket of fog, they encountered no resistance until they began to climb the ridge line of Hill 881 North. By then it was late in the morning. The fog had lifted, and the marines were exposed. Suddenly met by a deafening hail of automatic weapons fire and rocket-propelled grenades that cut down twenty men in thirty seconds, they threw themselves to the ground, returned fire, and called for additional fire support. Within minutes ninety-five pound shells from 155s on the base were pulverizing enemy positions. By afternoon the marines had regained the initiative and were preparing to assault the hilltop when, suddenly, the battle was called off. Colonel Lownds had received new intelligence that made it imperative for all units to be at their assigned posts. Company I was ordered to pull back immediately to Hill 881 South.

The source of the colonel's new information was a North Vietnamese soldier who had materialized at the eastern end of the airstrip at 2:00 P.M., holding a white flag in one hand and an AK47 in the other. Identifying himself as First Lieutenant La Than Tonc, the defector told his marine interrogators that regiments of the NVA 325C and 304th Divisions were preparing to overrun Khe Sanh. He then described the battle plans of both divisions, as well as other units that had infiltrated across the DMZ. According to Tonc, Khe Sanh was just the beginning. The North Vietnamese were preparing to sweep across the two northern provinces and seize the city of Hue. The first attacks would come that very night. At 12:30 A.M., Hill 881 South, Hill 861, and the base itself would be hit.

"He willingly gave a wealth of information to his interrogators with more detail than would be expected of an officer in his position," the marines would later note. But Tonc's claims accorded closely with other allied intelligence, and General Rathvon McCall Tompkins decided "that if we accepted it as valid we had nothing to lose, and stood to gain a great deal." Tompkins passed the information along to General Cushman, Cushman contacted Westmoreland, and that night Westmoreland cabled Washington with the new information: "The enemy will soon seek victories essential to achieving prestige and bargaining power."

At precisely 12:30 A.M., January 21—right on schedule—a heavy barrage of mortar rounds, rockets, and rocket-propelled grenades slammed into the marine outpost atop Hill 861. A half-hour later 300 NVA soldiers, led by an elite unit of combat engineers, charged through sustained artillery and machine-gun fire and breached the defensive wire with satchel charges, bangalore torpedoes, and bamboo ladders. But the marines of Company K, 3/26, had been waiting for them. Before the enemy could fully exploit their initial success, the marines counterattacked down the trench lines and overran the attackers in brutal hand-to-hand fighting. By 5:15 A.M. Hill 861 was once again secure.

The predicted attack on Hill 881 South never materialized. But fifteen minutes after the battle for 861 ended, hundreds of 82MM mortar rounds, artillery shells, and 122MM rockets slammed into the combat base, sending the marines scrambling into their bunkers and trenches. One of the first incoming rockets hit the main ammunition dump at the eastern end of the runway, and 1,500 tons of ordnance burst into a mammoth, blinding explosion. Helicopters tumbled across the base, buildings and tents collapsed, fuel roared into flames, and thousands of burning rifle, mortar, and artillery rounds rained down inside the perimeter. Some of the shells detonated upon impact; others "cooked off" and exploded later in the day. Another enemy round hit a cache of tear gas, releasing thick clouds of choking vapor that soon enveloped the entire base. The landing lights along the airstrip were knocked out, and the operable length of the runway itself was reduced from 3,900 to 2,000 feet.

As the day dawned, fires still burned at the base. A few supply planes landed on the battered airstrip, bringing some 24 tons of fresh supplies. But Colonel Lownds had estimated that it would require a minimum of 160 tons of supplies per day to sustain the combat base, and now he had just lost more than 90 percent of his ammunition. He also needed more men. The following day, January 22, the 1st Battalion, 9th Marines—veterans of the siege of Con Thien and nicknamed "The Ghost Battalion"—arrived at Khe Sanh. Four days later they were joined by the ARVN 37th Ranger Battalion. Lownds now had some 6,000 troops to defend Khe Sanh against an estimated enemy force of 20,000 to 40,000 "hard-hat" NVA regulars.

Supplying the combat base posed critical problems. The principal overland road into the base, Route 9, had been cut off by the enemy in August 1967, and all ammunition and provisions had to be airlifted. Now the northeast monsoon was rapidly closing in, the airstrip was heavily damaged, and the North Vietnamese were littering the skies above Khe Sanh with antiaircraft fire. General Westmoreland and his staff nevertheless remained confident that they could get supplies in, that with sheer firepower they could crush even a major assault, that they could hold Khe Sanh until the weather cleared. On January 22, after personally selecting the targets for his B–52s, Westmoreland ordered the onrush of Niagara II.

The decision to hold

Not everyone shared Westmoreland's belief that Khe Sanh could, or even should, be successfully defended. Since mid-December, when national security adviser Walt Rostow reported that the Communists "intend to reenact another Dien Bien Phu," President Johnson had closely monitored the situation, increasingly preoccupied by the possibility of a major military setback. Soon after the siege began he started making nightly visits to the White House Situation Room. Defending Khe Sanh was a gamble, and the president wasn't sure he liked the odds.

Every day the president pored over his maps, read the latest cables from the war zone, and conferred with his advisers on the Khe Sanh situation. Every day he questioned the chairman of the Joint Chiefs about the wisdom of the decision to hold Khe Sanh, and every day General Wheeler echoed Westmoreland's confidence. Then he asked each member of the JCS to endorse the decision personally, an unprecedented request for a written guarantee from the nation's highest-ranking military officers. On January 29 the Joint Chiefs complied.

The president, however, still had serious misgivings. So did his chief military adviser, retired General Maxwell D. Taylor, former ambassador to South Vietnam and General Wheeler's predecessor as chairman of the JCS. Noting the similarities between Khe Sanh and Dien Bien Phu, emphasizing the isolation of the base and the poor weather conditions, and pointing out that any defensive position can be taken if the enemy is willing to pay the price, Taylor suggested that withdrawal ought to be considered.

While Lyndon Johnson pondered that advice, the enemy struck—not at Khe Sanh, but almost everywhere else in South Vietnam. With the shock of the Tet offensive the debate over whether or not to hold Khe Sanh came to an abrupt halt. "It was apparent," General Taylor later recalled, "that the die was cast and we would have to fight it out on this line . . . we ourselves had done a great deal to build up the importance of Khe Sanh in the minds of the public, and it was going to be difficult to explain to our own people or anyone else that Khe Sanh was a minor outpost and the outcome of the battle unimportant." The president now felt that he had little choice but to accept

Westmoreland's gamble. Khe Sanh could not fall. There could be no American Dien Bien Phu.

During the first days of February, discussion in the White House turned to alternative courses of action that might relieve the pressure of the beleaguered combat base. A diversionary amphibious landing along the coast of North Vietnam was considered, as was the possibility of a drive westward through the DMZ, but it was ultimately decided that too much time would be required for either operation to exert any effect on the Khe Sanh battlefield. These were not the only options under consideration. On February 1 General Wheeler sent a top-secret cable to General Westmoreland raising the question of "whether tactical nuclear weapons should be used if the situation in Khe Sanh should become that desperate." Westmoreland promptly replied that "the use of tactical nuclear weapons should not be required in the present situation." But, he added, should the situation change dramatically, "I visualize that either tactical nuclear weapons or chemical agents would be active candidates for employment."

By his own admission, Westmoreland did not fully appreciate the atmosphere of crisis and gloom that gripped Washington in the wake of the Tet offensive. Unlike his

North Vietnamese soldiers charge up a shell-scarred hillside northwest of Khe Sanh. Although rarely visible to allied troops, the NVA kept alive the threat of a full-scale assault with periodic attacks against outlying American positions.

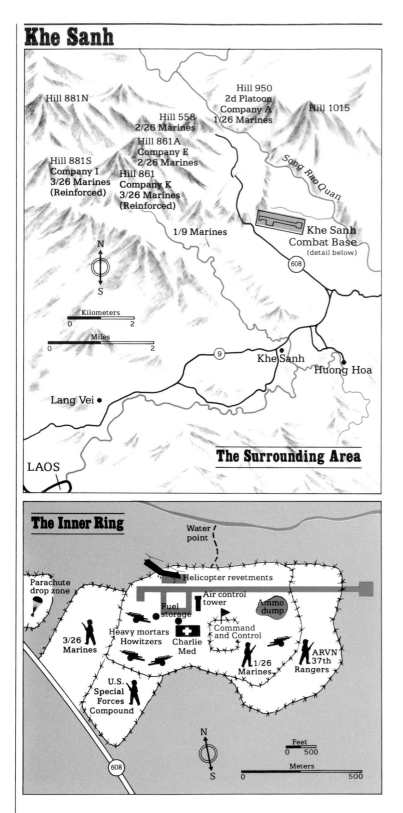

Khe Sanh

Hill 881N

Hill 950
2d Platoon
Company A
1/26 Marines

Hill 1015

Hill 558
2/26 Marines

Hill 861A
Company E
2/26 Marines

Hill 881S
Company I
3/26 Marines
(Reinforced)

Hill 861
Company K
3/26 Marines
(Reinforced)

Song Rao Quan

1/9 Marines

Khe Sanh
Combat Base
(detail below)

608

Kilometers
0   2

Miles
0   2

9

Khe Sanh

Huong Hoa

Lang Vei •

LAOS

The Surrounding Area

The Inner Ring

Water point

Parachute drop zone

Helicopter revetments

Air control tower

Fuel storage

Ammo dump

3/26 Marines

Heavy mortars
Howitzers

Charlie Med

Command and Control

1/26 Marines

ARVN 37th Rangers

U.S. Special Forces Compound

608

Feet
0   500

Meters
0   500

moreland was confident it would stay that way. The French had had few aircraft and only fair artillery support; American firepower differed "by orders of magnitude over that at Dien Bien Phu."

Waitin' and diggin'

Toward the end of January allied intelligence detected heavy and sophisticated radio traffic emanating from a site inside Laos. Believing that he had pinpointed "the North Vietnamese headquarters controlling forces around Khe Sanh, if not the entire northern region," suspecting further that General Giap himself might be there to direct the operation personally, Westmoreland ordered the single largest "Arc Light" strike of the war. On January 30, thirty-six B-52s crossed the Laotian border and dropped 1,000 tons of bombs on the specified coordinates. Later in the day, nine more B-52s struck the same site. The radio signals stopped.

Whether the bombings of January 30 forestalled a major attack on the combat base may never be known. But when the Tet offensive erupted the day after the strike, Khe Sanh was quiet. According to several captured NVA officers, it was these bombings that triggered the premature attacks on the cities of I Corps and II Corps. For the marines stationed at Khe Sanh, it mattered little. They had been expecting a full-scale enemy assault every day since January 21, and every day they had had to prepare themselves for that possibility. Every day they endured the shocks of 50, 200, or 500 North Vietnamese shells, and every day they reinforced their positions—digging their trenches a foot deeper, laying down another roll of barbed wire, adding another sandbag to each bunker. "Just waitin' and diggin'," one marine lamented. "That's all we're doing. Just waitin' and diggin'."

Waiting and digging and watching took a toll on the marines, many of whom developed a blank look in their eyes known as "the 1,000 yard stare." At night, to contend with the strain, they talked and sang, played cards and listened to music, smoked pot and shot rats for target practice. They stuck lucky playing cards in their helmet bands and wrote slogans on their helmet covers and flak jackets: "GOD WALKS WITH ME," "VC GO HOME," the name of a girl friend, or even "WHY ME?" They marked their calendars and established daily routines. On Hill 881 South the day began with a ceremonial flag raising, accompanied by a cacophonous bugle rendition of "To the Colors," and then, in the distance, the sound of the first incoming shells of the day. The marines of I Company knew that they had precisely twenty-one seconds before the rounds hit, but they stayed at attention until the flag had fully ascended the radio antenna that served as its pole. Then they scattered into their trenches and foxholes as the shells pounded their position. Minutes later another banner went up, a pair of red panties called "Maggie's Draw-

commander in chief, he was not haunted by the specter of Dien Bien Phu. The analogy between the two sieges was perhaps inevitable, but in the general's view, it was false. Both bases were isolated, but Dien Bien Phu had been in a valley while Khe Sanh rested upon a plateau. The French had held no high ground, while the U.S. Marines commanded most of the important hills surrounding their base. The French airstrip had been closed on the first day of the siege; at Khe Sanh the runway was open and West-ers," the traditional sign of a miss on the training camp firing range.

If the defenders of Khe Sanh taunted their adversary, they also respected him. Most of the time he was invisible to the marines, concealed in the thick vegetation and impenetrable gray mists beyond the base perimeter. Occasionally, however, NVA troops could be seen at night through "Starlight" scopes, moving furtively across the terrain or digging fresh trench lines. Then, during the day, the marines watched the American bombers, artillery, and helicopter gunships pummel the enemy positions and wondered how the NVA could take it.

One particularly brave NVA soldier even became the camp pet. Dug into a spider hole some 180 meters from the perimeter, he raked the marines daily with .50-caliber machine-gun fire, aiming at anything that moved. The marines retaliated with their own marksmen, mortars, and thousands of beehive rounds from 106MM recoilless rifles, but the sniper kept popping up and firing back. Eventually a napalm strike was called in, inundating the position in liquid red-orange fire that burned for ten minutes. As the flames died out, the sniper again popped up and fired off a single round. The marines cheered. They nicknamed him "Luke the Gook," and after that they hoped that nothing would happen to him.

The marines resented their defensive posture. It was contrary to their training, contrary to their style, contrary to the heritage of the corps. For the record, in fact, the marine command refused to concede that Khe Sanh combat base was under siege, pointing out that troops continued to patrol beyond the perimeter. The patrols, however, were under orders to proceed no farther than 500 meters. Most of the time the marines stayed inside the wire, waiting for the enemy to strike.

Lang Vei

On February 2, an enemy rocket from Hill 881 North hit the U.S. Army Signal Corps bunker at the main base, instantly killing four soldiers and temporarily severing all contact with the outside world. Tension mounted, then subsided; there was no follow-up attack.

Three days later the NVA mounted a night assault on Hill 861 Alpha and seized a portion of the hilltop before being halted by a thunderous artillery and mortar barrage. At the base and on nearby hills marines stared into the night, searching the shadows for evidence of enemy troops massing at the wire. Nothing happened.

During the night of February 7, the enemy struck again. At half-past midnight Sergeant Nikolas Fragos detected movement at the wire of Lang Vei Special Forces camp. Perched atop an observation tower above the TOC, he peered into the flickering light of the flare that had been set off by the enemy advance and immediately radioed the command bunker: "We have tanks in our wire!" Cap-

tain Frank C. Willoughby, the camp commander, was incredulous. There had been recent reports that the enemy was moving armored vehicles into the area, but no one knew that the North Vietnamese had tanks. He ran up the steps to see for himself. Two Soviet-made PT76 tanks slowly clanked forward, scanning the compound with mounted searchlights, flattening bunkers, blasting away. Behind them came two NVA platoons armed with AK47s and flame throwers. Soon a third tank appeared, then two more.

Inside his underground command post, Captain Willoughby contacted Khe Sanh. He wanted a flareship, artillery support, air strikes—anything that was available and fast. Fifteen minutes later the first artillery shells from Khe Sanh smashed just outside the camp perimeter; ten minutes after that the fighter-bombers arrived. By then, however, the situation at Lang Vei had already become desperate. The defenders had immobilized the first three tanks, but the other two now rumbled freely inside the camp, destroying bunkers and gun emplacements at pointblank range. Another two tanks assaulted the base from the north, while four more penetrated the wire to the west. Two of the tanks began firing at the command post from a range of about ten meters, then one of them rolled onto the roof. Sappers threw grenades and satchel charges down the vents and stairwells. Willoughby ordered all lights extinguished and called in artillery near his own position. He asked the marines to put into operation a contingency plan to relieve Lang Vei. Fearing ambush if they tried to reach the camp by land, unwilling to order a heliborne assault in the dark against enemy tanks, the marines refused. The defenders of Lang Vei would have to hold out until morning.

The fighting continued for several hours, but ultimately the camp was overwhelmed. A few survivors fought their way out during the night, crept through NVA lines, and made it to Khe Sanh by morning. Others, including Willoughby, were evacuated by helicopter the following day. Of the 500 troops at Lang Vei, most of them CIDG irregulars, 200 were dead or missing and 75 wounded. Of the 24 Americans there, 10 had been killed. The camp itself had been reduced to a bleak, smoldering shell.

Officially, the marine command denied that there was any direct connection between the assault on the Special Forces camp and the battle for Khe Sanh. But, as journalist Michael Herr observed, "After Lang Vei how could you look out of your perimeter at night without hearing the treads coming?" The fall of the nearby outpost stirred the most deep-seated fear of the men at Khe Sanh: If the enemy wanted to take Khe Sanh they would come, and come, and keep on coming until the combat base became as empty and dark as Lang Vei.

Yet after Lang Vei, the NVA ground probes abated, and the battle for Khe Sanh reverted to "a contest of supporting arms." Every day North Vietnamese shells and rockets hammered the base; and every day the Americans countered with another Niagara torrent.

The most formidable threat to the base came from big 130MM and 152MM guns high atop Co Roc Mountain in Laos. Concealed beneath camouflaged netting or mounted on tracks inside caves, firing erratically so that muzzle flashes would not betray their precise location, and vulnerable only to air strikes because of their distance from the base, the batteries escaped destruction throughout the siege. Other enemy positions proved equally difficult to pinpoint. Although a computerized Fire Support Control Center made it possible to direct artillery fire on any particular spot with forty seconds' notice, the terrain, the fog, and the movement of enemy troops compelled the Americans to resort to "area fire." After selecting a particular target "box"—500 meters square for a "micro-Arc

Light," a rectangle four times that size for a "mini-Arc Light"—fire coordinators at the base inundated the area with high-explosive shells.

Air strikes intensified the manmade firestorm. Tactical aircraft—F-4 Phantoms, F-105 Thunderchiefs, A-4 Skyhawks, and A-6A Intruders—flew approximately 300 sorties per day over Khe Sanh, dropping a total of 35,000 tons of bombs on suspected enemy positions. Even more devastating was the firepower of the B-52s. Flying from U.S. air bases in Guam, Thailand, and Okinawa, two cells of B-52s emptied their payloads every three hours, twenty-four hours a day. The bombs fell in numbers that were high even by World War II standards, with total estimates ranging from 59,000 to 96,000 tons. The aircraft flew so high over the arc of the earth that the pilots never saw

Lang Vei

On the night of February 6, 1968, Camp Lang Vei, eight kilometers west of Khe Sanh, was manned by 24 U.S. Special Forces troops, a South Vietnamese Special Forces group, and approximately 500 montagnard CIDG troops. In the early morning hours of February 7, the NVA attacked the base with a force of eleven Soviet-made PT76 tanks and approximately 400 infantry troops with artillery support.

Among the American defenders at Lang Vei was First Lieutenant Paul R. Longgrear, Mobile Strike Force company commander, who provided this record of the radio transmissions from the besieged outpost that night. (See glossary, below,

Lang Vei

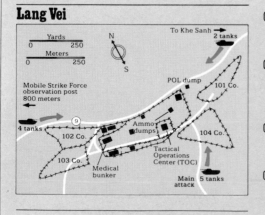

for explanation of numerical designations and terms.)

February 6

2230 *Outposts report sporadic mortar and artillery fire incoming.*

2310 *Several stations communications check—no activity.*

February 7

0030 *MSFOP to transmission station 06: "I think I have VC below me."*

0035 *Sergeant Nikolas Fragos in TOC observation tower to 06: "They've got tanks!"*

0039 *Fragos to 06: "I don't know how many but they have tanks out there!"*
06: "Where in the hell are they?"

0043 *Fragos to 06: "We have two tanks in our wire!"*

0047 *Unknown station: "We've got five tanks on line right at our wire!"*

0054 *Same unknown station: "We've got tanks inside our wire—I said inside our wire!"*

0056– *Many transmissions from all sta-*
0100 *tions of noise, small arms fire, and track vehicles.*

0101 *09 to 06: "There's one tank on the hill with us and a total of seven tanks in all."*

0102 *06 to FAC: "Request air strike or anything else you can give us at coordinates ... [north and west of camp]."*

0103 *06 to FAC: "We need Spooky to work the south edge of the perimeter."*

0109 *06 to marine artillery: "We have tanks coming up the road. Request fire number five. Keep it working*

up and down the road [to the north of the camp]."

0120 *Bomber to FAC: "Got a B-57 with funny bombs."*

0124 *FAC to 06: "Where do you want the bombs?"*
06 to FAC: "All over the south side of the hill and along the road."
FAC to 06: "Where those flares are?"
06 to FAC: "Yes."
FAC to 06: "Any friendlies?"
06 to FAC: "No."

0128 *28B to 06: "Troops are moving up on this position from two directions."*

0130 *09: "Uh-oh, the POL dump just went up!"*

0132 *28B to 06: "I think the enemy is in our old bunkers. Get some HE in there."*

0133 *06 to marine artillery: "Fire ... [garbled]."*

0134 *Marine artillery to 06: "What kind of fuse?"*
06 to marine artillery: "Oh hell! Mixed quick and delay, I guess."

0136 *Many stations transmit, at times cutting each other out.*
FAC to 06: "We've got two F-100s with 750-pounders on standby."
32B: "Christ, a bomb just fell on our position!"
40: "There are two tanks on the main road by the mess hall on the road to Khe Sanh."
Unknown station: "Can you get the LAW over here?"
Unknown station: "We don't have any more LAWs left."

their targets, and no one on the ground ever saw the B–52s. "All you saw," one marine recalled, "was the air being ripped apart and the ground tremoring underneath you—and you bouncing in the air." Yet they could strike with extraordinary precision. Toward the end of February, as the NVA began to extend their trench lines, the B–52 strikes edged ever closer to the perimeter. "One hiccup," said one air force commander, "and we would have decimated the base."

Equally vital to the survival of the base, and far more dangerous, were the missions flown by the pilots of the supply aircraft. Hampered by poor weather, exposed to "flak alley" as they approached the airstrip from the east, and even more vulnerable when they landed, the big C–130 cargo planes and C–123 "Providers" swept in and out of Khe Sanh as quickly as possible. Some pilots could land, unload, and be off again in less than three minutes. Others skimmed along a few feet above the runway while parachutes yanked large cargo pallets and sent them skidding into the base. All told, 455 planes managed to land at the base between January 21 and April 8. The North Vietnamese destroyed only 4.

The cargo planes, however, were able to supply the marines with only 35 percent of their needs. Most supplies and ammunition had to be parachuted in or, when "zero–zero" (zero visibility–zero ceiling) weather set in, brought by helicopter. During February helicopters ferried some 465 tons of supplies to the main base.

The terror of the airstrip, the persistent enemy shelling, the ebb and flow of anxiety and adrenalin, all made life at

---

0145 *FAC to 06:* "Where do you want that fire?"
06 to FAC: "All over the area."

0150 *FAC to marine artillery:* "Fire the preplanned fires right on his position."

0151 *FAC to bomber:* "I want you to put those hard bombs to the east of the camp entrance right on the road. Jacksonville, 06 wants you to keep those flares coming!"

0157 *FAC to 09:* "I've got one more bomb. Where do you want it?"

0200 *06 to 09:* "I think we got a tank down by the dispensary. There is another by supply. We didn't get it. There's one by supply."

0208 *FAC to 09:* "I only have soft bombs. They spread out. Do you want them on the eastern end?"

0209 *FAC to Spooky:* "Put your fire on the eastern end of the perimeter."
09 to FAC: "We have a very active tank on each end of the perimeter."

0210 *09 to FAC:* "Tanks and a lot of infantry are coming into the camp!"

0215 *09 to FAC:* "They are coming in from each end of the camp. We will have to do something soon!"

0216 *Marine artillery to FAC:* "Can we help?"
FAC to 09: "Can Jacksonville help?"
09 to FAC: "Yes! Flares! Flares! Flares!"

0218 *09 to FAC:* "There are more tanks coming! We've got to do something!"

0220 *FAC to 09:* "We've got bombs. Do you want them on the eastern end of your position?"

0221 *09 to 06:* "Those tanks are tearing up 104 Company!"

0222 *FAC to 09:* "Fighters are coming down to take a look at it now."

0223 *09 to 06:* "Tanks coming our way!"

0225 *FAC to second FAC:* "I'm out of rockets. Can you mark the trail at the east entrance of the camp?"
Second FAC to first FAC: "Let me get oriented and I think I can get it."

0227 *09 to FAC:* "There is a tank coming up on the TOC!"

0230 *09 to 06 to FAC:* "There is a tank right on top of the TOC and it's giving us fits! We knocked one out."

0230– *FAC attempts to contact 06 and 09.*
0238

0238 *FAC to 09:* "Do you want us to put something on that tank?"
09 to FAC: "No!"

0239– *FAC cannot contact any element at Lang Vei.*
0245

0245 *FAC to 09:* "Where do you want the bombs?"
09 to FAC: "Put the bombs just south of the green star cluster to get the tank. We're moving off the hill."

This was the last transmission monitored from any station in Camp Lang Vei.

TRANSMITTING STATIONS
06: Captain Frank C. Willoughby, in the TOC
09: Sergeant First Class Michael W. Craig
28B: Specialist 5 William G. McMurray and staff Sergeant Dennis L. Thompson
32B: Sergeant Richard H. Allen

40: Sergeant First Class Earl F. Burke
FAC: forward air controller (airborne)
Marine Artillery/"Jacksonville": artillery headquartered at Khe Sanh
MSFOP: Mobile Strike Force observation post, manned by Sergeant First Class Kenneth Hanna and Sergeant First Class Charles W. Lindewald

TERMS
FFE: "fire for effect"—aim and fire artillery at a directed target.
funny bombs/soft bombs: fragmenting explosives, sometimes with variable time fuses, also known as cluster bomb units (CBUs).
hard bombs: conventional nonfragmenting explosives.
HE: high explosive artillery.
"number five" & "number eight": artillery targets preplanned in case of attack.
POL: petroleum, oil, and lubricants.
shifting fires: moving artillery target.
Spooky: call sign of AC–47 gunship with Gatling guns and illumination flares.

Lieutenant Longgrear is helped to an evacuation helicopter at Khe Sanh. He was one of fourteen American survivors of the North Vietnamese attack on Lang Vei.

Khe Sanh something to be endured. Overcrowding added to the burden. The entire area of the main base was less than two miles long and a mile wide, and by early February the place was a mess. Buildings lay in pieces. Debris littered the perimeter. Everywhere there were piles of empty shell casings, C-ration cans, splinters of wood, and chunks of shrapnel. Bunkers reeked of mold and decay, sweat, and urine. Rats skittered around, and sometimes on, sleeping marines. Khe Sanh, one reporter observed, looked "like a shanty slum on the outskirts of Manila."

At the end of February a marine patrol discovered a network of enemy trench lines, some more than a mile long, leading toward the combat base. Fearing that the Communists might attempt to tunnel under Khe Sanh as they had at Dien Bien Phu, and dynamite the marines from below, General Westmoreland declared an "immediate emergency," dispatched a seismographic team to the base, and called in the B-52s. But the enemy kept on digging, adding as much as 90 meters a night, until some of the trenches extended to within 320 meters of the base perimeter. Others began to branch out into Ts, usually the final stage of preparation before assault ramps were put in place. March 13, the anniversary of the first attacks on Dien Bien Phu, was only two weeks away. It was beginning to look as if history would repeat itself.

The marines once again steeled themselves for a full-scale NVA assault. But March 13 passed quietly. So did the weeks that followed. The shelling continued, but patrols were finding that some of the enemy trenches had been abandoned weeks before. The threat had suddenly dissolved. The defenders were alone.

Pegasus

Why the North Vietnamese decided to withdraw from Khe Sanh remains a matter of conjecture. According to one interpretation, by early March it had become clear to the Communist high command that they could never overrun the base and that any further sacrifice of men and materiel was pointless. Other analysts contend that the abandonment of Khe Sanh was directly related to the collapse of Communist efforts to hold Hue and gain control of Quang Tri and Thua Thien provinces. Still another possibility is that the Communists never intended to overrun Khe Sanh and withdrew because they had achieved their objective: to divert allied forces away from the cities.

Whatever the reason, as the NVA moved out and the weather began to clear, General Westmoreland decided that the time had come to relieve Khe Sanh. Since the marine command had insisted all along that the base was not

A B-52 Stratofortress headed for Khe Sanh on an Operation Niagara run takes off from Guam. Flying in cells of three and striking every ninety minutes on average, the bombers made the 5,500-mile round trip in twelve hours.

Arc Light strike. Each B-52 carried up to 54,000 pounds of bombs, with a combined force so devastating that the concussion could kill even those hiding in deep caves and underground shelters.

besieged, he was careful to point out that the operation involved "not relief in the sense of rescue . . . but relief in the sense of reopening ground contact and eliminating the enemy with mobile operations." The army and the marines would coordinate offensive operations and eventually link up outside the base.

The U.S. Army 1st Cavalry Division (Airmobile) spearheaded the operation, code-named Pegasus, with an air assault east of Khe Sanh on the morning of April 1. Charged with the task of reopening Highway 9 and eliminating any enemy troops still lingering in the area, the 1st Air Cav met only token resistance. They did, however, discover traces of the enemy, including caches of unopened enemy supply crates and neat rows of abandoned AK47s, as well as ample evidence of the destructiveness of American firepower. "The place was absolutely denuded," General Tompkins later remarked, "The trees were gone . . . everything was gone. Pockmarked and ruined and burnt . . . like the surface of the moon." They also found hundreds of enemy corpses, some buried in shallow graves, others lying where they had fallen.

On April 11, four days before Pegasus came to an end, General Westmoreland flew to Washington to confer with the president. Standing on the White House lawn, he announced that Route 9 was once again open; the battle

of Khe Sanh was over. In his official report, the general lavished praise on every branch of the American military for its role in the victory: the marines for their "heroic defense"; the combat engineers for their "herculean" efforts in reopening the main road to the base; and the supply units for having performed "the premier logistical feat of the war." The highest approbation, however, was bestowed upon those who had contributed to "one of the heaviest and most concentrated displays of firepower in the history of warfare." Army and marine artillery units had fired 158,891 rounds during the siege, establishing a ratio of more than 10 outgoing rounds to every 1 incoming. The air force had flown 9,691 bombing sorties over Khe Sanh, the marines 7,078, and the navy 5,337. Yet the "key to success, the big gun, the heavyweight of firepower," was the B-52 strikes. As Westmoreland later told B-52 pilots and crews stationed on Guam: "Without question, the amount of firepower put on that piece of real estate exceeded anything that had ever been seen before in history by any foe, and the enemy was hurt, his back was broken, by airpower . . . basically the fire of the B-52s."

Two months later, on June 17, the marines at Khe Sanh began to dismantle their base, blowing up bunkers, filling in trench lines, trucking supplies and ammunition down Route 9. The news provoked immediate criticism in the

Part of the 30,000-man task force committed to Operation Pegasus, a U.S. tank points the way west down Route 9 toward Khe Sanh.

In a classic display of airmobility tactics, fleets of helicopters swept westward carrying men and supplies to relieve the marines at Khe Sanh in the first two weeks of April. Here a CH–54 Tarhe helicopter delivers ammunition to a U.S. Army artillery unit.

Operation Pegasus

Mission accomplished. Soldiers of the 2d Battalion, 7th Cavalry, 1st Air Cav, relax after reaching their destination on April 8.

U.S. press. Journalists wanted to know why the "western anchor" of allied defenses in I Corps, the gateway to the main NVA infiltration route into South Vietnam, the major Communist objective of the Tet campaign, had suddenly become so dispensable. They were told that the enemy had changed his tactics and reduced his forces; that the NVA had carved out new infiltration routes; that the allies now had enough troops to carry out mobile operations; that a fixed base was no longer necessary. "We don't want any more Khe Sanhs," said one marine junior officer. "To defeat an enemy, you've got to keep moving. We're through sitting in one place and taking our lumps."

Questions of strategy

The relief and subsequent abandonment of Khe Sanh left many crucial questions unanswered: questions about the relationship between the siege of the remote marine outpost and the countrywide attacks on the cities; questions about Hanoi's short- and long-range motives in launching the Tet offensive; questions of strategy.

From the outset General Westmoreland had maintained that the Communists would mount their "main effort" in northern I Corps. The Tet attacks represented a "diversionary effort," a "desperate gamble" designed to lure allied troops from I Corps, pave the way for a takeover of Quang Tri and Thua Thien provinces, and possibly, precipitate a negotiated settlement. The key to that campaign, according to Westmoreland, was the battle of Khe Sanh. Had the North Vietnamese succeeded in overrunning the combat base, not only would they have inflicted a major defeat upon the Americans, but they would also have freed three full NVA divisions to reinforce units operating in the populated coastal lowlands, including Hue. By holding their ground, the Americans had instead inflicted "one of the most damaging, one-sided defeats among many that the North Vietnamese incurred."

Fifteen years later, military analysts and historians still could not agree about the accuracy of Westmoreland's assessment. On the one hand, the overall pattern of Communist operations in northern I Corps—the heavy build-up of NVA forces along the Laotian border and inside the DMZ, the initiation of the siege of Khe Sanh, the simultaneous Tet attacks on allied communication and supply lines, widespread village takeovers and the establishment of a "revolutionary" government in Hue, the shift of three NVA regiments from Khe Sanh to Hue in mid-February—suggests a concerted, coordinated effort to gain control of Quang Tri and Thua Thien provinces. It is also clear that Westmoreland's reinforcement of allied defenses in the north, particularly the timely deployment of the 1st Air Cavalry Division to Quang Tri just before Tet, severely disrupted Communist plans. On the other hand, there is reason to believe that Westmoreland misjudged the role of Khe Sanh in the enemy's tactical planning. According to many analysts, including the authors of the MACV Command History for 1968, the siege of Khe Sanh was a "feint" designed to divert U.S. military resources and attention away from the populated regions before Tet. Others liken the siege to an "option play." The NVA, they argue, was prepared to overrun the base if the opportunity arose but was content to hold its positions as long as MACV maintained an investment in the defense of Khe Sanh.

A variety of evidence tends to support these "diversion" theories. To begin with, the North Vietnamese initiated the siege ten days prior to the onset of the Tet offensive. If Khe

Sanh were really a primary target, the late Brigadier General S. L. A. Marshall observed, it was unlike the Communists to "telegraph punches this way." Nor did the NVA attempt to exploit the dire ammunition shortage caused by their opening rocket attack. Subsequent enemy shelling never approached the dimensions of other sieges. At Dien Bien Phu, Vietminh gunners pounded the French with an average of 2,000 rounds per day; at Khe Sanh the daily average was 105 rounds. Similarly, the ominous network of trenches at Khe Sanh was "nothing like the maze of diggings that strangled Dien Bien Phu." Perhaps most telling of all, the enemy never touched Khe Sanh's sole water source, a stream more than 500 meters from the base. According to General Tompkins, had they contaminated the stream the allies would not have been able to provide Khe Sanh with enough water.

Yet to suggest that the enemy never intended to overrun Khe Sanh does not necessarily mean that the allies failed to achieve their own purposes. Among Westmoreland's principal reasons for holding the base was that it offered an unprecedented opportunity to kill large numbers of enemy troops at minimal cost in American lives. If Giap was willing to expose 20,000 to 40,000 NVA regulars to the fearsome might of the U.S. arsenal, Westmoreland was more than willing to call his bet. When the American command later announced that 10,000 Communist soldiers had been killed at Khe Sanh, it seemed that Westmoreland had been right all along. The accuracy of that figure, however, remains open to question.

Estimates of enemy losses, like the original intelligence estimates of the number of NVA troops at Khe Sanh, were established almost exclusively by indirect means: sensor readings, sightings of secondary explosions, reports of defectors or prisoners of war, inference, and extrapolation. Feeding these findings into their computers, together with data on the expenditure of allied firepower, MACV systems analysts concluded that 49 to 65 percent of the besieging force had been killed or seriously wounded—between 9,800 and 13,000 men. Presumably these estimates took into account shifts in NVA troop deployments during the siege, such as the three regiments that surprisingly materialized outside Hue. What remains unclear is whether they also allowed for evasive enemy action. Two NVA officers who defected to the allies, and four other captured prisoners, all claimed in separate interviews that their units had received advance warnings, including takeoff times and tentative coordinates, of American B–52 strikes. The source of the timely alerts, which provided between two and twenty-four hours' notice, was unknown. But American officials later speculated that they came either from Russian trawlers in the western Pacific or from intercepted messages originating at Tan Son Nhut. "The heavyweight of firepower," it seemed, had been misdirecting a lot of its blows.

Although the "kill ratio" at Khe Sanh may not have been so favorable as the American command maintained, Communist losses throughout South Vietnam during the first three months of 1968 were staggering. The official estimates of more than 72,000 enemy soldiers killed provoked a good deal of skepticism. But even if that total were reduced by half, it would still represent an enormous sacrifice of troops, the vast majority of whom came from the ranks of the Vietcong.

The question is, to what end? What did the Communist high command hope to achieve by launching the Tet offensive in tandem with the siege of Khe Sanh, hurling tens of thousands of soldiers into a single battle destined to fall short of "final victory"? Was the Tet campaign an act of desperation on the part of the North Vietnamese, a "go-for-broke" effort to bring about a rapid political solution because "protracted" warfare wasn't working? If so, why did the NVA commit so few of its own troops to the attacks on the cities, thereby virtually insuring that many VC units would be decimated in the allied counterattack? Were they held back because the initial assaults had been less successful than anticipated? Or rather, as some have speculated, was the sacrifice of the VC a devious ploy intended to insure Hanoi's control of the southern insurgency? Did North Vietnam's leaders believe that they would break the back of ARVN, foment a General Uprising in the cities, and seize the two northern provinces at a single blow? Or were their actual objectives more modest?

The full scope of Hanoi's plan—the details, the priorities, the contingencies—remains shrouded in uncertainty. The general outlines, however, are clear. They chose to attack when the allies least expected—during the Tet holiday when half of all ARVN troops were on leave and a cease-fire was in effect everywhere but in I Corps. They struck where the allies were most vulnerable—in the cities, which had previously been spared the trauma of battle and were under the protection of South Vietnamese forces. And they directed their efforts primarily against RVNAF and GVN installations, not at the Americans.

Driving the Americans out of South Vietnam had been the chief tactical goal of Communist military strategists since 1965, and as recently as September 1967 General Giap had reaffirmed that objective in his annual review of the war, a tract entitled "Big Victory, Great Task." Acknowledging that the Americans had proved a far tougher foe than the French, that the superiority of U.S. firepower and mobility posed serious problems for his own troops, and that Communist tactics were in need of revision, Giap in effect conceded that the Communists were not winning the war. But neither, in his view, were they losing it. For all their failings, they had succeeded in depriving the Americans of the one thing the U.S. wanted, and needed, most: a quick victory. They had forced the Americans to commit themselves to a protracted war, and in so doing they had tipped the odds in their own favor. The war might last

55

"five, ten, twenty or more years," he wrote, but as long as the Communists kept on fighting, eventually the Americans would leave.

But if time were truly an ally of the Communists, why should they launch so bold, and so risky, a venture as the Tet offensive? The turgid prose of Giap's tract reveals nothing about the decision that had already been made in Hanoi. Nor does the general discuss the extent to which U.S. efforts had forced the North Vietnamese to reshape their strategic thinking. In the North, the "Rolling Thunder" bombing campaign had not broken Hanoi's will to fight or appreciably diminished the flow of NVA troops and supplies into South Vietnam. But it had seriously disrupted the country's industrial base and transportation system, forced the government to allocate hundreds of thousands of workers to repair bomb damage, and necessitated a heavier reliance on Russian and Chinese aid. In the South, the unexpectedly large American build-up had compelled Hanoi to commit ever-increasing numbers of its own troops, while allied pacification efforts were beginning to make some headway in the countryside.

Far more threatening to the Communists than rural pacification was the process they called *gom dan*, or "herding in"—the flight of refugees from the countryside to GVN relocation camps and the cities. One 1967 NVA report from Phu Yen Province in the central highlands admitted the loss of 200,000 villagers from Communist control attributing it to "enemy sweep operations and [the allied] plan of settlement of the people." Total estimates ranged between 500,000 and a million people per year. Not only did this mass migration bring large numbers of people under the control of the Saigon government, but it severely cut into the Communists' principal base for recruitment and supply.

The Communists thus found themselves in a difficult position. Committed in principle to a strategy of protracted warfare, they had fought the allies to a military stalemate and possessed enough human and material resources to keep the war going indefinitely. But in the decisive battle for control of the South Vietnamese population they were losing ground.

The Americans, meanwhile, seemed more confident than ever of their ability to win the military struggle. All that was needed was time: time to grind the Communists into submission; time to strengthen the newly elected Saigon government; time to win the allegiance of the South Vietnamese people.

By the end of 1967, the Vietnam War had become a race against time, not only for the allies, but for the Communists as well. In launching the Tet offensive, Hanoi decided to accelerate the pace. By attacking the cities in force, the Communists transformed the entire country into a battle zone: shattering the illusion of security for millions living under GVN control; inviting the Americans to unleash their awesome firepower on the homes of those they sought to protect; and causing painful social and economic dislocation everywhere. By striking at ARVN and the seats of government authority, and directing only secondary attacks against U.S. bases, they heightened tensions between the South Vietnamese and their American allies and provoked doubts about the quality of American intelligence. By forcing Revolutionary Development teams to retreat to the cities, they created a virtual vacuum in the countryside and set back the timetable of allied pacification. And by raising the stakes once again, they compelled the American government, and the American people, to reevaluate their commitment to South Vietnam.

Yet for all their successes, the Communists did not achieve their optimum goal: to instigate a popular national uprising against the GVN that would open the way to a coalition government. What ultimately undermined the Communists' strategy was the unexpected resiliency of ARVN, compounded by the deficiencies of their own troops. Despite extensive preparations, and despite the advantages of secrecy and surprise, Communist units time and again failed their assigned missions. Only in a few cities were they able to hold on long enough to reinforce their positions, and only in Hue were they able to establish a working, if short-lived, revolutionary government. That they benefited from some degree of popular support is undeniable, but for the most part that support was passive. People did not report to allied authorities on Communist troop movements and infiltration prior to Tet, and during the battles most complied with Communist demands rather than resist. Yet only in a few instances did they heed the calls to "rise up" against the Saigon regime and the Americans. ARVN did not buckle, the GVN did not fall, and the vaunted General Uprising did not occur.

On February 4, Westmoreland cabled Washington with his assessment of the impact of the Tet offensive:

From a realistic point of view we must accept the fact that the enemy has dealt the GVN a severe blow. He has brought the war to the towns and cities and has inflicted damage and casualties on the population. Homes have been destroyed; distribution of the necessities of life has been interrupted. Damage has been inflicted to the LOCs and the economy has been disrupted. Martial law has been invoked, with stringent curfews in the cities. The people have felt directly the impact of the war.

It was a sobering appraisal, but it was also, as he points out, "realistic." In the wake of the Tet offensive the myth of steady "progress" dissolved, and the "light at the end of the tunnel" dimmed. What the final outcome of the current campaign would be, no one could say for sure. But this much was clear: the war would go on. And while questions of military strategy and tactics would be decided by the politicians and generals, questions of victory or defeat would be decided by those who "felt directly the impact of the war"—the people of South Vietnam. In the meantime, the people of the United States rendered their own verdict.

Seventy-Seven Days

Sitting atop an Ontos, a marine stares into the dawn mists at Khe Sanh, looking for signs of enemy movement one week before Tet.

"Incoming!" Curled up in a trench near the airstrip, marines brace against the impact of enemy shells.

A marine scrambles across ammunition pallets looking for burning debris as enemy rounds slam into the base.

Dienbienphu, Dienbienphu. Look, it's not always true that history repeats itself.

Khe Sanh didn't try to be, nor could it have been, a Dienbienphu. Khe Sanh wasn't that important to us. Or it was only to the extent that it was important to the Americans—in fact, at Khe Sanh their prestige was at stake.

Because just look at the usual paradox that you will always find with the Americans: As long as they stayed in Khe Sanh to defend their prestige, they said Khe Sanh was important; when they abandoned Khe Sanh, they said Khe Sanh had never been important.

Besides, don't you think we won at Khe Sanh? I say yes.

—*General Vo Nguyen Giap*

Khe Sanh will stand in history, I am convinced, as a classic example of how to defeat a numerically superior besieging force by coordinated application of firepower.

—*General William C. Westmoreland*

Vast mounds of empty shell casings testify to the volume of artillery hurled back at the enemy.

The enemy was supported not only by the usual rockets and mortars but also modern artillery up to and including 130mm guns and the 152mm gun howitzer. This was the only place in Vietnam where the enemy was equipped with artillery. ... We were never able to silence [it].

—General Rathvon McC. Tompkins, commander, 3d Marine Division

They were hitting us with rockets, day after day, after day. All we could do was take it, and call in close air support. They wouldn't let us go after them.

—Corporal William Huston

Being in Khe Sanh is like sitting in an electric chair and waiting for someone to pull the switch.

—Airman Second Class Allen Belcher

We huddled together in the bunker, shoulders high and necks pulled in to leave no space between helmet and flak jacket. There is no describing an artillery barrage. The earth shakes, clods of dirt fall from the ceiling, and shrapnel makes a repulsive singing through the air.

—Newsweek reporter John Donnelly

Some of our guys have to be out in the open, even when the incoming is heavy. They have to make sure the ammo gets to the guns so we can fire back. That's the trouble.

—Staff Sergeant Sam Pearson

Everything I see is blown through with smoke, everything is on fire everywhere. It doesn't matter that memory distorts; every image, every sound comes back out of smoke and the smell of things burning.

—Journalist Michael Herr

You never know when it's coming, so why worry about it. If it's got your name on it, you won't know what hit you anyway.

—unidentified marine at Khe Sanh

We didn't know from day to day what was going to happen. We never asked ourselves, "Why didn't they come in?" We didn't want to know why they didn't.

—Lance Corporal Robert Houck

Marines seek cover as an enemy rocket roars into one of the base's ammunition dumps, triggering a blinding secondary explosion.

Top and above. Survivors of a thirty-man patrol ambushed by the NVA struggle back to the main base, dragging their wounded to cover.

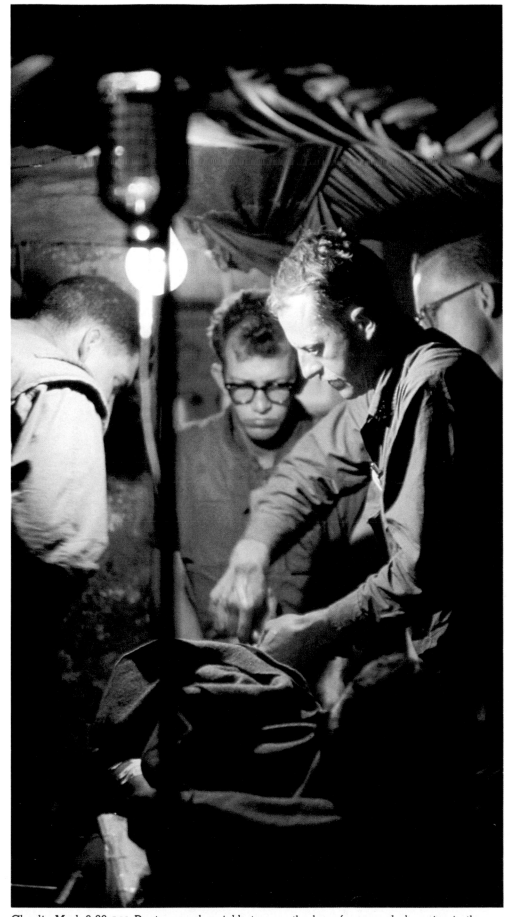

Charlie Med, 3:00 A.M. Doctors work quickly to save the leg of a wounded marine in the underground medical bunker. More than 1,500 men were treated during the siege.

The term "siege," in the strictest sense of the word, was somewhat of a misnomer because the Allies conducted a number of daily patrols, often as far as 500 meters from their own lines.

> —*Captain Moyers S. Shore, II,*
> *The Battle for Khe Sanh*

They would go out on patrol, to do what I don't know, and they were promptly slaughtered. It didn't seem to me to prove anything. I mean, we have airplanes, why send out a foot patrol? It just struck me as a waste of human beings ... I thought it was damn silly.

> —*Corpsman Richard Heath*

There were three doctors and about twelve corpsmen attached to Charlie Med. There really weren't any operating tables. We had about six stretchers. When they came in, the stretcher became the table.

We helped treat men in great pain and grave danger. Men with legs nearly amputated from shrapnel wounds and with arms severed off at the shoulder; others with brain damage and ugly head wounds. And pale-faced men who never knew that their time on earth was over.

> —*Corpsman Heath*

When I get back, I'm going to open a bar especially for the survivors of Khe Sanh. And any time it gets two deep at that bar, I'll know someone is lying.

> —*Lieutenant C. J. Stack*

It was a shocking image. With the sound of small firearms crackling in the background, a slight man is led up a Saigon street by Vietnamese marines. Hands tied behind his back, the man is identified by the correspondent on the scene as a Vietcong officer, yet he wears no uniform or military insignia—only a short-sleeved plaid shirt, black shorts, and sandals. He has obviously been beaten. As he moves closer to the hand-held camera, another man comes into view: General Nguyen Ngoc Loan, chief of South Vietnam's National Police. Loan draws a revolver and begins waving away onlookers as the prisoner is brought to a halt. Then, with unexpected suddenness, the general's spindly right arm extends toward the prisoner, the barrel of his revolver seemingly inches from the man's right temple. Loan squeezes the trigger. The prisoner's face grimaces in anguish. He falls backward to the ground, blood spurting from the open wound in his head.

The grisly sequence lasted only fifty-two seconds. But it left an indelible impression upon the minds and memories of the estimated 20 million Americans who watched the NBC "Huntley-Brinkley Report" on February 2, 1968. Like most television news clips, edited and packaged for rapid mass consumption, it told an incomplete story. The viewing audience did not know that the battle sounds they heard in the background had been added in the studio for effect; that the wide-angle lens had distorted the actual distance between executioner and victim; that the shot itself had been edited out because a passer-by had stepped in front of the camera at the moment of firing. Nor were they told anything about the enigmatic General Loan, a self-described "romantic" more popularly known as the "terror of Saigon," or about the anonymous Vietcong officer whose moment of death had been electronically projected into their living rooms. What the American public saw was only an imperfect representation of reality, one small fragment of a complex war removed from its context and frozen in time. Yet that small fragment also conveyed an undeniable truth about the cruel and brutal character of the Vietnam War.

"I thought we were winning the war!"

By 1968, of course, most Americans had grown accustomed to images of death and destruction emanating from Vietnam. They littered the pages of daily newspapers and weekly news magazines and provided common fare for network news shows. They reminded Americans that the nation was at war and that the war continued.

With the onset of the Tet offensive, however, media coverage of the Vietnam War changed dramatically. If the 179 accredited U.S. correspondents in-country were overextended in normal circumstances, the unanticipated magnitude of the attacks as well as the dizzying pace of developments strained American news organizations to their technical and human limits. Where previous coverage had tended to present a well-ordered vision of the war—with on-the-scene reports providing representative glimpses of organized operations, features on new American weaponry, and periodic assessments of political and military progress—early reports of the countrywide Communist offensive reflected nothing so much as a pervasive sense of chaos.

Saturated with wire reports from the war zone and under constant competitive pressure to get the story out first, newspapers printed confusing and sometimes contradictory accounts. Television correspondents crouched down to comment on the "raw footage" that flickered across the

TV screen, as bullets ricocheted and shells exploded in the background. Some of the scenes, like those showing refugees fleeing their burning homes or American jets swooping out of the sky, were familiar enough. But many were not: the bodies of VC sappers strewn across the grounds of the U.S. Embassy compound, fighting in the streets of Saigon and Hue, large portions of South Vietnamese towns shattered by allied bombs, and, in a significant departure from previous practice, American soldiers falling in battle. While it is difficult to gauge the overall impact of this avalanche of war news upon the general public, many Americans shared the reaction of TV newsman Walter Cronkite. "What the hell is going on?" he exclaimed as initial reports of the offensive reached the CBS news room. "I thought we were winning the war!"

Cronkite's alarm was understandable. For years, U.S. officials and many reporters in Washington and Saigon had been reporting progress in South Vietnam, and in recent months the Johnson administration had made a concerted effort to "get the message out" that "we are winning." Concerned about the increasingly widespread view that the war was a military "stalemate," the administration had launched an all-out public relations campaign during the fall of 1967 to "sell" its war policy to the American public. Under the direction of presidential adviser Walt W. Rostow, chief of the White House Psychological Strategy Committee, the "Success Offensive," as it came to be called, inundated the major news media with a wave of effusive optimism. Every statistical index of progress, from "body counts" and "kill ratios" to "overland road haul (in thousands of short tons)," was fed to selected organs of the popular press. The charts and graphs, statements and statistics, all pressed the same story. "We are beginning to win this struggle," asserted Vice President Hubert Humphrey on NBC's "Today" show in mid-November. "We are on the offensive. Territory is being gained. We are making steady progress."

The campaign reached its peak in mid-November, when the president summoned Ambassador Ellsworth Bunker, pacification chief Robert W. Komer, and General Westmoreland to Washington for what was officially billed as a "high-level policy review." While Bunker and Komer both echoed the code words "steady progress," Westmoreland was more emphatic. "I am absolutely certain that whereas in 1965 the enemy was winning, today he is certainly losing," he declared in a speech at the National Press Club on November 21. "We have reached an important point when the end begins to come into view."

To some extent the "Success Offensive" achieved its intended purposes. By the end of the year the polls showed a 6 percent increase in popular approval of the president's Vietnam policy. Yet for all its efforts, the administration was unable to close the "credibility gap" between its own rosy assessments and the pessimistic press reports issuing from the war zone. As one *New York Times* editorial pointed out in late November, "The long road the United States had traveled to its present heavy involvement in Southeast Asia is littered with similar expressions of official expectations that were never fulfilled."

More confused than convinced, more doubtful than despairing, most Americans on the eve of 1968 adopted a similar "wait-and-see" attitude. While doves continued to call for a negotiated settlement and hawks urged stronger military measures, both groups were united in the desire to end the war as soon as possible. For the most part, neither was yet prepared to recommend the abandonment of South Vietnam. Then came Tet.

Widening the "credibility gap"

If the initial press response to the outbreak of the Tet offensive was marked by shock and confusion, the hasty assessments put forward by officials in Washington and Saigon only raised more questions than they answered. General Westmoreland's claim that the "enemy's well-laid plans went afoul," the president's assertion that "we have known for some time that this offensive was planned by the enemy," the repeated official description of the attacks as a "complete failure," all seemed to many observers to perpetuate the same myths that had characterized the sanguine progress reports of the previous fall. "If we expected attacks," the *Baltimore Sun* wanted to know, "why were we caught utterly by surprise?" "Some

thing enormous has gone wrong," declared the *Cleveland Press*, "and it cannot be shrugged off with the kind of flimsy explanations given so far."

In the absence of a persuasive official interpretation, many newspapers delivered their own judgments. What the attacks demonstrated, according to the *St. Louis Post-Dispatch*, was "the hollowness of the Saigon government's pretensions to sovereignty in the cities, the fraud of our government's claims of imminent victory, and the basic untenability of the American military position." "The psychological damage," said the *New York Times*, "is tremendous." Perhaps most biting of all, however, was Art Buchwald's satire, "We Have the Enemy on the Run, Says General Custer at Big Horn." "It's a desperation move on the part of Sitting Bull and his last death rattle," Custer asserts, in an "exclusive interview."

As the fighting persisted through the first week of February, the credibility gap widened into an unbridgeable chasm. Official references to the battles of Saigon and Hue as "mopping up operations," the stark photograph of the Loan shooting, the offhand remark of an American major at Ben Tre that "it became necessary to destroy the town to save it," all magnified the disparity between official claims of victory and the firsthand observations of the U.S. press. Shock soon yielded to anger and dismay, heightening tensions between the administration and the media to an unprecedented level. Subjected to relentless questioning and criticism, government officials began to

Accompanied by aides and reporters, Ambassador Bunker (light shirt, light pants) surveys the grounds of the U.S. Embassy on January 31 following the Communist attack. Even though the VC never entered the chancery, many Americans were shocked to learn that the enemy had penetrated the embassy compound.

characterize the Communist offensive as a test of America's will and to blame the press for undermining public confidence in the nation's leadership. "There gets to be a point when the question is, 'Whose side are you on?' " the usually imperturbable Secretary of State Dean Rusk snapped at an American reporter in a background press session on February 9. "None of your papers or your broadcasting apparatuses are worth a damn unless the United States succeeds."

The Johnson administration had good reason to worry about the national resolve in the aftermath of the Tet attacks. Although the first polls recorded a slight surge of hawkishness, consistent with a traditional tendency of Americans to rally round the president in times of crisis, subsequent samplings showed an inexorable erosion of public support for the administration and for the war. A Gallup survey conducted in early January had indicated that 47 percent of the public disapproved of the president's handling of the war. By mid-February that figure had climbed to 50 percent and by the end of the month to 58 percent. There was also an increase in the percentage of people who believed that the U.S. had made a "mistake" in sending troops to fight in Vietnam: from 45 percent in December 1967 to 49 percent in late February 1968. The same uncertainty and pessimism marked responses to the question, "Do you think that the U.S. and its allies are losing ground in Vietnam, standing still, or making progress?" Between November 1967 and late February 1968, perceptions of progress fell from 50 percent to 33 percent, and belief that the U.S. was losing ground in Vietnam soared from 8 percent to 23 percent.

Although gloomy news reports contributed to the pessimism that swept across America during the first weeks of February, the principal trends of public opinion had been well-established long before the Communists launched their attacks. The Tet offensive coverage did not so much cause a change in popular attitudes toward the war as accelerate the downward spiral of doubt, disenchantment, and disapproval that had begun in 1966. What it did alter, however, were the terms of the public debate over the war. By mid-February, the central issue was no longer the credibility of the government's optimistic war reports but the validity of the president's entire Vietnam policy.

More of the same won't do

The Tet offensive "has finally shattered the mask of official illusion with which we have concealed our true circumstances, even from ourselves," declared Senator Robert Kennedy. We must recognize "the basic truth" that "a total military victory is not within sight or around the corner; that, in fact, it is probably beyond our grasp." "From the outset," said Senator Mike Mansfield, "it was not an American responsibility, and it is not now an American responsibility, to win a victory for any particular Vietnamese group, or to defeat any particular Vietnamese group." The time has come, affirmed Senator William Fulbright, for a "full-scale examination of the purposes and objectives of our policy in Vietnam."

Congressional calls for a change in American policy in Vietnam were not altogether new. Ever since U.S. combat troops were first introduced into the conflict, a growing number of doves had urged the president to cut back on the bombing and seek a peaceful political solution, while a vociferous group of hawks called for further escalation to bring the war to a rapid end. Until Tet, however, opposition from the right and left had never seriously threatened Johnson's command. Now, as public opinion began to swing decidedly against the president, as the economy began to show signs of the war's strain, and as American casualty figures reached record levels, many members of Congress demanded a change in policy. "A year ago," observed Senator Thruston Morton, a Kentucky Republican who had gained national attention when he joined the antiwar camp in late 1967, "one couldn't count ten doves in the Senate." Yet by late February he estimated there were twenty-five antiwar voices in the Senate and another sixteen "leaning to the doves."

The new antiwar sentiment on Capitol Hill proved to be a boon to Eugene McCarthy, the scholarly, introspective senator from Minnesota who had announced in December that he would challenge Johnson for the presidency. Initially his chances of wresting the Democratic nomination from an incumbent president as powerful and politically astute as Lyndon Baines Johnson were considered negligible. But after Tet the senator's lonely crusade rapidly gained momentum. By mid-February the Democratic regulars were becoming worried about the McCarthy insurgency, as major polls revealed what appeared to be a growing "peace vote" in New Hampshire. Subsequent studies have shown that many of McCarthy's supporters knew little or nothing about his antiwar position. A majority, in fact, considered themselves hawks rather than doves. "The only common denominator," a research report prepared at the University of Michigan later concluded, "seems to have been a deep dissatisfaction with the Johnson administration."

The same "deep dissatisfaction" was manifesting itself in other ways and in some rather unlikely places as well. On February 23 the *Wall Street Journal*, the voice of the American financial community and a long-time, if not uncritical, supporter of the war effort, published an editorial entitled "The Logic of the Battlefield." "We think the American people should be getting ready to accept, if they haven't already, the prospect that the whole Vietnam effort may be doomed," wrote Joseph Evans, the conservative chief editorial writer for the *Journal*. "We believe that the Administration is duty-bound to recognize that no battle and no war is worth any price, no matter how ruinous."

The War and Public Opinion

Beginning in 1965, American pollsters regularly sought to gauge public attitudes toward the Vietnam War. The questions they posed ran the gamut from speculation about the eventual outcome of the conflict to evaluations of America's moral right to intervene in Southeast Asia. In the view of many public opinion analysts, however, the single best indicator of popular support for the war was the question: "In view of the developments since we entered the fighting in Vietnam, do you think the U.S. made a mistake sending troops to fight in Vietnam?"

The results of the "mistake sentiment" surveys (Figure 1) show that a majority of Americans supported the initial deployment of U.S. combat troops to Vietnam in 1965. Over the next three years support for the war effort declined steadily while opposition rose, finally surpassing support during the third quarter of 1967—*before* the Tet offensive. Surveys taken after Tet suggested for the first time that a majority of Americans opposed the war. But when viewed over four years, the Tet offensive only reinforced a growing public perception that American involvement in Vietnam was a mistake.

Another key survey concerned President Johnson's handling of the war. From 1965 to mid–1967, the figures from this poll (Figure 2) roughly paralleled responses to the "mistake" question. Although the administration's "success offensive" in fall 1967 aroused additional support for the president by the end of the year, Tet and its aftermath plunged Johnson's "war approval rating" to an all-time low of 26 percent by the end of March 1968.

Underscoring the mounting disapproval of the president's war policies were the findings of a Gallup poll that asked respondents to identify themselves as either hawk or dove (Figure 3). When this question was first posed in December 1967, a majority of those sampled described themselves as hawks, while 35 percent considered themselves doves. During the next two months the number of hawks increased, peaking at 61 percent during the first days of Tet. In ensuing weeks, however, the hawk figure fell precipitously, the number of doves rising proportionately. By mid–March, the two opposing groups were virtually equal in size. Yet, when considered in light of the president's war approval rating (Figure 2), both hawks and doves seemed to share one sentiment: dissatisfaction with President Johnson's handling of the war.

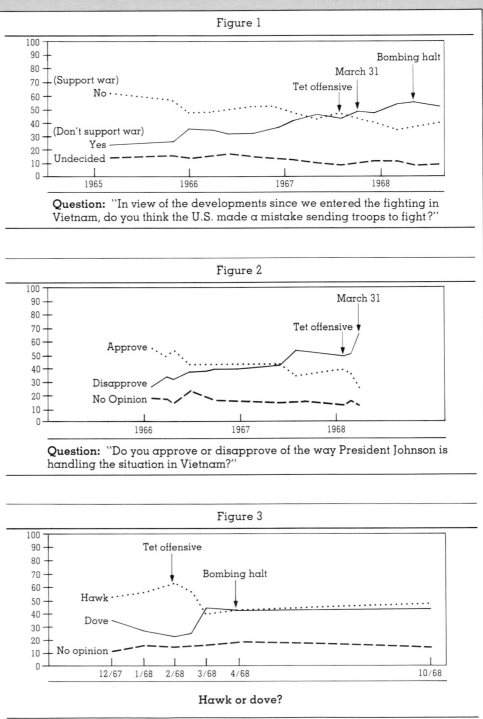

Figure 1

Question: "In view of the developments since we entered the fighting in Vietnam, do you think the U.S. made a mistake sending troops to fight?"

Figure 2

Question: "Do you approve or disapprove of the way President Johnson is handling the situation in Vietnam?"

Figure 3

Hawk or dove?

Four days later, in the first clear-cut editorial statement on the war by a major network newscaster, Walter Cronkite expressed a similarly bleak view. Skeptical of official assessments of the impact of the Tet offensive, Cronkite had gone to Vietnam for two weeks in February and interviewed hundreds of officers and officials. What he learned only reinforced his disillusionment. "We have been too often disappointed by the optimism of the American leaders," he told an estimated audience of 9 million Americans, "to have faith any longer in the silver linings they find in the darkest clouds." Characterizing both the Tet offensive and the siege of Khe Sanh as "standoffs," he contended that "the only realistic, yet unsatisfactory, conclusion" was that the U.S. was "mired in stalemate." "The only rational way out then," he said, "is to negotiate, not as victors, but as an honorable people who had lived up to their pledge to defend democracy, and did the best they could."

By early March the chorus of criticism directed at the Johnson administration had reached a deafening crescendo. Throughout the country editorial writers hardened their lines, with the hawks calling for further escalation and a widening of the war while the doves urged the government to de-escalate and negotiate. Whatever their differences of opinion, whatever their hopes for the future, all shared with the editors of *Newsweek* magazine the conviction that "More of the Same Won't Do."

"After three years of gradual escalation, President Johnson's strategy for Vietnam has run into a dead end," wrote the editors of *Newsweek*, introducing the cover story of their March 18 issue, "The Dusty Agony of Khe Sanh." Not only had the American military strategy failed, but the political goal of creating a democratic, stable South Vietnamese government seemed as distant as it had ever been. The GVN was a "political morass," riddled with corruption, hamstrung by ineptitude, bereft of the will necessary to earn the allegiance of its people. What was needed, the editorial concluded, was "the courage to face the truth"—that "the war cannot be won by military means without tearing apart the whole fabric of national life and international relations. . . . A strategy of more of the same is no longer tolerable."

206,000

But "more of the same" seemed to be precisely what the administration had in mind. On March 10, two days before the New Hampshire primary, the *New York Times* reported that General Westmoreland had requested 206,000 more troops for Vietnam, stirring "a divisive internal debate within high levels of the Johnson administration." The following day Secretary of State Rusk made a scheduled appearance before the Senate Foreign Relations Committee, beginning what was to be "the most prolonged questioning of a cabinet officer ever broadcast to the

American people." Over the course of the two-day, eleven-hour grilling he repeatedly sidestepped the issue of a possible troop increase. "There is no specific recommendation in front of the president at the present time," Rusk affirmed. "[The] entire situation is under consideration from A to Z."

The request for an additional 206,000 American troops for Vietnam originated in a series of back-channel cables between General Wheeler and General Westmoreland during the first two weeks of February. Conveying the president's continuing concern about the possible fall of Khe Sanh, the chairman of the Joint Chiefs asked Westmoreland on February 3 "if there is any reinforcement we can give you." The commanding general immediately replied that the defense of Khe Sanh was solid and that his only requirements were a few more supply aircraft and faster delivery of other materiel. The following day, Westmoreland received another cable from Wheeler, indicating that the White House was actively considering diversionary attacks, either north of the DMZ or in eastern Laos, to relieve the pressure on Khe Sanh. On February 5 the same message was reiterated by Admiral U.S. Grant Sharp, CINCPAC, who informed Westmoreland that there might be some inclination in Washington "to relax the military ceiling." Noting that outgoing Secretary of Defense Robert McNamara had not ruled out a troop increase in a recent interview on "Meet the Press," Sharp strongly suggested that "it may be timely now to estimate any additional needs."

Westmoreland was puzzled. From the very beginning of the siege of Khe Sanh through the first chaotic days of the Tet offensive, he had repeatedly and emphatically reassured Washington that he had the situation "well in-hand." The sense of urgency reflected in the latest cables seemed unwarranted. Yet he was also enticed. Like the Joint Chiefs of Staff, he had been urging the president for years to remove the constraints on military operations in Southeast Asia. The possibility that Johnson might at last be willing to authorize an expansion of the ground war, not only into Laos but even into North Vietnam, was an opportunity not to be missed. He ordered his staff to prepare a study of additional military requirements for the coming year and on February 8 informed Wheeler of the results. Listing the modernization of ARVN as his number one priority for 1968, he noted that another American division would be needed later in the year "if operations in Laos are authorized."

That was not, however, what Wheeler wanted to hear. He promptly, and rather testily, told the MACV commander to focus on his "immediate requirements stemming from the present situation in Vietnam," not his "longer range" needs. Another cable on February 8 spelled out Wheeler's thinking more clearly. It also implicitly challenged Westmoreland's assessment of the enemy's intentions. Calling attention to the "theory, which could be

CBS anchorman Walter Cronkite interviews a Hue University professor during his tour of the war zone in February 1968. Soon after returning to the U.S., the influential newsman declared the war a "stalemate."

logical, that overall enemy strategy is to attack and attrite the ARVN" and that the "massive Khe Sanh build-up is [an] alternative threat to enforce a siphoning off of troops from the South," he pointed out that the Communists might "attack in force along the DMZ if you do not respond by a build-up of your forces in I Corps." "The United States is not prepared to accept a defeat in South Vietnam," said Wheeler bluntly. "In summary, if you need more troops, ask for them."

Although Wheeler's promptings reflected a far gloomier view of the situation than General Westmoreland's, fear of defeat was not his sole motive in urging an immediate reassessment of U.S. troop strength. Along with the other members of the Joint Chiefs of Staff, Wheeler had long been concerned about the strain of the war on American military resources throughout the world. Since the summer of 1965 he had repeatedly recommended that the president order a "national mobilization," not only to prepare for possible intensification of the Vietnam War effort but to insure that the nation's strategic military reserve did not become depleted. But Johnson, recalling the public outcry that followed President Kennedy's reserve call-up during the Berlin Crisis and knowing that mobilization would require cutbacks in his Great Society programs, had steadfastly refused. By early 1968, however, United States forces outside of Vietnam had been so depleted by the war that, in Wheeler's view, another troop increase could not be authorized without a concomitant call-up.

Sensing the president's growing bellicosity in the wake of the Tet offensive, Wheeler and the Joint Chiefs once again pressed their case for "national mobilization" and for widening the war in Vietnam. This time Johnson seemed more attentive.

"I do not like what I am smelling from these cables from Vietnam," said the president, addressing his senior foreign policy advisers at a White House meeting February 9. "I want you to lay out for me what we should do in the minimum time to meet a crisis request from Vietnam if one comes. Let's assume we have to have more troops. . . . If it takes more men to avoid defeat let's get them. . . . Get the JCS to review all the options and let's review them together," he told General Wheeler. "Let's consider the extensions, call-ups, the use of specialists. . . . Should we ask for a declaration of war?" Secretary of State Dean Rusk adamantly advised against it. Moments later, Lyndon Johnson's newly appointed secretary of defense, Clark Clifford, interjected his own views into the discussion for the first time: "There is a very strange contradiction in what we are saying and doing," he pointed out. "I think we should give some very serious thought to how we explain saying on one hand that the enemy did not take a victory and yet [we] are in need of many more troops and possibly an emergency call-up." "The only explanation I can see," replied the president, "is that the enemy has changed its tactics. . . . We have to be prepared for all that we might face."

71

**FELLER CALLS
ERS OF PARTY
ARLEY TODAY**

to Exchange Views
uation Following
awal of Romney

ASSESS SUPPORT

Those Invited Have
ed Their Support of
nor for President

THOMAS P. RONAN

or Rockefeller will
e today with top-rank-
blicans from many
he country "to ex-
vs on the situation
y" following Gov.
mney's withdrawal
Presidential race.
s the reason for the
en yesterday by Les-
he Governor's press
But informed Repub-
they believed Mr.
would explore with
the amount of sup-
ld expect if he de-
active candidacy for
nomination.
to expected him to
ders' advice on the
o pursue if he did

NATURAL DEFENSE IN NORTH VIETNAM: One of the many caves in the country being used as cover against U.S. bombing raids. This one, photographed by a Japanese newsman, shelters small factory. Sign expresses determination.

Nihon Denpo News via Associated Press

Johnson and Nixon Given Big New Hampshire Edge

By WARREN WEAVER Jr.
Special to The New York Times

CONCORD, N. H., March 8—President Johnson and Richard M. Nixon are prohibitive f-   --es in their separ-

700 CONVICTS RIOT AT OREGON PRISON

11 Are Held as Hostages
Under Th—

Warsaw Students Battle Policemen 2d Day in a Row

By JONATHAN RANDAL
Special to The New York Times

WARSAW, March 9—Polish
shouting "L—

WESTMORELAND REQUESTS 206,000 MORE MEN, STIRRING DEBATE IN ADMINISTRATION

Enemy Hammers 7 Sites On the Outskirts of Saigon

By TOM BUCKLEY
Special to The New York Times

SAIGON, South Vietnam, Sunday, March 10—The Viet-cong made coordinated attacks early yesterday against seven targets on the southern edge of Saigon.

The district police head-quarters and the militia post at Caykho, about three miles from the capital, repelled ground assaults. Two police substations, a housing com-pound for the families of po-licemen about a mile and a half from the United States Embassy, and military outposts at Nhabe and Longthanh were struck in the 30-minute mortar and rocket barrage.

Nhabe, on the Saigon River about four miles southeast of the city, is an important pe-troleum storage area where oceangoing tankers pump out their cargoes. The South Viet-

namese police said that 4 per-sons had been killed and 10 wounded, all civilians, in the attacks.

The Navy reported that planes from the carrier Bon Homme Richard had escorted transport planes into Khesanh, the Marine outpost in the northwestern corner of South Vietnam, to suppress antiaircraft fire that has claimed three cargo aircraft and damaged many others.

The pilots reported that the North Vietnamese trenches had been dug within 500 yards of the runway. Lieut. Comdr.

Continued on Page 2, Column 3

FORCE NOW 510,000

Some in Defense and State Departments Oppose Increase

The following dispatch was written by Hedrick Smith and Neil Sheehan, assisted by Max Frankel and Edwin L. Dale Jr.

Special to The New York Times

WASHINGTON, March 9 — Gen. William C. Westmoreland has asked for 206,000 more American troops for Vietnam, and the request has touched off a divisive internal debate with-in high levels of the Johnson Administration.

A number of sub-Cabinet civilian officials in the Defense Department, supported by some senior officials in the State De-partment, have argued against General Westmoreland's plea for a 40 per cent increase in his forces "to regain the initia-

Government officials were distressed and the American public startled when the New York Times *revealed a proposed major troop increase in Vietnam.*

The next day, February 10, General Westmoreland once again cabled Wheeler, this time emphasizing that "additional forces from CONUS would be most helpful" in meeting the continuing enemy threat in I Corps. On Feb-ruary 11 Wheeler responded. He explained that West-moreland's latest message had been "interpreted" as ex-pressing less than "a firm demand" for more troops. By that point, Westmoreland later recalled, the "signals from Washington" had become so strong that "it seemed to me that for political reasons or otherwise, the president and the Joint Chiefs of Staff were anxious to send me reinforce-ments. With General Wheeler's encouragement, I made, on February 12, a formal request for reinforcements."

General Westmoreland's lengthy cable of February 12 presented a far different view of the post–Tet situation than any he had previously forwarded to Washington. Where earlier communications had been rich in the language of confidence, optimism, and resolve, he now talked of "rein-forcements, which I desperately need . . . to cope with the situation at hand." He described the current moment as one of "great opportunity" but also stressed the "height-ened risk." "I have been promised 525,000 troops," he said. "I need these 525,000 troops now. . . . Time is of the

essence." He urged immediate deployment of a marine regiment and a brigade of the 82d Airborne Division.

So striking was the change in Westmoreland's tone that General Taylor dashed off a memorandum to the presi-dent expressing his astonishment that it had been "written by the same man." He nonetheless agreed with West-moreland that "we should meet this challenge by a com-mitment of all necessary resources." The Joint Chiefs, how-ever, did not agree. For the first time in the course of the Vietnam War, the nation's highest-ranking military offi-cers refused to endorse the immediate deployment of troops requested by COMUSMACV, a request their chair-man had carefully coaxed from him. Having created a lever to move the president toward mobilization, the JCS now tried to use it: Unless the president called up some 120,000 army and marine reserves, they advised, "deploy-ment of emergency reinforcements should not be made." The commander in chief overruled them. Deferring once again a decision about the reserves, he authorized imme-diate deployment of the "emergency augmentation" that Westmoreland requested—a total of 10,500 troops.

Several days later President Johnson flew to Fort Bragg, North Carolina, to visit with some of the departing paratroopers of the 82d Airborne, and then to El Toro, California, to call on a detachment of marines. "These visits with brave men," he later wrote, "were among the most personally painful meetings of my presidency. . . ."

I remember vividly my conversation with one soldier. I asked him if he had been in Vietnam before. He said: "Yes, sir, three times." I asked if he was married. He said: "Yes, sir." Did he have any children? "Yes, sir, one." Boy or girl? "A boy, sir." How old is he? "He was born yesterday morning, sir," he said quietly. That was the last question I asked him. It tore my heart out to send back to combat a man whose first son had just been born.

"A very near thing"

By the time the president authorized the "emergency augmentation," he had already decided to send General Wheeler to Vietnam to evaluate the situation firsthand and to confer with the MACV commander about possible future needs and actions. On the morning of February 23, Wheeler arrived in a Saigon still tense from a recent "second wave" of rocket attacks and ground probes.

During his two-day visit, he deliberated with Westmoreland about the opportunities and potential pitfalls of the current military situation: the "plausible possibility," in Westmoreland's words, that the administration might at last approve a more ambitious military strategy now that the hawkish Clark Clifford was about to become secretary of defense; the forces that would be required to carry out

such a strategy; and the need to reconstitute the strategic reserve in the United States if any sizable new deployments were approved. In the end, the generals hammered out a proposal for three "force package requirements" totaling nearly 206,000 additional troops. The first increment of 108,000 troops was to be deployed by May 1; the second, some 42,000 men, by September 1; and a third, of 55,000 men, by December 1. Both Wheeler and Westmoreland acknowledged a "clear understanding" that only the first increment was earmarked for Vietnam. Deployment of the remaining two was contingent upon unanticipated Communist successes or the approval of a more aggressive ground strategy. Otherwise they would be added to the strategic reserve.

The report that Wheeler filed on February 26, however, said nothing about contingencies or new strategies or building the strategic reserve. Instead he painted a somber picture of the impact of Tet upon South Vietnam, contradicting Westmoreland's earlier reports and clearly suggesting that the proposed troop increase was a matter of vital military necessity. Although the enemy had suffered enormous losses, Wheeler told the president, the Tet offensive was "a very near thing." More important, it had not yet run its full course. With the enemy still surrounding Khe Sanh and once again poised to hit in the central highlands and around Saigon, "MACV will be hard pressed to meet adequately all threats," he reported. "[W]e must be prepared to accept some reverses." In order to meet the

Vietnam-bound jeeps in Okinawa. By early 1968 the war was costing the United States more than $20 billion per year.

President Johnson says good-bye on February 17 to marines bound for Vietnam as part of the "emergency augmentation" he had just authorized.

continuing danger in I Corps and at the same time restore security in the cities and countryside, Wheeler concluded, more men will be needed: 206,000 more, in three increments.

Why did the chairman of the Joint Chiefs of Staff neglect to mention that his "clear understanding" with Westmoreland was contingent upon approval of a new ground strategy? Westmoreland, in his memoir *A Soldier Reports,* implies that General Wheeler deliberately concealed the truth in order to force the issue of the strategic reserve.

The Chairman of the Joint Chiefs has a difficult job living with his civilian bosses . . . striving to convince them in terms they can understand of matters that he views as military necessity . . . . If he could gain authority to raise the troops, exactly what was to be done with them could be decided once the troops were actually available . . . . [He] saw no possibility at the moment of selling reinforcements in terms of future operations.

If that was General Wheeler's intention, the ploy did not work. Rather than compelling the president to replenish the strategic reserve in order to meet General Westmoreland's apparent needs, the troop request set in motion the most searching government debate over American purposes, policies, and military strategies in Vietnam since the summer of 1965. National Security Adviser Walt Rostow recommended that the president appoint an "intensive working group" to study the matter. His candidate

to head the group was the new secretary of defense, Clark Clifford. Believing that "a new pair of eyes and a fresh outlook should guide the study," the president heartily endorsed Rostow's suggestion.

The Clifford task force

A man of quiet brilliance and consummate charm, a superb lawyer, and a pragmatic negotiator, Clark Clifford, wrote one reporter, was "one of the most elegant men alive." If his eloquence and ease disarmed the powerful, his unshakable self-possession often dominated them. His secret, said a colleague, "is that he intimidates people. He doesn't make statements, he pronounces judgments. It's a lot like talking to God—or listening to God."

By 1968, Clifford had been making pronouncements in Washington for more than twenty years. Presidents since Truman had listened and counted on his advice. President Johnson, who had known Clifford since the late 1940s, considered him "an old and trusted friend whose advice was always cogent, clear, and effective," and he had consulted Clifford on every major policy decision of his administration, including the decision to escalate the war in July 1965. Clifford had voiced some early misgivings, but by 1966 he was convinced of the necessity of the war effort. Doubts had resurfaced in September 1967, when Clifford talked with representatives of America's allies and discovered that they seemed far less concerned about Vietnam than the United States. Despite his uncertainties, he recalled, "I continued to be a full supporter of our policy." And when Lyndon Johnson asked him to succeed Robert McNamara as secretary of defense, Clifford accepted.

If the president believed that Clifford would prove a loyal advocate of his Vietnam policies, so did most people inside and outside the government. Many Pentagon officials considered him a confirmed hawk, while the press greeted the news of his nomination as evidence of Johnson's resolve to see the war through to the end. Clifford himself saw things differently. The president, he observed, "had nothing I wanted. I was older than he. Our relationship was on an entirely different basis than some of his other advisers." Clark Clifford would make up his own mind about the merits of the administration's war policy.

His first job, the president told him, would be to head a task force looking into General Westmoreland's latest troop request. "Give me the lesser of evils," Johnson said. "Give me your recommendations."

The Clifford task force gathered for its initial meeting February 28. Among those in attendance were Treasury Secretary Henry Fowler, Deputy Secretary of Defense Paul Nitze, CIA Director Richard Helms, Dean Rusk, Robert McNamara, Walt Rostow, and General Taylor. According to Clifford, the group's charge was to determine

how, not whether, the troop request could be met. As the deliberations proceeded, however, the group found it impossible to stay within the narrow parameters of their assignment. "Fundamental questions," said Clifford, "began to recur again and again." What were the ultimate objectives of the United States in Vietnam? How would additional military forces contribute to the achievement of those goals? What would be the impact of a major mobilization on the American public and economy? Was there a definable limit to the American commitment to South Vietnam? How much blood and treasure would have to be spent before the price became too high? "The question," Clifford observed, had "quickly changed from 'How could we send the troops to Westmoreland?' to 'What was the most intelligent thing to do for the country?'"

During the next three days officials at the State, Treasury, and Defense departments, as well as staff members of the JCS and CIA, worked feverishly on a series of reports analyzing the implications of the troop request and examining alternative courses of action. By March 2, fifteen study papers lay before the task force. Although the Joint Chiefs, backed by General Taylor, reaffirmed their recommendation that the troop request be fulfilled, most of the reports recommended denial. "The financial considerations alone," Clifford noted, "were appalling." According to Treasury Secretary Fowler, any large increase in mili-

Shortly before departing for Vietnam, young conscripts phone home. By March 1968 more than half a million American soldiers were serving in that country.

tary expenditures would mean spending an additional $2.5 billion in fiscal 1968, $10 billion in 1969. It would add $500 million to an already acute balance-of-payments deficit and possibly necessitate wage, price, and credit controls. The political implications, concluded Philip Goulding, assistant secretary of defense for public affairs, were equally grim. Unless accompanied by some other move, either a fresh peace initiative or an escalation of the bombing, a troop increase would satisfy no one. The best option, he argued, was to deny the request and alter the American strategy in Vietnam.

Goulding was not the only one to raise the issue of strategy. To one extent or another, all of the Defense Department papers assailed the inadequacy of American military policy in South Vietnam. Even General Taylor suggested that "new strategic guidance" be given to COMUSMACV. Perhaps most damning of all was the paper on "Alternative Strategies," written by Alain Enthoven, assistant secretary of defense for systems analysis. "Our strategy of attrition," he asserted flatly, "has not worked." Despite a "massive influx of 500,000 U.S. troops, 1.2 million tons of bombs a year, [and] 20,000 U.S. KIA," the enemy "shows no lack of capability or will to match each new U.S. escalation."

We became mesmerized by statistics of known doubtful validity, choosing to place our faith only in the ones that showed progress. We judged the enemy's intentions rather than his capabilities because we trusted captured documents too much. . . . In short, our setbacks were due to wishful thinking compounded by a massive intelligence collection and/or intelligence failure.

"We have achieved stalemate," Enthoven concluded, "at a high commitment."

Jolted by the Pentagon's sweeping repudiation of U.S. military strategy in Vietnam, Clifford began to ask some hard questions, only to discover that "there was no military plan for victory."

Our plan seemed to be that continual attrition hopefully would force the enemy at some unknown time in the future to come to terms. But when I attempted to find out how long it would take to achieve our goal, there was no answer. . . . I couldn't find out how many more guns and planes, how much time was needed. It was a dead end.

As an alternative to the search and destroy tactics employed by MACV since 1965, most members of the task force favored an urban-centered "population control strategy." General Wheeler, however, vigorously opposed the idea, arguing that such a strategy contained "two fatal flaws": It would mean increased fighting near the cities, and hence higher civilian casualties, and it would concede the initiative to the enemy. The civilians in the Pentagon countered by pointing out that the current strategy had effectively invited the enemy to strike the cities at no small cost in South Vietnamese civilian casualties.

On March 4 the Clifford task force filed its report. Born

of compromise between Pentagon civilians and the American military command, it contained a number of specific recommendations: that the president immediately authorize the deployment of 22,000 new troops to Vietnam; that he approve a call-up of 245,000 reservists; that he link any future increases in American military strength to improvements in the performance of both ARVN and GVN; and that he make some "general decision on bombing policy"—either "a substantial extension of targets" or a "seasonal step-up through the spring." While the main thrust of the report seemed to accord closely with the views of the Joint Chiefs, eight appendices explicitly pointed out the need for "new strategic guidance" and for the determination of a finite "limit" to the American involvement in Vietnam. "Big questions remained," remembered William Bundy, assistant secretary of state for Far Eastern affairs. "There were stop signs—caution signs—all over this draft. This was quite deliberate. We had fulfilled our mandate, but there were all sorts of questions remaining. . . . Anybody could see that this was perfectly clear, that no president would decide on the basis of these recommendations."

Crisis

The findings of the Clifford task force troubled Lyndon Johnson. Despite the gathering storm of public opposition to his war policy, the president had been encouraged by the most recent MACV assessments of the situation in Vietnam. Not only had the GVN and ARVN continued to improve, according to Westmoreland, but American forces throughout South Vietnam were "moving to a general offensive." Now some of his most trusted advisers were telling him that U.S. military strategy had failed and that a new strategy was needed. Walt Rostow tried to mitigate the underlying pessimism of the report, attributing it to disgruntled Pentagon officials who had long ago soured on the war. Noting the initial surge of public hawkishness that had followed the Tet attacks, he urged the president to rally the American people for an all-out effort to win the war. Johnson was unpersuaded. He was more disturbed by the futility and despair reflected in the faces of many members of the task force than by the words of their report.

Although the question of the troop increase was still officially unresolved, soon after the task force presented its report General Wheeler cabled Westmoreland and told him "to forget the 100,000." A second cable followed on March 8. Speaking on behalf of the new secretary of defense, Wheeler said, he wanted the MACV commander to know that "your request for additional forces . . . would be hard, perhaps impossible, to sell if we do not adopt a sober and conservative attitude as to the political, economic, and psychological situation in South Vietnam." Unaware of the manner in which Wheeler had presented the

request, equally unmindful of the crisis of confidence that it had precipitated in Washington, Westmoreland shot back an angry reply. He told Wheeler to inform the secretary that he would conform to his guidance in so far as it was "consistent with intellectual honesty as to my appraisal of the situation." Two days later, the Sunday edition of the *New York Times* reported that Westmoreland had requested 206,000 more troops for Vietnam. Believing the story to be wholly erroneous, Westmoreland was furious. "I was shocked to later learn that my recommendation was portrayed as an urgent request."

What followed was a week of startling political reversals that propelled Lyndon Johnson toward the most agonizing crisis of his presidency. On March 12, two days after the *Times* story appeared, the citizens of New Hampshire went to the polls. The results of the Democratic primary shook the White House and reverberated across the country: McCarthy 42.4 percent, Johnson 49.5 percent. Even though Johnson's name did not appear on the ballot, the organizers of his write-in campaign had anticipated a comfortable margin of victory. The unexpectedly strong showing of the "Peace Candidate" from Minnesota made it clear that the incumbent president, the man who four years before had been elected by the widest margin in American history, was in serious political trouble. On March 16 Senator Robert Kennedy announced his candidacy for the Democratic nomination. Two days later 139 members of the House of Representatives sponsored a res-

olution calling for an immediate Congressional review of American policy in Southeast Asia.

As the political fabric of Johnson's presidency unraveled, the economic stays of his Great Society also began to splinter. The president had always believed that "a rich nation . . . can afford to make progress at home while meeting obligations abroad." But by early 1968 the combined weight of his two-front war against communism in South Vietnam and against poverty in America threatened to send the economy into a tailspin. Rapid inflation, the first symptom of the growing strain, had been gathering steam since 1966. As a remedy the president had proposed a 10 percent surtax on income, but Congress had refused approval unless the tax hike were accompanied by cuts in domestic spending. As the dollar weakened, the American balance-of-payments surplus had dwindled, resulting in a deficit of $7 billion during the last quarter of 1967.

After Tet things got worse. Stock prices plummeted, interest rates soared, inflation continued unabated, and the prospect of additional increases in military expenditures without a proportional rise in taxes prompted foreign speculators to start a run on U.S. gold reserves. By mid-March the United States had lost $327 million to speculators, the London and Zurich gold markets had shut down, and Johnson had to act. Over the weekend of March 17 the financial ministers and heads of central banks from seven nations secretly met in Washington and worked out a tem-

My Lai

After the massacre, My Lai-4, March 16, 1968.

The men of Charlie Company, 1st Battalion, 11th Infantry Brigade, were tense as they boarded the army assault helicopters at LZ Dottie on the morning of March 16, 1968. Since their arrival in-country in December 1967, they had spent many weeks patrolling the coastal lowlands of eastern Quang Ngai Province. Snipers, mines, and booby traps had thinned their ranks, yet they had made little direct contact with the ever elusive enemy. Now, their commanding officer, Captain Ernest L. Medina, told them they would have a chance "to get even" with the VC.

Medina had assembled the entire company the night before to brief them on their mission and "to fire them up" for what "looked like a tough fight." Intelligence reports indicated that the Vietcong 48th Local Force Battalion, one of the enemy's best units, had established a base in My Lai-4, a subhamlet of the village of Son My some six miles northeast of Quang Ngai City. Charlie Company's objective, Medina explained, was to destroy the 48th Battalion as well as My Lai-4. The assault would begin at 7:30 A.M. By then the women and children would be on their way to the weekly market in the provincial capital, leaving a force of some 250 to 280 armed men in the

hamlet. The young soldiers of Charlie Company would be outnumbered two-to-one, the captain said, but he remained confident that his men would prove equal to the task.

Using a stick, Medina etched the plan of attack on the ground. Following a preparatory artillery barrage west of the hamlet, the 1st Platoon, under the command of Second Lieutenant William L. Calley, Jr., would lead the way. After clearing the LZ, they would move through the southern sector of My Lai-4, sweeping the enemy to the east. The 2d Platoon, led by Second Lieutenant Steven K. Brooks, had a comparable mission in the northern sector. The 3d Platoon and the weapons platoon were to follow behind and "mop up."

Echoing the orders he had received from his superiors, Captain Medina urged his men "to be aggressive and close in rapidly with the enemy." He also ordered them to burn the houses, kill all livestock, and destroy whatever crops and foodstuffs they found. According to many members of the company, Medina's message, implicitly or explicitly stated, was that nothing was to be left alive in My Lai-4.

★ ★ ★

It was sunny and already hot when the

first wave of helicopters touched down in a soggy rice field about 135 meters west of the hamlet at 7:30 A.M.—right on schedule. Mistakenly told that the landing zone was "hot," the men of the 1st Platoon came out firing but received no fire in return. Then one of the soldiers spotted an old man standing in the paddy, waving his arms. Thinking he was a VC guerrilla, they opened fire. The man fell in a hail of bullets. The troops went to retrieve his weapon. They found none.

Twenty minutes later Charlie Company launched its assault. As the soldiers approached the high bamboo grass and thick hedgerows that cloistered the settlement, a few Vietnamese began to flee across the open fields and were immediately gunned down. In one instance the victims turned out to be a woman and a baby; in another a woman and two small children. But most of the villagers, knowing that the Americans would shoot at anyone running, remained inside or in front of their homes, impassively awaiting the advancing soldiers.

No one remembers precisely when, or why, the killing started. There was still no hostile fire, still no sign of an armed enemy force. But as the squads of the 1st and 2d platoons swept into My Lai-4, some of the soldiers began to fire without warning into the thatch-covered huts and red-brick homes of the hamlet. Others set the dwellings ablaze and then shot or bayoneted the inhabitants as they attempted to escape. Still others ordered civilians into their family bunkers and then tossed in grenades. One old man was thrown into a well, followed by an M26 grenade. Two young women were raped and then shot at pointblank range. A group of "some old women and some little children," one soldier recalled, "were kneeling and crying and praying ... around a temple where some incense was burning" when several Americans "walked by and executed [them] by shooting them in the head with their rifles. The soldiers killed all fifteen or twenty of them."

The assault on My Lai-4 was the biggest operation of the day in the Americal Division. Expecting a major battle, headquarters had sent along two army correspondents—Specialist Five Jay Roberts, a reporter, and Sergeant Ronald L. Haeberle, a photographer—to record the action for the brigade newspaper. As Roberts and Haeberle followed the first two platoons into the hamlet, they saw dead bodies, dead animals, and burning huts everywhere, but no sign of fighting. One soldier was chasing a duck with a knife; another was butchering a water buffalo with his bayonet. Haeberle watched as a man and two children approached a group of soldiers. "They just kept walking toward us," he recalled. "You could hear the little girl saying, 'No, no....' All of a sudden the GIs opened up and cut them down." Later he saw a few soldiers grab a Vietnamese girl of about fifteen and attempt to tear off her blouse. An older woman, possibly the girl's mother, began flailing at the Americans but was knocked down by a rifle butt. Then one of the soldiers noticed Haeberle, camera in hand, and the struggle stopped. Other women and children quickly huddled around the young girl. As the photographer began to walk away, he heard a sustained burst of automatic weapons fire. Haeberle turned and saw that only a small boy had survived. Moments later he, too, was shot.

Other villagers were put under guard and led away. One group of twenty to fifty women, children, and old men were

taken to a clearing just south of the hamlet; another group of about eighty to a drainage ditch ninety meters to the east. Shortly after 8 A.M., Lieutenant Calley approached the first group and told his men, "You know what I want you to do with them." Ten minutes later he returned. "Haven't you got rid of them yet?" he asked. "I want them dead." The women, shouting "No VC!" or simply "No! No!" tried frantically but vainly to shield the children as the soldiers aimed their weapons. "We stood about ten to fifteen feet away from them and then he [Calley] started shooting them," one member of the squad later testified. "Then he told me to start shooting them. I used more than a whole clip—used four or five clips." Each M16 clip contained eighteen bullets.

Forty-five minutes later Calley arrived at the drainage ditch. By then, according to some witnesses, as many as 150 unarmed civilians, the majority of them women and children, had been herded into the ditch. When some of the villagers tried to crawl out, Calley opened fire and commanded his troops to join in. One of the soldiers refused, but the others dutifully complied. To conserve ammunition some switched from automatic fire to single shot. They fired and kept firing until the screams stopped and all of the bodies lay motionless. Then, miraculously, a two-year-old child emerged from the carnage, crying. When he began to run back toward the hamlet, Lieutenant Calley grabbed him, pushed him back into the ditch, and shot him. A few minutes later he told his men to take a break.

Warrant Officer Hugh C. Thompson, the pilot of a small observation helicopter assigned to the My Lai mission, was making a pass just south of the burning hamlet when he noticed several wounded civilians lying in a rice field. He ordered his door gunners to mark the location with smoke grenades and put in a request for medical assistance. When he returned to the same site an hour later, however, he discovered that all of the people he had marked were now dead. Continuing his flights over the village, he saw a small boy bleeding along a trench. Again he marked the spot with smoke, then watched in horror as an American officer casually walked up and shot the child.

Eventually Thompson came upon the

drainage ditch east of the hamlet. He decided to find out what was going on. Landing his helicopter near the ditch, he saw that some of the people were still alive. He asked a sergeant standing nearby what could be done to help the wounded. The sergeant told him that the only way he could help them was "to help them out of their misery." Thompson then returned to his helicopter and lifted off.

Soon he caught sight of a group of eight to ten women and children running toward a bunker about 180 meters northeast of My Lai, followed closely by a group of U.S. soldiers. Again he decided to land. This time, however, he ordered his crew to train their weapons on the Americans. Standing between the Vietnamese and the Americans, he asked the lieutenant in charge to help him get the civilians to safety. The lieutenant replied that "the only way to get them out is with a hand grenade." "You just hold your men right here," Thompson told the officer, "and I will get the women and kids out." A short time later two helicopter gunships landed and evacuated the people.

★   ★   ★

Between 300 and 400 people—most of them women, children, and old men—were slain in and around My Lai-4 on March 16, 1968. Captain Medina initially reported that his men had killed 69 Vietcong soldiers. The operation as a whole officially netted 128 enemy KIA. Charlie Company suffered only 1 casualty—a soldier who had accidentally or intentionally shot himself in the foot. On March 17 the *New York Times* told the story of a successful American operation the day before in Quang Ngai Province. "While the two companies of United States soldiers moved in on the enemy force from opposite sides, heavy artillery barrages and armed helicopters were called in to pound the North Vietnamese soldiers." There was no mention of any civilian casualties.

More than a year would pass before the American public learned the true story of the assault on My Lai-4.

Clark Clifford (right), who argued for de-escalation, meets with JCS Chairman Wheeler, who favored a call-up of the reserves and an expanded war effort.

porary solution. But the fundamental problem remained. Until the U.S. strengthened the dollar, either by cutting expenditures or by increasing taxes, the international monetary crisis would continue.

Caught in a maelstrom of conflicting pressures, Lyndon Johnson sought guidance from those he trusted most. On March 15 he met with Dean Acheson, the former secretary of state and a long-time supporter of the administration's war policy. Since late February, Acheson had been conducting an independent investigation of the war, interviewing officials at the State Department, the Defense Department, and the CIA. Johnson wanted to know what the elder statesman had learned. Acheson was blunt. He told the president that neither the time nor the resources necessary to achieve American military objectives were available. The American people would not stand for "more of the same," neither further escalation nor the continuation of the present level of effort over the period of time required—perhaps five years. He concluded that the ground strategy had to be altered, the bombing halted or greatly reduced, and the war brought to a close as quickly as possible.

But Lyndon Johnson was not yet ready to give up the fight. Heeding Rostow's earlier advice, he decided to take his case to the country and demand "a total national effort to win the war." "We must meet our commitments in the world and in Vietnam," he told the National Alliance of Businessmen in Chicago on March 18. "We shall and we are going to win!" Speaking to the National Farmers Union convention in Minneapolis the next day, he repeated the message. "We don't plan to surrender or let people divide our nation in time of national peril. . . . The time has come when we ought to stand up and be counted, when we ought to support our leaders, our government, our men, and our allies."

The truculent tone of Johnson's speeches, his apparent insensitivity to the public mood, deeply distressed many of his advisers. Telling the president he was "shocked" by the overwhelmingly negative public response to the speeches, James Rowe, Jr., a chief organizer of the Johnson reelection campaign, urged the president to do something "dramatic . . . before the Wisconsin primary" on April 2. "McCarthy and Kennedy are the candidates of peace and the president is the war candidate," he wrote to Johnson on March 19. "He must do something exciting and dramatic to recapture the peace issue." The following morning Johnson telephoned Clifford: "I've got to get me a peace proposal."

Dissonant voices

On March 20, and again on March 22, the president met with his senior advisers to discuss plans for a major television address on the Vietnam War. During the deliberations a consensus quickly emerged: The president should make a new peace initiative by limiting in some way the bombing of North Vietnam. As was commonly the case in the Johnson administration, however, underlying that broad consensus were fundamental differences of opinion. Dean Rusk and Walt Rostow advocated a partial cessation of the bombing for primarily political reasons. Recognizing the need to restore public confidence in the administration's war policy, yet convinced that negotiations would lead nowhere until the North Vietnamese realized they could not prevail militarily, both men favored an unconditional cutback in the bombing to the twentieth parallel because it involved few military risks. Only 5 percent of all bombing targets were north of the twentieth parallel, Rusk pointed out, and in any case the monsoon would inhibit air strikes throughout the spring. Moreover, if Hanoi rejected the offer, which Rusk fully expected, the United States would be in a much better position to continue the war with increased public support.

Clark Clifford, however, objected to Rusk's line of reasoning. The task was not to placate public opinion in order to permit a continuation, or even an escalation, of the conflict but to find a way out. What was needed was some gesture that would begin the process of negotiation, one concrete step that could be followed by a series of "de-escalatory steps" leading down the path of peace. Like Rusk, Clifford favored a limitation of the bombing, but he wanted every effort made to insure that the North Vietnamese would respond positively to such an initiative.

At the conclusion of the meeting of March 22, the president directed that the bombing halt proposal be removed from the draft of his speech and studied separately. Clifford, along with some of the president's other senior advisers, was discouraged. Johnson didn't seem to be listening. He seemed as determined as ever to pursue the same course. What Johnson required, Clark Clifford concluded, was "some stiff medicine to bring home to [him] what was happening in the country." He proposed that the president reconvene the same group of outside advisers, the so-called "Wise Men," who had met with him the preceding November. Johnson, recalling the strong support that these men had given him in the fall, welcomed the idea. He asked Rostow to set up a meeting as soon as possible.

The names Lyndon Johnson scribbled on his note pad on March 26 could have come from a "who's who" of the post–World War II American foreign policy establishment: Dean Acheson, George Ball, McGeorge Bundy, Arthur Dean, C. Douglas Dillon, Arthur Goldberg, Henry Cabot Lodge, Robert Murphy, Cyrus Vance, and Generals Omar

Bradley, Matthew Ridgway, and Maxwell Taylor. The list included former cabinet officers, undersecretaries of state and defense, presidential aides, ambassadors, and military commanders from the Truman, Eisenhower, Kennedy, and Johnson administrations. They were men Johnson trusted and respected, men experienced in the making of presidential decisions. He had brought them together in the past to sound out their views and to secure their endorsement of his policies. This time, the most decisive moment in his presidency, he hoped that these wise men would once again give him the guidance he needed.

In previous meetings, in April 1965 and in November 1967, their voices had rung with almost unanimous approval. Only George Ball had expressed any dissent from the collective judgment that the president was on "the right track," that the Korean War had been just as tough, if not tougher, and that if he just "stuck to it" he would ultimately prevail.

Now the voices were dissonant. In fact, "the majority feeling," said McGeorge Bundy, speaking on behalf of the group, "is that we can no longer do the job we set out to do in the time we have left and we must begin to take steps to disengage. When we last met," he explained, "we saw reasons for hope. We hoped then there would be slow but steady progress. Last night and today the picture is not so hopeful."

President Johnson meets with his advisers on March 22 to discuss his forthcoming speech to the nation. To his left is Defense Secretary Clark Clifford, to his right Secretary of State Dean Rusk.

"The picture" had been sketched out the previous evening in a discussion with the president's current advisers and in a series of briefings by officials of the State Department and the CIA and the staff of the Joint Chiefs. At one point C. Douglas Dillon, secretary of the treasury under Kennedy, asked how long it would take to win the war if the current level of effort were sustained. "Maybe five years, maybe ten," came the reply. An exchange between United Nations ambassador Arthur Goldberg and Major General William DePuy proved even more revealing. After the general noted that the enemy had lost more than 80,000 troops during the Tet offensive, Goldberg inquired about the killed-to-wounded ratio. The general told him that three-to-one would be a conservative estimate. Then Goldberg asked, "How many effectives do you think they have operating in the field?" DePuy cited the official MACV enemy order of battle figure of 230,000. "Well, General," said Goldberg, "I am not a great mathematician, but with 80,000 killed and with a wounded ratio of three to one, or 240,000, for a total of 320,000, who the hell are we fighting?"

The president's reactions to the discussions were veiled. He posed questions to each man around the table, probing for the cause of the dramatic shift in the majority view since the preceding November. At first he suspected that one of the briefers had "poisoned the well," but in the end he realized that the group had based its decision upon more fundamental considerations: the erosion of public confidence in the government, the dire state of the American economy, the plaguing uncertainties in South Vietnam, and the cost in lives and dollars of five to ten more years of war. As Johnson listened to Bundy's summary, he recorded on his note pad the verdict of his wise men. The phrases were broken, but the meaning was clear: "Can no longer do job we set out to do . . . Adjust our course . . . Move to disengage."

"I shall not seek . . ."

"Good evening, my fellow Americans." The red TV camera light switched on at precisely 9:00 P.M., Sunday, March 31, 1968. Bathed in the high-intensity television lights that surrounded his desk in the Oval Office, the president of the United States—his brow deeply furrowed, his eyes ringed by dark circles—looked every bit the weary man that he was. "Tonight I want to speak to you of peace in Vietnam and Southeast Asia. No other question so preoccupies our people. No other dream so absorbs the 250 million human beings who live in that part of the world. No other goal motivates American policy in Southeast Asia." He spoke of the "failure" of the Tet offensive, of the "widespread disruption and suffering" it had caused, of the mounting casualties "on both sides of the struggle," and of the need "to bring an end to this long and this bloody war." Then he returned to the issue of peace.

"Tonight, I renew the offer I made last August—to stop the bombing of North Vietnam. We ask that talks begin promptly, that they be serious talks on the substance of peace. We assume that during those talks Hanoi will not take advantage of our restraint. . . . We are reducing—substantially reducing—the present level of hostilities. And we are doing so unilaterally, and at once."

Johnson announced that he had already ordered "our aircraft and our naval vessels to make . . . no attacks around the principal populated areas" of North Vietnam. But in order to protect "forward allied positions," bombing would continue in "the area north of the Demilitarized Zone." He made no mention of the twentieth parallel or any other line of demarcation. Neither did he specify the duration of the halt nor list any conditions under which the bombing would be resumed. Instead he held out the possibility of "a complete bombing halt," depending upon future events. Yet if the terms of the president's new initiative came from Rusk's proposal, the emphasis echoed Clifford's.

"Now, as in the past, the United States is ready to send its representatives to any forum, at any time, to discuss the means of bringing this ugly war to an end. . . . I call upon President Ho Chi Minh to respond positively, and favorably, to this new step toward peace . . . the first in what I hope will be a series of moves toward peace."

The president then disclosed two other decisions—to send an additional 13,500 troops to Vietnam and to re-equip the South Vietnamese army—but their impact was overshadowed by the announcement of the bombing halt and the even more dramatic statements that followed.

For 37 years in the service of our Nation, first as a Congressman, as a Senator and as Vice President and now as your President, I have put the unity of the people first. . . .

And holding the trust that is mine, as President of all the people, I cannot disregard the peril to the progress of the American people and the hope and the prospect of peace for all peoples . . . .

What we won when all of our people united just must not now be lost in suspicion, distrust, selfishness and politics among any of our people.

Johnson had reached the formal end of his speech. He paused briefly. Even among his closest aides, few knew that at the last moment the president had appended another section to his text. Fewer still knew what he was about to say.

"Believing this as I do, I have concluded that I should not permit the Presidency to become involved in the partisan divisions that are developing in this political year," he asserted. "Accordingly, I shall not seek, and I will not accept, the nomination of my party for another term as your President."

The president's concluding words electrified the nation and the world. Even though he had not formally declared himself a candidate for reelection, it was generally assumed that he would run. Even though he told many of his close aides and friends that he might not, few took him seriously. Lyndon Baines Johnson was above all a creature of American politics and a master of its art. The son of poor Texas dirt farmers, he had climbed the "greasy pole" of democratic politics, as Benjamin Disraeli once described it, and attained the most powerful office in the world's most powerful nation. He had fought for what he got, and those who knew him best did not believe he would ever just give it up.

If he surrendered, however, it was not so much because he was beaten as because he recognized the futility of the fight. The American people had rendered a judgment, and he accepted that judgment. Brash, vulgar, domineering on the one hand, warm, generous, idealistic on the other, Lyndon Johnson was a man of contradictions. Yet in his feeling for his "fellow Americans," as he always called them, his egoism and his compassion converged.

He wanted to be remembered as a great president, and great because he had genuinely helped the people. Instead he had divided them and left divided judgments about his greatness.

None of the decisions that Johnson announced on March 31 was irrevocable. The duration of the bombing halt was contingent upon the response of the North Vietnamese; the future improvement of ARVN upon the will of the South Vietnamese to fight; and the new American troop ceiling upon developments that no one could then predict. The president also could have revoked the decision to withdraw from the presidential race. Yet there was more conviction and more finality attached to that decision than to any of the others. Consumed by the war he had chosen to fight, and by the war at home it had created, he withdrew from the battle in the hope of rising above it. To restore unity in America he would seek peace in Vietnam. The war, he realized, was tearing the nation apart.

Working late in the Cabinet Room, LBJ ponders the text of his March 31 speech.

America Divided

It was, declared the *New York Times*, "an astounding announcement." Scarcely had the president finished speaking before tributes began pouring into the White House from a stunned and grateful nation. "President Johnson's decision to sacrifice himself on the altar of peace and national unity," proclaimed the *Los Angeles Times*, "is an act of statesmanship which entitles him to the American people's deepest sympathy and respect." The *Washington Post* believed the president's "personal sacrifice in the name of national unity" entitled him to "a very special place in the annals of American history and to a very special kind of gratitude and appreciation." Even the *Chicago Tribune*, no friend of Democrats, could hardly restrain its admiration for "an act of self-abnegation unparalleled in American history."

The source of the national approbation that washed over Lyndon Johnson during the first week of April was only too apparent. "There is division in the American house now," the presi-

dent had declared from the Oval Office. "There is divisiveness among us all tonight." Inflamed by the war, a crisis of domestic harmony more profound than at any time since the Civil War gripped the people of the United States. No one person any longer seemed to speak for a common American purpose. No one any longer seemed confident that the social consensus forged out of depression and world war could endure.

Thus, it was with something close to exhilaration that the nation celebrated the president's call for unity. Throngs of well-wishers cheered Johnson's visit to New York for the investiture of Archbishop Terence Cardinal Cooke, while sixty blocks south the New York stock market recorded its greatest trading day in history, finishing with a twenty-point jump in the Dow Jones average. When Hanoi sent word on April 3 that it accepted the American offer and was prepared to talk, Johnson's gamble appeared to be on the verge of success.

But peace, whether abroad or at home, could no longer be purchased even at so great a cost. Johnson, more than most, understood the terrible dimensions of the problems he sought to resolve. "I put my last chips on the table," he

Preceding page. A demonstrator places pink carnations in the rifles of guards near the Pentagon. Soon after violence erupted; 27 persons were injured, 250 arrested.

told Postmaster-General Larry O'Brien the morning after his historic address. "But I don't think that's enough. I don't think even foregoing the presidency will be enough." It would prove to be a painfully accurate prophecy. The promise of negotiations would dissipate in weeks of wrangling over an acceptable site, and the hope of national reconciliation would explode in a murderous spring of political upheaval, civil disorder, and assassination.

The expansion of dissent

That explosion had been years in the making. As long as American military participation in the war remained relatively modest, public demonstrations against U.S. policy in South Vietnam were practically nonexistent. But with the escalation of the war in the spring of 1965, the implications of continued American involvement began to provoke vocal expressions of anger and dismay from a growing number of ordinary citizens.

The 20,000 protesters who rallied in Washington on April 17 of that year were one sign of the new anxiety. Another was the "teach-ins." The first took place on March 24 at the University of Michigan, an all-night marathon of speeches, songs, discussions, and seminars on the Vietnam conflict. Within weeks teach-ins on the war had taken place at over 100 colleges and universities. The

Above. As demonstrations against the war grew in size, so did the ranks of counterdemonstrators, like these taunting marchers at the April 1967 New York rally (shown on facing page).

Thousands of protesters jam the streets of Manhattan in a peaceful antiwar march, largest in the nation's history, on April 15, 1967.

administration attempted to respond by sending "truth teams" of government information officers to campuses, with little success. Thereafter the government was much more cautious in exposing its policies to public scrutiny. But the momentum of dissent could not be halted.

From the beginning, the antiwar movement was a counterpoint of radical and moderate impulses. Soon after the April 17 march, a group of independent leftists gathered thirty-three antiwar organizations into the National Coordinating Committee To End the War in Vietnam. One month later the California-based Vietnam Day Committee attempted to block troop trains. In October, the two groups mounted demonstrations in ninety-three cities in what organizers called the "International Days of Protest."

Yet the largest antiwar march of 1965 took place under the direction of SANE, a liberal, middle-class peace group that attracted some 30,000 people to Washington on November 27. Led by veteran Socialist Norman Thomas, pediatrician Dr. Benjamin Spock, and Mrs. Martin Luther King, Jr., they carried signs calling for an end to the bombing and a supervised cease-fire. "Middle-class Americans may not be any wiser than beatniks," commented Robert Sherrill in the Nation, "but they mean a lot more to Johnson, whose backbone of consensus is built right through the middle."

The most striking protest of 1965 took place during the October demonstrations when David J. Miller, a twenty-two-year-old Catholic pacifist, burned his draft card in defiance of a newly passed federal law making such action a felony. Miller was convicted and sent to prison, but draft resistance rapidly became a major part of the antiwar strategy. The decision in February 1966 to begin induction of college students "who were in the lower levels of their respective classes" brought a swift and angry response from college campuses, where selective service exams became a focus of protest. Draft resistance groups sprang up everywhere, their mood expressed by a lapel button: "Not With My Life You Don't." It was the first time that many college men confronted the prospect of conscription, and at many places the demonstrations attracted a much greater variety of students than had taken part in the past.

Dissent becomes respectable

During 1966 the antiwar movement expanded in a number of other ways. The resumption of American air strikes over North Vietnam on January 31, after a thirty-seven-day bombing pause, brought peace groups out in force. In Washington 100 members of Veterans and Reservists To End the War in Vietnam picketed the White House and tried to return their medals and campaign ribbons to the president. Four days later 5,000 American scientists, including seventeen Nobel Prize winners, begged the White House for a review of U.S. chemical and biological warfare in Vietnam. Numerous groups—physicians, lawyers, veterans, teachers, industrialists, clergymen, and entertainers—ran advertisements in the New York Times calling for an end to the war. Opening the Senate Foreign Relations Committee's hearings on the war on February 7, Chairman William Fulbright told reporters he had "never seen such dissent, reservation, groping, and concern."

The month-long Fulbright hearings made dissent respectable and paved the way for a flurry of nearly fifty "peace candidates" in fifteen states during the 1966 Congressional campaign. While most went down to defeat, some polled surprisingly well, including Robert Scheer, the editor of the radical magazine Ramparts, who received 45 percent of the primary vote against a liberal incumbent in Oakland's 7th district; and Alice Franklin Bryant, who won the Democratic nomination in Washington State's 1st Congressional district. In a local referendum held in Dearborn, Michigan, nearly 40 percent of the voters called for an immediate cease-fire and withdrawal of U.S. troops.

By 1967 antiwar activists were prepared to demonstrate that active opposition to the war was not limited to a few radicals and political idealists but included vast numbers of ordinary men and women. On April 15 some 300,000 Americans—"Quakers, Roman Catholics, Jewish war veterans, Episcopal seminarians, and students ... middle-class marchers in business suits, and housewives with children in baby buggies"—gathered in New York City in the largest antiwar rally in U.S. history. Two months later a national steering committee of adult pacifists, liberals, and academic radicals organized Vietnam Summer, an effort to bring the war literally to the nation's doorstep. Fanning out across communities all over the country, 20,000 students, housewives, ministers, and young professors canvassed their neighbors' attitudes on the war, built local antiwar organizations, held lectures and discussion groups, distributed leaflets, and organized "peace fairs." In September, pollster Louis Harris reported a 12 percent drop in support for the war over the previous two months. Despite the president's assurance that there were "no deep divisions" over his conduct of the war, Time magazine found instead "a clashing disharmony" ringing "loud and clear the length of the land."

Yet by the fall of 1967 antiwar forces were in a quandary. For all its growing size and energy, the movement had had little effect on the war. Draft calls continued to rise: 11,400 in April; 19,800 in June; 29,000 in August. So did casualty figures: August 13–19, 108 Americans killed; September 1–7, 157; September 8–14, 236.

The peace movement had succeeded in reaching out beyond the ranks of the demonstrators. But it had also provoked vocal assertions of support for the war and condemnation of the antiwar forces. Prowar activists picketed antiwar speakers, circulated petitions, and staged vigils in each of the fifty states. Rallies and parades designed to "Support Our Boys" flourished, as did prowar organizations like the National Committee for Responsible Patriotism and the California-based Victory in Vietnam Association. Public opinion polls revealed markedly negative attitudes toward antiwar activists. In a survey asking people to rate various groups and personalities on a 100-point scale, one-third of the respondents gave war protesters a zero. For many people, political scientist John Mueller discovered, "opposition to the war came to be associated with violent disruption, stink bombs, desecration of the flag, profanity, and contempt for American values."

Speaker of the House John McCormack called criticism of the war "a valuable mark of sympathy" for the Communist cause and excoriated dissenters, to a standing ovation from 100 House members. Accusing militant peace groups of "rebellion [that] verges on treason," former president Dwight D. Eisenhower refused to support any candidate advocating a withdrawal from Vietnam.

Moreover, the tenuous alliance between radical and moderate peace forces had begun to come apart. SANE spent much of 1967 arguing internally whether the organization should associate itself with groups like the National Mobilization Committee. A Mobilization cochairman thought of it as a "generational gap, with the older liberal organizations lagging behind the students." But SANE founder Norman Cousins saw it differently: "We couldn't

control what those people would say, and we didn't want SANE to be taxed with ideas that most of us didn't share."

For their part, the defeat of most peace candidates in the 1966 elections had turned many radicals away from the electoral process. Convinced that protest and education were not enough to halt the war, antiwar activists determined to confront directly the American military machine at the source of its manpower, the induction center, and at the Pentagon itself.

March on the Pentagon

During a week of protests, sit-ins, and running battles with the police, Stop the Draft demonstrators in Oakland, California, attacked the process of induction. On Monday, October 16, 120 pacifists were arrested following a sit-in at the Oakland induction center. The next day protest erupted into violence as 3,000 demonstrators throwing bottles and chunks of brick resisted a furious attack by Oakland riot police wielding nightsticks and Mace. With simultaneous antidraft actions underway in fifteen other cities, the Oakland clashes reached a climax on Friday, October 20, when 10,000 demonstrators, many wearing helmets and shields, battled police for hours over control of a

Police subdue a "Stop the Draft" protester in Oakland during a week of bloody antiwar demonstrations around the U.S. in mid-October, 1967.

twenty-two block area surrounding the induction center.

Three thousand miles away, it was Washington's turn. Within a month of the spring marches, the National Mobilization Committee had begun plans for a confrontation in the capital, eventually securing the cooperation of 100 separate antiwar organizations. To accommodate the variety of positions represented by these groups, the committee designed a two-part demonstration: for those interested in simply protesting the government's prosecution of the war, a rally; for those willing to challenge the government's authority, a march on the Pentagon. On Saturday, October 21, 75,000 people streamed into Washington and gathered in front of the Lincoln Memorial to hear speakers condemn Lyndon Johnson and the war, as blue and red Vietcong flags waved above signs demanding that the government "Bring Home the GIs Now!"

The marchers' numbers had been kept down by the government's own well-publicized preparations. Army patrols circled major government buildings. Speaker John McCormack ordered the House of Representatives closed against the possibility of invasion. Guards were heavily reinforced at the gates of the White House, while troops of the 82d Airborne Division—many of them Vietnam veterans—waited outside the capital. Military police ringed the Pentagon. On the roof, federal marshals and army riflemen, weapons at hand, scanned the approaches to the giant complex as helicopters flew back and forth monitoring the demonstration. The United States government had prepared for a confrontation of force with tens of thousands of its own citizens.

As the last speeches came to an end at the Lincoln Memorial, 30,000 demonstrators linked arms, crossed the Arlington Memorial Bridge, and advanced toward the Pentagon. They came, said a spokesman for the Episcopal Peace Fellowship, "to disrupt the center of the American war machine." Suddenly, hundreds of young people broke through a line of MPs and raced up the Pentagon's main steps. As thousands more followed, troops fired tear gas and struck the demonstrators with truncheons. A second charge carried a few protesters into the building before a wave of soldiers hurled them out. For the rest of the afternoon the demonstrators alternately taunted the troops in front of them and cajoled the soldiers to "join us." In the early October twilight someone held aloft a burning draft card; soon hundreds of such tiny flames flickered in the darkness. At midnight, after reporters had left, soldiers

"In the name of humanity we will call the warmakers to task." The first of some 30,000 demonstrators assemble outside the Pentagon on October 23, 1967.

and federal marshals began clubbing those protesters directly in front of the main entrance and hauling them away. By the time the demonstration came to an end twenty-four hours later, more than 700 people had been arrested and fully twice that number listed as casualties.

"The Pentagon [march] marked the end of the old ambivalence," wrote one antiwar observer, "now there are two sides, one right, one wrong. They were hopelessly mismatched, of course, but a sense of the quickening potential for upheaval in American society gave the movement new determination." In the last two months of the year thousands of demonstrators fought mounted police in New York City, while a bloody antidraft protest erupted at the University of Wisconsin. As 1,600 corporate leaders organized Business Executives Move for Vietnam Peace, protesters fought a five-day guerrilla war against 4,000 police guarding New York's Whitehall induction center.

But the war was not the only thing dividing Americans in the spring of 1968. The agony of racial violence, the hostility between the generations, and the growing isolation of the white working class all threatened to unravel the social fabric of the nation. For blacks, students, and workers alike the war acted as a powerful irritant, exacerbating

Above and top. As the demonstrations outside the Pentagon against "McNamara's War" turn to violent skirmishes, the secretary of defense watches from his office window.

Profiles in Protest

They all opposed the Vietnam War. It was really the only thing the three men had in common. They were unlikely activists, of different generations and backgrounds. Two took to the streets to protest the war on behalf of vastly dissimilar organizations, while the other tried to work at the heart of the system. Yet each man, in his own way, was instrumental in bringing war protest to the American people.

Antiwar doctor

He was the only famous pediatrician in America. His renown as an authority on children gave Dr. Benjamin Spock an advantage when he became a leading activist in a world far removed from babies. But some Americans must have wondered why Dr. Spock was marching with radical youths raised by the methods associated with his name.

At six-foot-four he was a striking image on the picket line, white hair, horn-rimmed glasses, "still brawny, even though he is sixty-four years old," a reporter noted. Educated at the finest schools, moving into a successful medical practice, and author of *Baby and Child Care*, one of the all-time bestsellers, Spock's career in the 1940s and 1950s was comfortable and decidedly conven-

tional. He had supported the war in Korea and stayed removed from most affairs outside of the hospital. Except for giving public support to John Kennedy's campaign in 1960, he was apolitical. But the resumption of nuclear testing in the early 1960s brought Benjamin Spock into the political arena as a concerned physician. He joined SANE, the moderate disarmament group, and marched in demonstrations to end nuclear testing.

In 1964, Spock worked hard for Lyndon Johnson, believing he offered the only hope for peace. Then escalation in Vietnam began. Spock felt betrayed, and when he looked into the facts of the war, he was outraged. He believed the war was not only immoral, it was hypocritical. The U.S. maintained that "our hearts bleed for the poor people of Vietnam," Spock argued, while at the same time "we bomb their homes . . . and kill and maim their children." His solutions were as clear and simple as his protest: stop the bombing, negotiate with everyone, including the NLF. One journalist said he sounded "no more radical than say, Robert F. Kennedy."

As a national officer in SANE, Spock organized some of the early protest marches against the war. He seemed willing to go anywhere, speak, march, sign anything that might bring the conflict to an end. And he did it all with a cheery, good-guy spirit that none could assail as wide-eyed fanaticism.

But there were other charges—that he had created an entire generation of undisciplined young men and women—"I'm not responsible for all those brats," he would snap; or that he was being duped by militant activists with little stake and less interest in American society—"How can I make people realize I'm doing exactly what I want to do?" he would ask. Whether he approved of the young people's idealism, or was manipulated by the more radical among them, his own moral convictions increasingly allied him with protests at the edge of the law. During 1967 he began to speak out forcefully on behalf of draft resistance, his actions eventually resulting in a federal indictment for conspiracy to help draft resisters and hinder the draft laws. As he

awaited trial Spock was undaunted: "I'd be *delighted* if the government would prosecute me! . . . I would be glad to have the opportunity to prove that we were right."

Accidental radical

From Benjamin Spock to Carl Oglesby is a leap across bounds of class, time, and experience. Even when Spock drifted toward the militants, he was still a moderate by temperament and conviction. Carl Oglesby became president of Students for a Democratic Society just as it took the first steps wholly outside the conventional American political spectrum.

He was a radical almost by accident. In 1964 Oglesby was a twenty-nine-year-old technical writer for Bendix Aviation in Ann Arbor, Michigan, an average fellow with a wife and kids, a house and a mortgage. His roots were in the working class in Ohio, and he had wandered the country trying to make it as an actor and playwright before returning to the Midwest.

While working part-time for a congressional candidate he later characterized as "a Cold War liberal," Oglesby drew the assignment of writing the candidate's position paper on the Vietnam War. By the time he was finished, he had become convinced that Vietnam was simply a proxy for America's cold war enemies. Even worse, he concluded, the U.S. was supporting the wrong side.

The candidate and his staff rejected the paper, calling Oglesby a radical; this surprised him because he didn't think of himself as one. But his open letter about Vietnam in a University of Michigan magazine drew the attention of local members of Students for a Democratic Society, and the one-time playwright was launched on a different career.

At the time he got involved with SDS, the organization had scarcely made a ripple on most college campuses. But Oglesby believed a student movement could be built to oppose the war in Vietnam. Within a year SDS had staged the first major protest against the war, and Carl Oglesby was its new president. Over the next twelve months he traveled the country: "big meetings, little meetings, just standing on a soap box trying to gather a crowd," at one university after another.

In a speech at a Washington rally in late 1965, Oglesby assailed not just the war, but the system "that creates and sustains the war in Vietnam." The men who planned and directed American involvement in Southeast Asia, who thought themselves technically and morally capable of suppressing revolutions in other countries, weren't *bad* men, he said, they were *liberals:* "good men" who had been "divided from their compassion by the institutional system."

His rejection of liberalism received the only standing ovation that day and established him as a national figure on the New Left. While Oglesby continued to travel and talk and organize—becoming "our only spellbinder," as one SDSer observed—he remained a reserved, thoughtful person off the speaker's platform, one of the few in the movement who seemed to spend time studying and considering his positions. And while he was never sure if his actions, or the surging antiwar movement, could end the war, he believed that "one thing you *could* do was save the soul of the middle class."

But even as Oglesby worried about America's soul, more militant antiwar activists began talking about revolution. Several years older than most of his fellow radicals, feeling more and more removed from the talk of rebellion, he looked at a divided country in 1968 with a growing sense of tragedy about the war and the movement against it he had helped create.

Democratic insurgent

He was always on the move—arriving out of breath, picked up at the airport by one of the young people who drove for him around the country. He would make his speech or attend a meeting—then go somewhere else, rarely stopping for sleep. A man in perpetual motion: That was how friends remembered Allard Lowenstein in 1967 when he built a movement to stop Lyndon Johnson's reelection as president.

One of Lowenstein's great gifts, they said, was his ability to communicate the sense of "urgency and importance of what he was doing": eyes darting behind thick glasses, intense, speaking with a moving eloquence. He believed that the right candidate could ride the wave of Democratic dissatisfaction over the administration's Vietnam policy and win the presidential nomination. Not many people in 1967 thought LBJ could be defeated at the ballot box. Lowenstein was used to being in the minority.

When he started talking about finding a Democratic alternative to Johnson, he was already known in liberal circles of the party and admired for his idealism, courage, and keen tactical sense. "If there was ever a man who seemed to be at one with history," someone who had known him since the civil rights days in Mississippi said, "it was Al Lowenstein in 1967."

David Halberstam had called him "a refugee from the New Deal." People knew him as a tough political pragmatist with a knack for finding underdog causes and fighting for them. He had gone South to help found the Mississippi Freedom Democratic party and the Freedom Vote, smuggled a black student out of South Africa and written a book on conditions there. He taught at universities, practiced law, became a leader in the liberal Americans for Democratic Action.

Now he saw a new danger. "If you foreclose the options of politics by saying you cannot oppose a sitting president . . . then the frustration has to spill over into nonpolitical or nonelectoral protest."

Lowenstein set out to demonstrate that dissent was not limited to long-haired peace marchers. But he had to start with the students, "because we had no money and therefore no hope of getting anybody else to work for us." With $2,000 and the help of Curtis Gans, an old colleague from ADA, Lowenstein crisscrossed the country, attending conferences of student leaders, recruiting lieutenants, and spreading the word that Johnson could be stopped by traditional political means. At a convention of the National Student Association on August 15, 1967, he formally christened his crusade the "Dump John-

son Movement."

Through the rest of the summer and into the fall Lowenstein expanded his network of dissent. What he needed were a few people: respectable, locally prominent Democrats who believed that the president could be beaten. He also needed a candidate.

His first choice was Robert Kennedy, but the senator was skeptical. He tried to entice Congressman Don Edwards of California, Senator Frank Church of Idaho, the economist John Kenneth Galbraith, and General James M. Gavin—all to no avail. Finally George McGovern of South Dakota suggested his fellow senator from Minnesota, Eugene McCarthy. To Lowenstein's surprise, Senator McCarthy accepted.

Three months later, McCarthy had come within an eyelash of winning the New Hampshire primary, and Lyndon Johnson had retired from the race. Allard Lowenstein had begun with a simple, some said naive, proposition, that antiwar sentiment could be harnessed to bring down an incumbent president. He wagered that the system could be made to work—and he won.

*   *   *   *   *

Benjamin Spock and three of his codefendants were found guilty of conspiracy to aid draft resisters and impede the draft laws. But a higher court reversed the conviction. During the mid-1970s, he revised *Baby and Child Care* to meet the demands of changing times and wrote a column for *Redbook* magazine. Carl Oglesby wrote for *Ramparts* and other magazines and continues to write and lecture. Allard Lowenstein served a term in Congress before returning to his life of free-lance crusading. He was murdered in 1980 by a former colleague from the civil rights movement.

Blacks join the April 15, 1967, peace march in New York City.

their sense of powerlessness and inflaming their discontent.

Two societies

Since 1955, when Martin Luther King, Jr., led Montgomery, Alabama, blacks against the city bus lines, the civil rights movement had recorded enormous gains. But neither the legal victories over segregation and discrimination nor LBJ's "war on poverty" proved sufficient to arrest a growing tide of black anger and alienation. Caught between rising expectations and the deterioration of their neighborhoods, between the promise of "freedom now" and the harsh reality of white backlash, blacks released their frustrations in annual cataclysms of violence: 1965—riots in Los

Angeles; 1966—riots in Cleveland and Chicago; 1967—riots in Tampa, Cincinnati, Atlanta, Detroit, Houston, Milwaukee, Nashville, New Haven, Phoenix, Dayton, and Newark.

In the wake of the 1967 riots, President Johnson appointed a special Commission on Civil Disorders chaired by Illinois governor Otto Kerner. Its report, issued on March 1, 1968, was frank and uncompromising. Citing a "clear pattern of severe disadvantage for Negroes," the commission painted a stark picture: inferior schools, decrepit housing, crime rates consistently higher than in white areas, poor sanitation conditions and substandard medical facilities, higher incidence of major diseases and a higher mortality rate, a growing legion of permanently unemployed, police brutality, and a double standard of justice and protection.

Pointing to white racism as the root cause of these conditions, the commission noted that little had been done in the aftermath of the riots to address the legitimate grievances of the black community. "Instead, in several cities the principal official response has been to train and equip the police with more sophisticated weapons," including automatic rifles, machine guns, and tanks, "weapons designed to destroy, not to control." The United States, concluded the commission, was rapidly moving toward two societies: one black, poor, shuttered in the decaying heart of the central cities; the other white, affluent, and suburban. To continue the present policies was to accept the inevitability of racial hatred and individual despair, to invite still greater outbursts of urban violence and social anarchy.

"Hell no, we won't go!"

One of the most disturbing aspects of the Kerner Commission report was its conclusion that black Americans were increasingly unwilling to pursue a strategy of peaceful reform. Growing frustrations were now leading many young blacks in particular to "the conviction that there is no effective alternative to violence as a means of achieving redress of grievances." It was out of this seed bed of alienation and hostility that militant advocates of immediate change raised the banner of "Black Power."

Confronted with the intransigence of white southern officials, and the failure of protest to solve the problems of the urban slums, young militants like Stokely Carmichael of SNCC (Student Non-Violent Coordinating Committee) began to part ways with more moderate black organizations. Carmichael and other Black Power leaders encouraged the establishment of black cooperatives, demanded community control of black schools, and exalted black pride. Along with such ultranationalist groups as the Black Panther Party in California, Carmichael called for "liberation" instead of integration, applauded the idea of "guerrilla warfare" in the ghettos, and described urban riots as political rebellions. Convinced that the white

The Black Panthers, like this group marching to an Oakland rally, emerged in the mid-1960s as a radical—some thought threatening—expression of black identity.

power structure would yield only to force, Carmichael urged his brothers to "execute the executioners."

With Carmichael's chant "Hell no, we won't go!" as its rallying cry, SNCC propelled Black Power advocates into the antiwar movement. In a statement released in January 1966, SNCC scoffed at the concern for Vietnamese freedom voiced by the Johnson government. Arguing that black draftees had been called upon "to stifle the liberation of Vietnam" in defense of a democracy that "does not exist for them at home," SNCC offered its support to those unwilling to accept induction.

For black militants the war in Vietnam appeared to confirm their belief that racism at home produced imperialist adventures abroad. But even among the mass of the black population there was growing disaffection with the war effort. Public opinion polls revealed that blacks were far more likely to oppose the war than whites. Even moderate and conservative black leaders feared that the escalation of the war meant that precious dollars that could have gone toward remedying the ills of their community were instead being used to purchase guns, tanks, and bombs. Others were more specific, calling the war racist, and pointing to the disproportionate number of black draftees and the high level of black casualties in the 1965–1967 period. Some simply didn't think their country was worth fighting for. Among the rioters in Detroit in

1967, 39 percent expressed this view to Kerner Commission investigators; in Newark the figure was 53 percent.

By 1968 black Vietnam veterans—nearly 120,000 strong—had become a particularly embittered group. Proud of the job they were doing and supportive of American goals while they were in Vietnam, many found themselves increasingly opposed to the war once they returned home. "The black veteran quickly gets to feeling that he has been seduced and abandoned by the man," said one former infantry officer. "That's why you won't find many black vets as hawkish at home as they were in Nam." "I'm ashamed of what I did in Vietnam," said George Armstrong, an Army Spec 4 who had fought the Vietcong at Dong Be near the South China Sea. "We did to yellow people what whites do to us." If the black veteran returned to his home town more disciplined, more self-assured, and better trained than other blacks his age, he also experienced a special kind of disillusionment. "The brother in Vietnam closed his eyes to the prejudice he knew existed and hoped against hope that America would change, would change because he fought for her," explained Ahmed Lorenc, a marine veteran of the siege of Khe Sanh. "But it didn't make a bit of difference, not a bit."

The angry cries of the black militants, the deepening concern of the other civil rights leaders, and the growing bitterness of the black veteran were all reflected in the

Martin Luther King, Jr., an outspoken critic of the war, delivers his last political address at a caucus of liberal Democrats in California in January 1968.

personal antiwar odyssey of Martin Luther King, Jr. As early as 1965 the domestic consequences of growing American involvement in Southeast Asia began to haunt King. "The war must be stopped," he declared. "There must be a negotiated settlement with the Vietcong." The statement made headlines and drew a chorus of disapproval—from members of Congress who said King was not competent to make such judgments; from southern legislators delighted that King had finally revealed his "Communist sympathies"; and from other black leaders who told him he was jeopardizing the whole civil rights movement with such talk. But King would not relent. By mid-1966 he had become a vocal opponent of the administration's war policies. Like the black critics who denounced his commitment to nonviolence, King had come to believe that the plight of the black man in America was only part of an enormous struggle between the poor of the world and those who would oppress them.

This was the message he brought with him on April 4, 1967, to New York's eminent Riverside Church. "A time comes when silence is betrayal," he declared. "That time has come for us in relation to Vietnam." He described his hope only a few years earlier, that white Americans had finally begun to deal seriously with the problems of the poorest among them. "Then came the build-up in Vietnam and I watched the program broken and eviscerated as if it were some idle political plaything of a society gone mad on war ... and I knew that I could never again raise my voice against the violence of the oppressed in the ghettos without having first spoken clearly to the greatest purveyor of violence in the world today—my own government."

During the preceding decade, King charged, the United States had sent military advisers to Venezuela and mounted counterrevolutionary activities in Guatemala. "This is the role our nation has taken—the role of those who make peaceful revolution impossible by refusing to give up privileges and the pleasures that come from the immense profits of overseas investment." Now the upheaval that the United States had tried vainly to suppress was everywhere. In the jungles of Vietnam and the slums of Chicago the choice was still ours to make, warned King, but no one should any longer misunderstand what was at stake: "nonviolent coexistence or violent coannihilation."

An indignant generation

With all its disruption and rage, the idea of black revolution was something many white Americans could at least comprehend, if not always agree with. When rebellion seized their own children, however, they were almost completely at a loss. A product of the postwar "baby boom," nurtured in affluence and concentrated in increasing numbers on college and university campuses, it was a generation marked by an unusual degree of political awareness and cultural alienation. Some shared with the beat writers and poets of the late fifties a deep disillusionment with the status quo, a restless yearning for something more than a "realistic" conformity. Others had been aroused by the southern sit-in movement, "the first hint," wrote a contemporary, "that there was a world beyond the campus that demanded some kind of personal response." Not so much ideological as moral, they were, in Jessica Mitford's words, "an indignant generation."

Speaking to the concerns of the most political among them, standing ready to provide both leadership and direction, were the youthful activists of the New Left. By mid-decade there was already a burgeoning group of radical student organizations. None proved more successful than the Students for a Democratic Society (SDS), led by two University of Michigan student leaders, Tom Hayden and Al Haber, and dedicated to the principles contained in a 1962 manifesto known as the Port Huron Statement.

"We are the people of this generation," the statement began, "bred in at least modest comfort, housed now in universities, looking uncomfortably to a world we inherit." Much of the document was devoted to a thoroughgoing critique of American society—its political parties, industrial corporations, labor unions, and universities. The manifesto demanded a greater democratization of American political life, greater popular control over economic institutions, and a massive "program against poverty." Coupling opposition to America's role in the Cold War with opposition to Communist totalitarianism, seeking social reform rather than social revolution, much of the Port Huron Statement was not a great deal further left than the liberal wing of the Democratic party.

What was radical about the Port Huron Statement was its insistence that America's problems were interconnected within a vast "system" of institutions and policies politically confused and morally bankrupt: "America rests in national stalemate, its goals ambiguous and tradition bound instead of informed and clear, its democratic system apathetic and manipulated rather than 'of, by, and for the people.'" SDS proffered instead a vision of American society based on humanism, individualism, and community, a "democratic society, where at all levels the people have control of the decisions which affect them and the resources on which they are dependent."

Within a year of their first convention, the young radicals were prepared to put participatory democracy to work on the streets. Inspired by the direct action expe-

A scene in Washington, D.C., 1965. Breeding grounds of poverty, crime, and drug addiction, the nation's urban black ghettos left some immobilized by despair, others mobilized toward violence.

97

"Burn, Baby, Burn"

Above and left. Riots in August 1965 in Watts, a black section of Los Angeles, shocked the country and provoked among blacks a new mood of defiance.

Above right. A small boy, wounded during the Newark riots of 1967, lies in a pool of his own blood.

Right. A burned-out block in Detroit following riots there in June 1967.

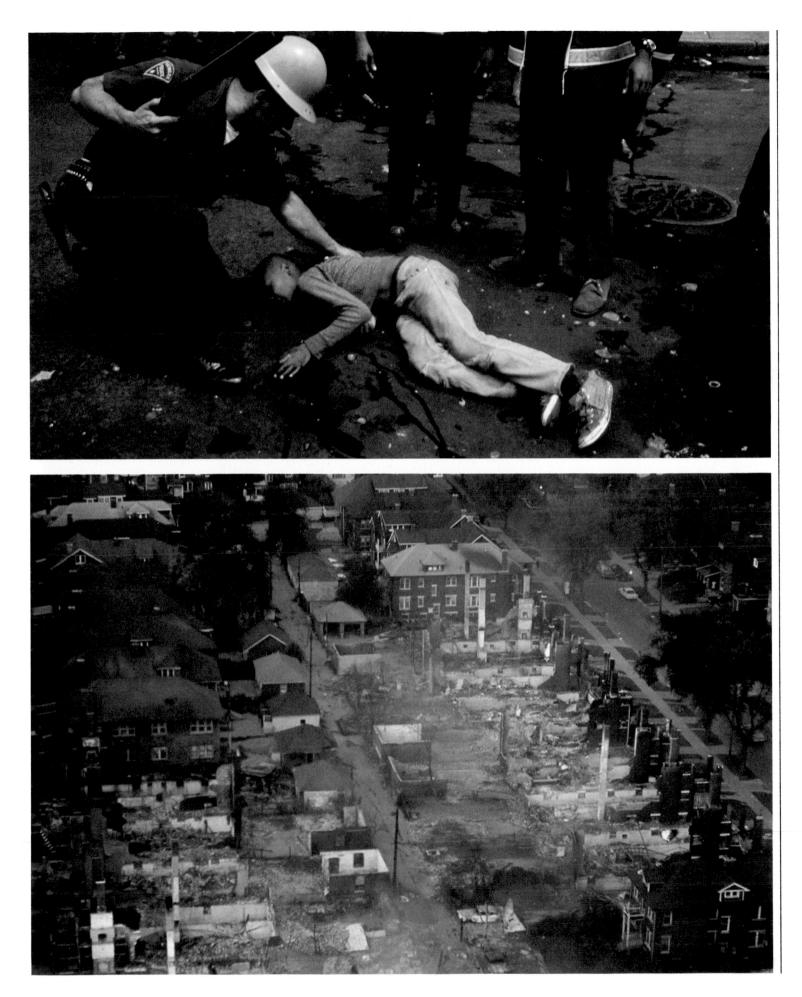

rience of SNCC in the South, SDS launched ERAP, the Economic Research and Action Project. "SDS still believed in the possibility of change within the framework of the formally representative institutions of American government," recalled ERAP veteran Richard Rothstein. "ERAP's goal was to goose those institutions a bit, to set up currents in American political life which would reverse the corruption of established liberal and trade union forces." SDS members established community organizing projects among the poor in Baltimore, Chicago, Cleveland, Boston, Newark, Philadelphia, and four other cities. In 1965 ERAP spread to San Francisco, New Haven, and elsewhere.

It soon became clear, however, that the experiment had failed. White, middle-class students found "the people" harder to reach than they had imagined and suffered mounting opposition from local officials. But ERAP had a profound effect on those who had taken part. Initially hopeful that labor unions and the liberal middle class could be prodded into action, they now viewed the liberal establishment with hostility and contempt. Next time out, they would not be content merely to challenge the system. They would resist it.

A revolutionary trajectory

The vehicle for that resistance was already waiting. On February 7, 1965, the American outpost at Pleiku was attacked. On the same day Lyndon Johnson ordered American bombers into the skies over North Vietnam. One month later the U.S. 9th Marine Expeditionary Brigade landed at Da Nang. The war had begun in earnest, and the relatively small Washington demonstration SDS had scheduled for April 17 turned into the largest peace march to date. The demonstrators paraded around the White House and then gathered behind the Washington Monument to hear SDS president Paul Potter decry the administration's war policies. "The incredible war in Vietnam has provided the razor," said Potter, cutting away "the last vestige of illusions that morality and democracy are the guiding principles of American foreign policy."

With the Potter speech the reformist tradition of SDS began to give way to more urgent demands for action. By the fall SDS was organizing directly against the draft, provoking the attention and condemnation of authorities. Mississippi's John Stennis rose in the Senate to denounce this "deplorable and shameful activity," urging the government "to jerk this movement up by the roots and grind it to bits before it has the opportunity to spread further." Columnists Rowland Evans and Robert Novak claimed that SDS had drawn up a "master plan" to "sabotage the war effort." More pointedly, Attorney General Nicholas Katzenbach announced that antidraft activity "begins to move in the direction of treason: There are some Communists in it and we may have to investigate. We may very well have some prosecutions."

The threats only brought new recruits. From 200 committed activists and 10 functioning chapters in 1962, SDS now counted 5,500 members in 151 chapters in thirty-seven states. By the fall of 1966 estimates of SDS membership ranged from 15,000 to 25,000—approximating the student body of no more than one large university, but exerting an influence out of proportion to their numbers. The enthusiasm of the new members brought SDS activities firmly back to the college campuses: In Florida, California, Washington, and Illinois, SDS put "free universities" into operation. At the University of Nebraska, SDS agitated for a student bill of rights. At New York University, the local SDS chapter staged a rally and student strike against a proposed tuition increase. And at Cornell, Brown, Columbia, Antioch, Wisconsin, Oberlin, Maryland, Kentucky, and Berkeley, SDS groups spearheaded protests against university complicity with the war effort, in particular the recruiting of students by the navy, marines, CIA, and Dow Chemical Company, the manufacturer of napalm.

It was this legion of young activists who in 1966 and 1967 hurled SDS forward on a revolutionary trajectory. The new stance appeared in escalating campus demonstrations. It took shape in the strongest antidraft program in the country. And it crystallized in an expanding rhetoric of resistance and confrontation. SDS members began to talk about a "radical rejection of American life and culture." As Dotson Radar, a Columbia University SDSer, recalled, the "meaninglessness of nonviolent, 'democratic' methods was becoming clear to us in the spring of 1967. The civil rights movement was dead. Pacifism was dead. Some Leftists . . . knew it early. But it took the rest of us a while to give up the sweet life of democratic Left for revolt."

The other dissenters

Watching the young soldiers and students stare at each other through the long Saturday afternoon of the march on the Pentagon, author Norman Mailer observed that they seemed to be looking "across the gulf of the classes, the middle classes and the white working classes," and he wondered at "the middle-class condemnation of an imperialist war . . . this working-class affirmation." The widespread belief that support for the war rested more firmly in the working class had received apparent confirmation only a few months earlier when more than 70,000 workers and their families—longshoremen, truck drivers, carpenters, seamen, mechanics, policemen—marched down New York City's Fifth Avenue to "Support Our Boys" in Vietnam. Attacking onlookers who held signs calling for an end to the war, their own banners displayed a contrary belligerence: "Down with the Reds"; "Escalate, Don't Capitulate"; "God Bless Us Patriots, May We Never Go Out of Style."

Unlike their middle-class counterparts, many working-class Americans had grasped only enough of the post–World War II economic boom to get, in the words of one historian, "a taste of comfort without the luxury of security." Those financially unable to escape from the decaying central cities endured rising taxes, received fewer social services, and suffered daily from the social dislocations of a rapidly changing society: crime, inflation, and the disintegration of their neighborhoods.

Not surprisingly, they fought back. They fought back against the blacks: resisting the desegregation of northern school systems, forming white paramilitary organizations, and elevating working-class spokesmen like Louise Day Hicks of Boston and Anthony Imperiale of Newark to political prominence. They lashed out against the long-haired hippies who turned their backs on the economic well-being that working-class families still struggled to achieve. They condemned student activism, bewildered at the readiness of middle-class youth to abuse the opportunities they could not provide for their own children, and furious at their noisy, sometimes irrational anti-Americanism. And they abandoned the liberal political leaders whose social programs rarely addressed their needs. By the late 1960s working-class Americans were looking instead for a Moses of their own to lead them out of the wilderness.

No one on the American political landscape spoke more forcefully to their fears and frustrations than George Corley Wallace, the once and future governor of Alabama. A shrewd populist, Wallace had built a following in the South with a strident defense of white supremacy and racial segregation. Leaping from provincial notoriety to national prominence with stunning showings in several 1964 presidential primaries, he proved as adept at appealing to northern workers as he had to poor southern whites. The self-styled champion of the "little guy," Wallace exploited blue-collar workers' growing sense of futility and cynicism. His impassioned rhetoric gave expression to their anger and in so doing helped raise the level of domestic heat to the boiling point.

Diminutive, intense, folksy, belligerent, he could rouse his audiences to a frenzy with demagogic attacks against "left-wing theoreticians, briefcase totin' bureaucrats, ivory-tower guideline writers, bearded anarchists, smart-aleck editorial writers, and pointy-headed professors." Promising to secure law and order, end school busing, and repeal open housing laws, he threatened to "have the Justice Department grab them by the long hair—these intellectual morons, these professors, these students tearing up their draft cards, raising money and blood for the Vietcong—and have them charged with treason, have them tried and put away. . . ."

Yet what drove the Wallace campaign forward was not hatred so much as despair. Like angry blacks, alienated students, and disenchanted intellectuals, working-class Americans increasingly thought of themselves as victims of a system that had someone else's interests at heart. And like those they condemned, they began to wonder whether Vietnam was worth the price.

In fact, studies of public attitudes revealed that support of withdrawal was significantly greater among workers than among those of higher economic and educational status. What obscured this phenomenon was the reluctance of blue-collar voters to publicize their views and the nature of their disenchantment: the conviction that they were being called upon to bear a disproportionate burden of the sacrifice required.

Class inequities in the draft and the distribution of combat assignments were widely recognized. The military required that all registrants pass the Armed Forces Qualification Test as well as a physical examination. Both eliminated many of the poor, both white and black. At the same time, student and occupational deferments enabled many privileged young men to avoid the draft for years, if not completely. The result was that men of the working and lower middle classes bore the brunt of the fighting and dying. One GI from Kansas recalled bitterly that "all but two of a dozen high school buddies would eventually

"Support Our Boys" parade in New York City, May 1967.

101

serve in Nam and all were from working-class families, while I knew of not a single middle-class son of the town's businessmen, lawyers, doctors, or big ranchers from my high school graduating class who made the trip over the big water." For a working-class mother whose boy had been sent to Vietnam it was difficult to understand how "the kids with the beads from the fancy suburbs—how they get off when my son has to go over there and maybe get his head shot off."

This sense of working-class victimization drove a deep wedge between blue-collar families and those most vocal in their opposition to the war. By 1968, however, what overshadowed all else was the terrible cost the war was exacting. Although they resented the college students thumbing their noses at the government, and abhorred antiwar protest as near treason, they had largely lost faith in those who said the war must go on. Watching the funeral procession for a local boy killed in Vietnam, a construction worker sitting in a Long Island tavern suddenly exploded in a rage shared by many of his friends: "For Christ's sake, how long are they going to let that slaughter go on over there?" he cried to no one in particular. "The whole goddamn country of South Vietnam is not worth the life of one American boy, no matter what the hell our politicians try to tell us. I'm damn sick and tired of watching those funerals go by."

A false spring

As though some great dam had finally given way under the pressure, all the accumulated troubles of a nation in turmoil rolled across the land in the spring of 1968. Amid scenes of mounting protest and riot the American people experienced a stunning series of shocks that left many wondering about the future of their country. But if it ended in tragedy, it began with hope, with the figure of a single man trudging across the hard winter landscape of New Hampshire.

To the few reporters who monitored his progress it seemed a futile quest. The candidate traveled at a lackadaisical pace exhibiting little energy and no emotion. "He seemed a nice enough man," an elderly woman remarked, but she could not for the life of her remember his name. Only a few young volunteers helped out, and polls predicted that the senator from Minnesota would receive no more than 11 percent of the vote.

Then came Tet and a startling shift of public opinion on the war. Doubt and concern had changed to bewilderment and, in some cases, outrage. In a speech in Manchester, New Hampshire, Eugene McCarthy captured exactly the feelings of many Americans.

In 1963, we were told that we were winning the war. . . . In 1964, we were told the corner was being turned. In 1965, we were told the enemy was being brought to his knees. In 1966, in 1967, and now again in 1968, we hear the same hollow claims of programs and victory. . . . Only a few months ago we were told that 65 percent of the population was secure. Now we know that not even the American embassy is secure.

For those who believed it was imperative to elect a candidate who would end the war, the McCarthy campaign had suddenly become the focus of national attention.

After Tet thousands of students traveled to New Hampshire from all along the East Coast, from as far away as Michigan, Wisconsin, and even California. Pundits called it the "Kiddie Crusade," but many of the kids were graduate and undergraduate students from the finest universities, suddenly given the opportunity to make a tangible contribution toward redirecting the course of American foreign policy. They were bright, hard working, and, equally important, could not have seemed more conventional: neatly dressed, their hair trimmed, their manners impeccable. The reaction was better than anyone had expected. "There are so many people who have kids of their own the same age, and they can't talk to their kids," said one local politician. "These kids knock on the door, and come in politely, and actually want to talk to grownups, and people are delighted."

In the astonishing political upset that resulted, it seemed as though Eugene McCarthy had single-handedly carried the antiwar movement out of the streets and into the polling booth. Now anything was possible. "Chi-ca-go! Chi-ca-go!" shouted cheering supporters, referring to the site of the Democratic National Convention to be held in August. "If we come to Chicago with this strength," McCarthy told them, "there will be no violence and no demonstrations but a great victory celebration."

With the president's call on March 31 for negotiations to end the war and McCarthy's victory in the Wisconsin primary two days later, the Minnesotan's bold vision seemed almost at hand. But there would be no peace. Four days after his historic address Lyndon Johnson once more had to plead with the nation for an end to hatred and violence. Martin Luther King, Jr., had been assassinated. The cities of America were on fire.

For fourteen years the commanding figure in the tortured struggle for racial justice, winner of the Nobel Prize for Peace, eloquent speaker, charismatic leader, King had been a transcendent symbol of nonviolent social reform. His murder by a white exconvict named James Earl Ray, reported one national news magazine, "seemed to threaten the onslaught of race war."

King's death did ignite the most widespread racial violence in the nation's history. Rioting broke out in 169 cities causing some $130 million in property damage, bringing nearly 24,000 arrests, and taking forty-three lives, thirty-six of them blacks. In Detroit, Baltimore, Philadelphia, and Toledo, black crowds broke windows, looted stores, and set fire to scores of ghetto businesses. Black colleges boiled with rage, while high schools in one city after an-

In his home state of Alabama, George Wallace addresses a rally during his 1968 presidential campaign.

Inset. A Wallace supporter.

other closed down in the face of violent racial confrontations. In Baltimore, Detroit, and four southern cities, overwhelmed local officials called out the National Guard. In New York, an angry Harlem crowd taunted Mayor John Lindsay when he arrived at the scene of disorders. In Minneapolis, a black man vowed to kill the first "honky" he saw, then shot his white neighbor to death. "My King is dead," he sobbed, firing repeatedly. "My King is dead."

Hardest hit were Washington and Chicago. Within minutes after news of King's death, bands of teen-age blacks began roaming through downtown Washington. By midafternoon the next day, with looting in full swing only a few blocks from the White House, a pall of smoke fed by more than 700 fires hung over the Capitol. On the ground, rampaging blacks of all ages cleaned out store after store. If the looters acted more like Mardi gras revelers than revolutionaries, others sounded a more ominous

note. "Go home and get your guns," shouted black militant Stokely Carmichael to a group of young rioters. "When the white man comes he is going to kill you. I don't want any black blood in the street. Go home and get you a gun and then come back because I got me a gun." With the situation rapidly getting out of control, the president ordered 6,500 army and National Guard troops into the city. One contingent took up positions on the grounds of the White House itself. But only after the addition of 5,000 more federal soldiers and another day and night of chaos did the rioting end.

The situation was even worse in Chicago, where whole blocks of the West Side ghetto went up in flames, and young blacks promised an orgy of destruction. Police, fearful of armed confrontation, let looters carry arm loads, then carloads, of clothing, food, jewelry, and TV sets from shattered store windows. Three thousand National

Residents watch a Chicago drugstore go up in flames during riots following the assassination of Martin Luther King, Jr.

Guardsmen armed with carbines and M1 rifles patrolled the streets in four-man jeeps. But they had no more success than the police in halting the rioting, which was brought under control only with federal troops.

Columbia

As the turmoil subsided, students and faculty at New York's Columbia University gathered in the campus chapel for a memorial service to the fallen civil rights leader. Columbia's vice president David Truman had just begun his eulogy when Mark Rudd, the newly elected chairman of the Columbia SDS chapter, strode to the lectern. How, he demanded, could the leaders of a university that for years had fought the unionization of its own black workers, that had stolen land from the people of Harlem, presume to memorialize King's death? "Dr. Truman and [Columbia's] President Kirk are committing a moral outrage. We will therefore protest this obscenity."

Rebellion had been brewing at Columbia for some time when Rudd and his "action faction" took over control of Columbia SDS promising a new politics of confrontation. Seizing upon King's death, Rudd called for a rally to protest the construction of a new gym on city land and the university's participation in the Institute for Defense Analysis (IDA), a multimillion dollar consortium founded in 1955 to test weapons and military strategy.

The nearly 1,000 students at the rally on April 23 had no plan of action until Bill Sales, a leader of the Student Afro-American Society, threw down a gauntlet to the white radicals: "If you're talking about revolution," shouted Sales, "if you're talking about identifying with the Vietnamese struggle . . . you don't need to go marching downtown. . . . You strike a blow at the gym, you strike a blow for the Vietnamese people."

Chanting "IDA Must Go! IDA Must Go!" the crowd seized the administrative offices at Hamilton Hall, barricading Dean Henry Coleman in his office. Within hours SDS leaders went to Low Library to open up a "second front." Once inside, they made their way to President Grayson Kirk's office where they sipped his sherry, smoked his cigars, and rifled his files looking for documents linking the university with the war effort. Over the next three days more buildings were occupied by other student groups and a "strike central" was established under the SDS leadership.

While counterdemonstrators threatened to end the occupation of the buildings by force and teen-age blacks stormed the campus, the faculty attempted to negotiate a solution to the crisis. But the protesters would not budge from their demands. After seven days the increasingly violent confrontations between demonstrators and counterdemonstrators convinced the administration that the students would have to be removed. On April 29, New York City police peacefully escorted the black students from Hamilton Hall into waiting vans, then forcibly cleared the other occupied buildings.

Three weeks later President Kirk called the police back to Columbia with far bloodier results. After demonstrators staging a new sit-in at Hamilton Hall had been taken away, roving bands of students and nonstudents erected barricades, broke windows, set fires in university buildings, and assaulted the police with bricks, bottles, and obscenities. Ordered to clear the campus, some 500 men of the city's Tactical Police Force smashed through piles of debris, then began kicking and clubbing fleeing students. After their first charge, the TPF gave way to several hundred plainclothes men armed with billy clubs and blackjacks. Although they had express orders not to enter any of the university residences, a group of plainclothes men carrying handguns burst into two dormitories, breaking into rooms and beating students. A faculty investigative panel later concluded that the police had "engaged in acts of individual and group brutality for which a layman can see no justification unless it be that the way to restore order in a riot is to terrorize civilians."

The rebellion at Columbia resulted in nearly 900 arrests, 180 injuries (34 to police), and the suspension of 73 students. The demonstrations provoked hundreds of protests at campuses around the country, including at least forty major confrontations, and unleashed a torrent of criticism against the students.

Grayson Kirk went on national television to castigate "those who are out to wreck the university." Lyndon Johnson labeled the militant students "young totalitarians," while the editors of Fortune magazine warned that SDS was "acting out a revolution—not a protest . . . but an honest-to-God revolution." It was an assessment welcomed by those who had led the Columbia uprising. "Liberal solutions . . . are not allowed anymore," declared Mark Rudd. "We are out for social and political revolution, nothing less."

RFK

But for the most revolutionary young ideologue, the most angry black, the most dissatisfied worker, there still seemed an alternative. The radicals had called it the "Liberation Ticket"—Kennedy and King. One had been gunned down, but the other remained.

Although an image of arrogance, even ruthlessness, had followed him from his early days as counsel to a Senate committee investigating labor racketeering, Robert Kennedy had shown a remarkable capacity to understand the suffering of others. More than this, he had demonstrated an untiring commitment to the welfare of those who had gotten little more than the crumbs of the great American banquet. In fact, Kennedy appealed most strongly to precisely those groups most disaffected with American society in 1968. They believed in him with a

Senior David Shapiro, an SDS radical, lights up one of Columbia University president Grayson Kirk's cigars during student occupation of his and other administration offices for a week in late April.

passion unmatched for any other national political figure, in part for what he had done, but also for the kind of man he was.

Yet even as dissatisfaction with Johnson's policies grew within the Democratic party, the senator from New York had been reluctant to run. He despised Johnson and had come to hate the war, but he was also a loyal and ambitious Democrat looking to the party's presidential nomination in 1972. Months of soul-searching and poll scanning had convinced him that by challenging the president he would divide the party, perhaps destroy his own political future, and assure victory for Richard Nixon. Tet and the New Hampshire primary changed his mind. On March 16, citing the depth of "the present division within our party and country," he announced his candidacy for the Democratic presidential nomination.

Kennedy's late start made it difficult to raise money and set up a campaign organization. Even more important, his tardy entrance into the race infuriated many potential

supporters who admired Eugene McCarthy's lonely stand against the war. Newspaper cartoons skewered the "Bobby-come-lately," as Senator Robert Byrd called him. Others could see little humor in the situation. The *Washington Post* called the senator a "demagogue"; and as far as liberal columnist Murray Kempton was concerned, Kennedy simply allowed McCarthy to carry the battle, then came "down from the hills to shoot the wounded."

McCarthy's crusade against the war had won him many admirers. But the narrowness of his cause was also his greatest vulnerability. He condemned the war for what it was doing to the United States, "what it's doing to us around the world today." For Kennedy, the tragedy of the Vietnam War was far more profound—it was destroying something precious in the American spirit, robbing those who most needed them of the resources necessary to help themselves, and tearing at the social bonds that held the nation together.

Without an organization, without delegates, Kennedy

had to "win through the people. Otherwise I'm not going to win." Hurling himself through sixteen states in twenty-one days, he spoke to the people at airports, college campuses, street corners, and shopping centers. They replied, wrote one reporter, with "an intensity and scope that was awesome and frightening." Everywhere the scenes repeated themselves: Kennedy's impassioned indictments of the president's policies; surging crowds clutching, grabbing at him; his fist pounding away to the rhythm of his rhetoric; shouting, chanting supporters screaming his name.

Robert Kennedy went to the people, and the people responded: victory in Indiana on May 7; victory in Nebraska on May 14. Then in Oregon on May 28, the first electoral defeat for any Kennedy—McCarthy 45 percent, Kennedy 39, Johnson 12. Now California became the crucial test. There would be determined who would challenge the Johnson-Humphrey forces at the convention in August for the leadership of the party, and perhaps of the nation. And there, on June 4, Kennedy prevailed. On the same day he won a landslide victory in rural South Dakota.

In his victory statement to cheering campaign workers at the Ambassador Hotel in Los Angeles, Kennedy asserted that his victories were more than ordinary political triumphs. They proved that "the violence, the disenchantment with our society; the divisions, whether it's between blacks and whites, between the poor and the more affluent, or between age groups or on the war in Vietnam" could be overcome. "We can start to work together." As he made his way to a press conference in another part of the hotel, a small, dark man raised a snub-nosed .22-caliber pistol and fired. The gunman was Sirhan Bishara Sirhan, a Palestinian Arab angered over Kennedy's support of Israel. Twenty-five hours later Robert Kennedy was dead.

They brought the senator's body back from California to New York City, where it lay in state at St. Patrick's Cathedral. Throughout a stifling day and the long night that followed, an endless line of somber mourners filed past the coffin, making the sign of the cross, touching the dark mahogany casket. Chicago mayor Richard Daley came, his head bowed, crying unashamedly. So did Tom Hayden, sitting in the back pew, weeping quietly.

Jack Newfield, a former SDS member and later a speech writer for the Kennedy campaign, felt a despair shared by all those who had for eleven brief weeks risen above their fears and discouragement, believing that in one man at least remained the hope of national reconciliation. For those who had endured "the murderous spring of 1968," thought Newfield, there had been a terrible lesson. "Things were not really getting better ... we shall *not* overcome. ... We had already glimpsed the most compassionate leaders our nation could produce, and they had all been assassinated. And from this time forward, things would get worse: Our best political leaders were part of memory now, not hope."

Robert Kennedy on the presidential campaign trail in Indiana.

"You Can't Trust Anyone Over Thirty"

Beneath the turmoil that rocked the country during the 1960s was the emergence of a youthful culture of opposition unprecedented in American history. Composed neither of the deprived nor the dispossessed, the vocal minority of dissenting young was by and large the product of affluence and education. "Never before," wrote sociologist Kenneth Kenniston, "have so many who had so much been so deeply disenchanted with their inheritance."

Skeptical of their parents, alienated from the political process, hostile toward authority, millions of young people adopted a posture of defiance toward society. The questions they posed and the "lifestyle" they flaunted became a source of division beyond their opposition to the war in Vietnam.

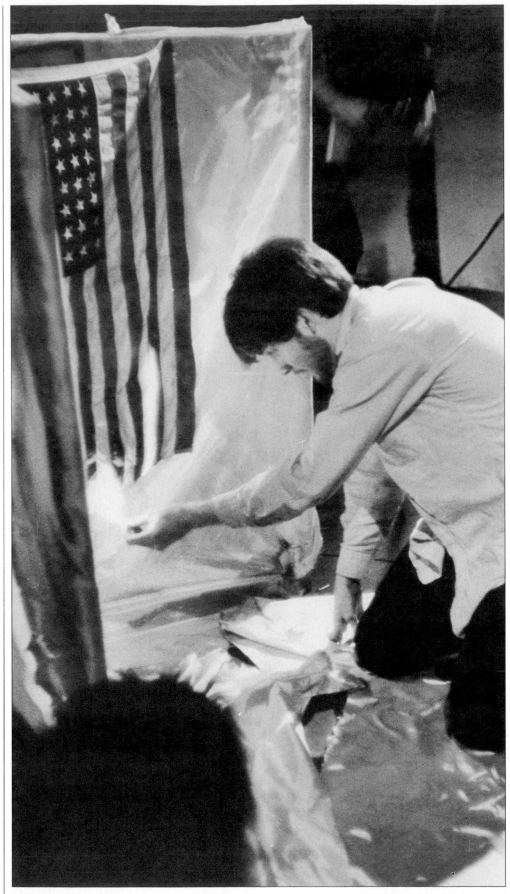

Jose Rodriguez-Soltero, an artist and filmmaker, burns an American flag to the background music of "Ballad of the Green Berets," a song popular at the time. Soltero's anti-American statement was part of a performance called "Live–Multiscreen–Scrambled–Love–Hate–Paradox USA" given at a theater in New York City's East Village in April 1966.

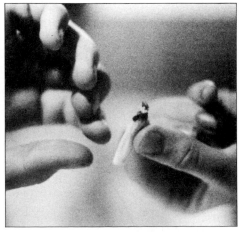

Marijuana, one of the hallmarks of 1960s youth.

Signs of the times. Protesters rally beneath a flag bearing the peace symbol at the 1968 Democratic convention in Chicago.

Allen Ginsberg dances at the "Human Be-In," a gathering of 10,000 to 20,000 radicals and hippies in San Francisco's Golden Gate Park on January 17, 1967. Ginsberg's poetry-writing and social activism took him from the Greenwich Village coffee houses of the 1960's "beat generation" to the street scene of Haight-Ashbury's flower children.

The young were not satisfied merely to attack the inequities and what they saw as the hypocrisies of American society. By the late 1960s they had created something akin to their own culture: a "counter-culture" centered in the universities, with its own dress, its own music, its own prophets, its own press, and its own attitudes about personal relationships.

Suspicious of those in power and impatient with traditional values, many young people looked outside the bounds of conventional culture for inspiration and guidance. They resurrected the mystical dreams of beat poet Allen Ginsberg, followed theologian Alan Watts through the disciplines of Zen Buddhism, and vibrated to the electric rhythms of rock-and-roll.

The "Merry Pranksters"—a hippie troupe that traveled the West staging LSD-induced "happenings"—perch atop their bus. On the hood is Ken Kesey, author of One Flew Over the Cuckoo's Nest and leader of the Pranksters.

Although not primarily an intellectual movement, the revolt of America's young was informed by the ideas of a number of radical thinkers: like sociologist C. Wright Mills, who argued that the concentration of power in major institutions had left decision-making in the hands of small, self-perpetuating elites; philosopher Herbert Marcuse, who maintained that technology had combined culture, politics, and the economy into a system that restricted independent thought and suffocated the hope of genuine freedom; classical scholar Norman O. Brown, who asserted that the only path to happiness was the liberation of man's sexual sensibility.

The most visible examples of the rejection of the majority culture and youthful rebellion were the hippies.

Bob Dylan at the 1963 Newport Folk Festival, where his music brought him stardom and his protest lyrics, like those of "Blowin' in the Wind," made him a favorite of the young.

Their music was a backdrop to the generation; their dress, hairstyle, adoption of Eastern religion—and almost everything they did—inspired others to follow. Here, the Beatles and friends sit with their guru, the Maharishi Mahesh Yogi, September 1967.

The media called them flower children; bearded and beaded, their long hair clasped in leather headbands, they wandered through San Francisco's Haight-Ashbury district, the Sunset Strip in Los Angeles, or New York's East Village, turned on, tuned in, and looking for a way out of a repressed, commercialized culture they wanted no part of. More concerned with "being" than "doing," they looked to drugs, especially marijuana, but also hallucinogens like LSD. More impressed with spiritual enlightenment than material accumulation, they practiced a phantasmagoria of Eastern religions in search of higher truths. More committed to utopian dreams than pragmatic accommodations, they banded together on New England farms and New Mexican mountains, hoping to find in the land what had been corrupted by the city.

In all this they were regarded by their elders as preposterous, ridiculous, bizarre. Yet beneath their somewhat outlandish surface, the hippies gave expression to an alienation shared to a greater or lesser degree by many of their peers.

Rejecting science and technology, elements of the youth culture began to diverge radically from the values of the postwar world. In place of the goal-oriented achievement society of the 1950s, young people sought a new consciousness based on imagination, spontaneity, and love. In place of the politics of interest groups, they sought a politics of democratic participation. In place of formally structured roles and bureaucratic patterns of authority, they sought the direct, personal relationships of the small community. And in place of an aggressive defense of Western interests around the world, they demanded support for national liberation movements and an end to the nuclear arms race.

Although their vocal denunciations of American society angered the older majority, what mattered in the end was less the specifics of their indictment than their posture of opposition. "You can't trust anyone over thirty," they said. And, many of them meant it.

Beyond the drugs, demonstrations, and anger, many alienated young Americans sought new ways of living which might take them away from the city and toward the land and, they hoped, a simpler self-sufficiency. This family lives in a tepee on a West Coast commune.

Picking up the Pieces

In a cabinet in his office at the presidential palace, Nguyen Van Thieu kept a prized war souvenir. It wasn't a weapon or some other combat booty from his years of military service. It was a tape recorder captured from the Vietcong, along with tapes announcing the General Uprising. One recording even proclaimed the death of President Thieu. The reports of his demise were premature. But if the tape was a source of ironic amusement for the president, the catastrophe of the Tet offensive was all too real.

What Thieu saw as he surveyed South Vietnam was a nation in shock. Wherever he looked the picture was the same: urban devastation, civilian casualties in the thousands, refugees in the hundreds of thousands, the threat of epidemics, social and economic programs abandoned, communications cut, transportation at a standstill, a pacification program in apparent shambles, and a government administrative apparatus virtually inoperative.

Destruction lay at every hand. More than 70,000 homes had been destroyed in the fierce fighting, perhaps 30,000 more were heavily damaged. Of the forty-one cities attacked, ten suffered major devastation. In Ban Me Thuot, the capital of Darlac Province, residents slept in doorways rather than risk having the roofs of their battered homes collapse on top of them. In Saigon, where the most severe devastation was limited to the poorer sections of the city, 20,000 homes lay in ruins, including much of the Chinese section of Cholon. All that was left of four hamlets near Ben Tre, reported Bernard Weinraub, was "a zig-zag row of bricks." But the worst destruction had been reserved for Hue, once Vietnam's most beautiful city, now in many sections little more than shattered stucco houses, burned-out shops, and block after block of rubble, wreckage, and dust.

Refugees and mourners

While the physical damage was staggering, the human cost of the Tet offensive was even greater. As the fighting died down, official estimates put the number of civilian dead at 14,300, with an additional 24,000 seriously wounded. Never in more than twenty years of conflict had the people of South Vietnam suffered such a blow. Weeks after the worst of the fighting had ended, the sixty-three public hospitals in the country were packed with wounded and dying victims of Communist attack and allied counterattack.

The situation was also grave for the 630,000 new refugees generated by the fighting. Even before the offensive the government had struggled vainly to deal with nearly 800,000 displaced persons. Now 1 out of every 12 South Vietnamese was in a refugee camp. While some families in the worst-hit areas camped in the ruins of their bombed-out homes, others crowded into universities, local high schools, churches, and makeshift camps, or wandered through their neighborhoods looking for missing relatives. And everywhere there was the stench of decay, the stacks of unburied coffins, and the sight of white-clad mourners burying their dead.

The disruption of transportation made food distribution an arduous task. Continuing Communist sabotage of Route 4 leading south from Saigon cut off virtually all shipments of produce and hogs from the delta. Although rice was readily available in the capital and in the refugee camps that ringed the city, milk and meat were in short supply. In Hue, survivors of the fighting went hungry for days until an armed convoy reached the city with 2 million pounds of provisions. How long they would last no one could be sure.

What food was available in the cities had nearly doubled in price. Within a few weeks farmers rushing to take advantage of the situation drove prices back down, but they remained 15 percent higher than before the widespread urban fighting. High prices, a decline in tax receipts, and fear in the business community all put tremendous pressure on the already shaky South Vietnamese economy. "Because people are frightened, they're hoarding cash and not spending very much money," reported one official. The lack of spending exacerbated short-term unemployment. What it foretold for the future, according to U.S. economists in Saigon, was an eventual spending spree by both businessmen and consumers that threatened to drive prices upward as much as 55 percent. The necessity of significantly increased military expenditures by the government only added to the dire predictions of further inflation.

Compounding the government's difficulties were the breakdown of its administrative machinery and the disintegration of city services. By the end of February only 150 out of 3,000 civil servants were back on the job in Hue, their work rendered almost impossible by the Communists' destruction of public records. Most of the civil servants in Ban Me Thuot refused to return to work for fear of VC assassination squads still roaming the city. In Saigon, government workers ignored instructions to forego the traditional midday siesta so that they could leave work in time to conform with the ongoing curfew. They continued to take their siesta and left early anyway. The city's public transportation system operated only sporadically, mail piled up undelivered, schools remained closed, gravediggers could not be found, and garbage service only slowly recovered after weeks during which uncollected mounds of refuse became a breeding ground for rats and flies. Outside the major cities and district capitals, the government bureaucracy scarcely worked at all.

The collapse of communications made it impossible to determine the fate of the pacification program, but most assessments were pessimistic. When the Communists launched their attacks the government pulled nearly half of the 550 Revolutionary Development teams out of the hamlets to help defend the cities, along with eighteen of the fifty-one army battalions assigned to protect the pacification teams. In so doing, Saigon abandoned the countryside and dealt the pacification program what many felt was a considerable setback. "There always was a semi-vacuum in the countryside," said one U.S. pacification worker. "Now there's a complete vacuum." By the end of February orders had gone out for pacification teams and some troops to return to the hamlets, but progress was slow. Although 95 percent of the 5,000 RD workers in the Saigon region reported back to their assigned locations once the capital had been secured, by mid-March only 80 out of 300 RD teams had returned to the countryside in I Corps, while in the delta entire provinces had to be temporarily abandoned to the Vietcong.

The ruins of Tet surround a woman burning incense at a hastily dug grave in Hue. Over 14,000 civilians were killed and at least a half million left homeless by the Communist offensive.

Young recruits. These draftees were part of the 25 percent increase in military forces called for in the GVN's new national mobilization plan.

The effect upon rural South Vietnamese, many pacification workers feared, would be profound. "The peasants have seen that when it came to the crunch, they were left to the mercy of the VC," remarked an American official. "It's shot our credibility all to hell. We may get our teams back in the hamlets in a month or two—if the VC let us— but it will be years before the peasants trust us again. As far as they're concerned we bugged out once and we might do it again."

The reasons for the delay in resuming the Revolutionary Development program were all too clear. "There's no sense in returning these teams to the countryside with no security," declared a CORDS representative. "It would be suicide." In the aftermath of their nationwide assault, the Communists remained within easy range of most major population centers, distributing leaflets warning of new attacks, and harassing cities, airfields, and allied installations with rocket and mortar fire. Saigon, struggling by day to regain a sense of normalcy despite continued infiltration of enemy cadres and pockets of stubborn VC commandos, retreated at night into a state of siege as allied

artillery pounded along the outskirts of the city and searchlights scanned the dark sky. Fearing a second attack, officials in Hue postponed rebuilding efforts while they hurried to erect a new defense system. American correspondent Flora Lewis reported that Can Tho and other delta cities endured nightly assaults. "Recovery, repair, rehabilitation . . . remains beyond the horizon."

Whatever they may have lost in men and equipment, the Communists had gained at least one victory at Tet: The offensive had shaken the confidence of millions of ordinary South Vietnamese that there really was any safety from attack. "We are very, very frightened," an aged woman said as she stirred her noonday rice in a Hue refugee camp. "We cannot sleep at night for worrying."

Running scared

Yet amid the chaos and destruction there was also evidence of fresh determination. If the Communist offensive had shaken the confidence of the South Vietnamese people in their government, it seemed to shake the government out of the lethargy that had gripped it for more than a decade. "The government is running scared," said a somewhat surprised official, "but it's running." And no one seemed to be running harder than Nguyen Van Thieu.

On February 1 President Thieu declared a nationwide state of martial law and nine days later called for implementation of a vigorous program of national military mobilization. The plan included a 65,000-man increase in the armed forces, an end to student deferments, the call-up of eighteen- and nineteen-year-olds, and the abolition of military discharges except for medical reasons. Reiterating his willingness to negotiate with Hanoi at "any time," but warning that the enemy would seek peace only when he was convinced that he could not win, Thieu announced plans to give military training and arms to all government officials under the age of forty-five, as well as a program of military instruction in the schools to students seventeen years of age or older. On March 21 he ordered an additional force increase of 135,000 men, and on June 15 the National Assembly passed the president's general mobilization bill providing for the induction of 200,000 draftees into the armed forces by the end of the year. The new measures would bring South Vietnam's overall military strength to more than 900,000 men.

By March, Ambassador Ellsworth Bunker could report that in the month following the Tet attacks more than twice as many men had reported for the draft as had during February 1967 and that the number of volunteers had gone up fivefold. The results, said the ambassador, were a tangible indication of "a greater determination on the part of the GVN" in the face of unprecedented crisis.

Integral to the president's plan for full military mobilization were the reorganization of the army and the creation of civilian self-defense groups. Moving against the entrenched power of the army high command, the former general dismissed IV Corps commander Major General Nguyen Van Manh, widely criticized for his tolerance of corruption and lack of aggressiveness, and II Corps commander Lieutenant General Vinh Loc who, American military commanders reported, had lined his pockets with U.S. aid money. To restrain further the independent power of senior officers, Thieu stripped the four corps commanders of the authority to appoint province chiefs, reserving that responsibility for himself. Along with steps to tighten up ARVN, the president established a new civilian self-defense directorate that organized 495 local units in Saigon and twenty-eight of the nation's forty-four provincial capitals. According to the government, by March 21 more than 10,000 of the 69,000 volunteers had already received weapons.

Financing the cost of arms and men, said the president, would require a 20 percent increase in income and business taxes, plus additional levies on gasoline, beer, and cigarettes. As part of the new austerity program, Thieu ordered the closing of all bars, nightclubs, and dance halls

Black markets like this, which had operated with impunity throughout the war, were an early target of the Saigon government's post-Tet crackdown on illegal activities.

and instructed government agents to suppress the "open black markets" selling stolen American commissary goods and relief supplies.

A new resolve

If many Americans had been shocked to learn that after ten years of fighting the Saigon government was only now prepared to order a general mobilization, American officials in South Vietnam were gratified by Thieu's vocal support for a crackdown on the corruption that had plagued both military and government administrations since 1954. On March 1 the president replaced six province chiefs, including Lieutenant Colonel Phan Van Khoa, chief of Thua Thien Province and mayor of Hue. By the end of the month six more had been relieved of their duties, five army officers had been sentenced to death for embezzlement of public funds, and eight others had received terms at hard labor.

Everywhere the official watchwords were unity and reform. Hoping to unite government and opposition forces into a single anti-Communist front, Thieu gave his blessing to a multitude of unity organizations that emerged in the face of the national crisis, among them the Free Democratic Front and the Front for the Salvation of the People. On July 4, the two groups were welded into the People's Alliance for Social Revolution, which vowed to "wipe out corruption, do away with social inequalities, and root out the entrenched forces of militarists and reactionaries who have always blocked progress."

Responding to the renewed spirit of national resolve, the National Assembly passed measures liberalizing press laws and making it easier for new political parties to be formed. Thieu announced the formation of two new groups "to improve the efficiency of the governmental machinery" and called for a major reform of the national police administration.

Military mobilization, anticorruption drives, demonstrations of political unity, and administrative reforms represented to American officials a welcome change in the attitude of the Saigon regime. But for the people of South Vietnam, what mattered most was recovery: how fast and how adequately the authorities would provide relief, rebuild homes, repair bridges, and, most of all, achieve some measure of security from future attacks.

On February 2, President Thieu announced that Vice President Nguyen Cao Ky had established a National Recovery Committee. In the weeks that followed, the committee set up food distribution centers and mapped plans to rebuild the most heavily damaged cities. Each refugee family was promised—and within weeks some had already received—roofing, cement, lumber, and cash to rebuild their shattered homes. While small-arms fire still crackled on the outskirts of Saigon, 2,500 Revolutionary Development cadres went to work collecting garbage and manning refugee centers. Trucks dispensed rice throughout the city, while officials promised the reconstruction of 10,000 to 20,000 homes for refugees on a twenty-year loan plan. In Tay Ninh Province local officials moved quickly to provide refugee relief, distributing building materials and food supplies provided by Saigon. The government launched an ambitious plan to rehouse thousands of delta refugees and undertook an emergency program of inoculations in Hue to head off a threatened cholera epidemic.

Some American officials, like pacification chief Robert Komer, pronounced themselves "most impressed" with the government's reconstruction plans. What encouraged the Americans even more was a new determination among the ordinary citizens of South Vietnam. Indignant that the VC had launched their attack during Tet, many city dwellers in particular shared what General Westmoreland called an "attitude of outrage." The surprise and audacity of the Communist blow had left some South Vietnamese with a new respect for the enemy's military capabilities. But it drove others into active support of government ef-

forts to repel enemy units from the vicinity of the cities and to rebuild areas that had been destroyed.

Although there had been fierce opposition to increased military mobilization in the fall of 1967, now journalists, political figures, and religious leaders alike—even the militant Buddhists—professed confidence in the government's plans. Some of the RD cadres returning to rural hamlets found the people more receptive than before the attacks, and in sharp contrast to the pre-Tet silence, police now reported an unprecedented number of informants identifying Vietcong positions and arms caches.

Some civilians volunteered for relief work, like girls from a Catholic youth organization in Hue who sawed boards for refugee barracks, or high school students in Ben Tre who formed a refugee relief force that dug bunkers, tended children, and distributed food. Others created local self-defense patrols, like the people of Bui Phat, a section of northwest Saigon, who armed themselves with hammers, axes, bicycle chains, and kitchen knives, built barbed-wire fences around their neighborhood, and mounted nightly patrols.

Yet the new militance of South Vietnamese civilians reflected, in many cases, as much pessimism as it did resolve. If the people of Bui Phat had little use for the Communists—"With Communism we have no right to use the things we have," explained one area youth. "We don't have our property. We don't have our freedom"—they also had little confidence in their elected leaders. "We are fighting for ourselves with what we have," declared a neighborhood leader grimly. "The Government cannot protect us, so we must protect ourselves."

Old problems

Indeed, for all the apparent tenacity and resolution, old problems continued to bedevil South Vietnam. The burst of activity with which Saigon had responded to the Communist offensive had been in large part an attempt to appease the Americans. Led by Ambassador Bunker, the U.S. put pressure on the GVN to push forward with military mobilization, to create the National Recovery Committee, to encourage the formation of unity groups, to enact administrative reforms, and to launch an anticorruption campaign. While the initial response had been encouraging, within weeks frustrated embassy officials were complaining that the Thieu government was moving far too slowly and, in some cases, in the entirely wrong direction. The Americans were not alone in their disappointment. "Vietnamese I have known for many years are as frank as they are sad these days in their prognoses," reported the American journalist Robert Shaplen. "They sound more and more like men who know they are suffering from an incurable malady."

In a situation of crisis demanding national unity, efforts at concerted action quickly gave way to factional bick-

A casualty of reform. Accused of expropriating 2 million piasters ($160,000), a young ARVN battalion commander is executed before a crowd of 1,000 spectators.

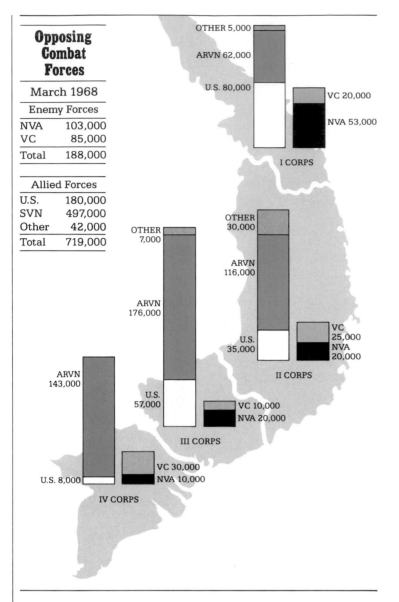

Opposing Combat Forces

March 1968

Enemy Forces	
NVA	103,000
VC	85,000
Total	188,000

Allied Forces	
U.S.	180,000
SVN	497,000
Other	42,000
Total	719,000

OTHER 5,000
ARVN 62,000
U.S. 80,000
VC 20,000
NVA 53,000
I CORPS

OTHER 30,000
ARVN 116,000
U.S. 35,000
VC 25,000
NVA 20,000
II CORPS

OTHER 7,000
ARVN 176,000
U.S. 57,000
VC 10,000
NVA 20,000
III CORPS

ARVN 143,000
U.S. 8,000
VC 30,000
NVA 10,000
IV CORPS

ering. The government itself showed little of the unity it trumpeted in public announcements. Within the executive branch alone, Thieu, Ky, Secretary General Nguyen Van Huong, and Premier Nguyen Van Loc vied with one another for political leverage. General Nguyen Ngoc Loan, chief of the National Police and head of the Military Security Service, was a separate power in his own right. And despite steps taken by Thieu to restrict their power, the four corps commanders retained considerable influence. The legislature was similarly fragmented into Buddhist and Catholic blocs, nationalist parties, and factions representing a variety of southern interest groups.

Nor did the promising nationalist groupings prove more than an ephemeral gesture toward real unity. The National Salvation Front was from the start riven with mutual suspicions and hampered by the nonparticipation of many Buddhists, militant Catholics, and Cao Daists. More opposed to the way things had been than united behind a program for the future, more preoccupied with parochial interests than with the preservation of the country, the front

had little success as a rallying point for an anti-Communist crusade.

Nothing disrupted these incipient coalitions as much as a series of political arrests harkening back to the fearful days of Ngo Dinh Diem. All through February, South Vietnamese police took labor leaders, Buddhist monks, intellectuals, lawyers, professors, and students into "protective custody," citing the appearance of their names on captured NLF assassination lists. Among them were three prominent political figures: Truong Dinh Dzu, runner-up in the 1967 presidential election; Ho Thong Minh, a former Diem cabinet member; and Thich Tri Quang, the leader of the militant Buddhists. After six weeks of incarceration, four of the political prisoners published an open letter condemning the Saigon government's "contempt for the constitution." Describing "protective custody" as a "sugar-coated word camouflaging illegal arrest and detainment," they warned that South Vietnam was rapidly becoming "a police-state society."

Even for those less drastically affected, the post-Tet months brought little relief from the chronic disabilities of South Vietnamese life. With the government issuing a billion piasters ($8.5 million) in new currency each week, inflation soared. Food prices climbed steadily, and with police deployed elsewhere to guard against Communist troop infiltration, vandalism and robbery became so commonplace in Saigon that many doctors, lawyers, and dentists simply abandoned their downtown offices.

Old habits reasserted themselves in other ways as well. Despite strong warnings from the government about corruption, graft hampered relief efforts at every level. Most of the chickens brought into the country to restock flocks decimated during the Tet offensive, reported *Newsweek* magazine, "ended up in back-yard poultry farms improvised by wives of local officials," while the majority of the supplies sent to Hue by the government never reached the refugees. Reconstruction efforts faltered when Vice President Ky, under pressure from Thieu partisans, abruptly resigned from the National Recovery Committee on February 20. Four months later a U.S. Senate subcommittee reported that "rampant and inconceivable corruption" had frustrated American refugee aid and deprived the country of more than half the medical supplies sent by the United States. Meanwhile, the government discouraged civilian initiatives, jailing one Hue student leader trying to organize help for that city's homeless.

While most of the province chiefs replaced by Thieu clearly deserved their fate, critics noted that other corrupt officials remained untouched. Secretary General Nguyen Van Huong defended the policy of selective replacement, observing that if the government removed everyone guilty of malfeasance "we wouldn't have enough people left to run the country and we haven't enough jails to put all the corrupt officials in." But many Vietnamese, originally heartened by the president's anticorruption campaign, be-

Refugees bid for "free" rice furnished by the USAID as South Vietnamese troops supervise. For all the talk of reform, graft and corruption continued to flourish in South Vietnam.

came increasingly cynical about its likely results. "The dung heap is the same," observed one Saigon resident. "Only the flies are different."

Much the same complaint was directed toward the National Assembly, which despite the urging of Ambassador Bunker, showed little inclination to address the ongoing problems of the peasantry. Even as legislators called for change, a study released in Washington by the House Government Operations Committee blasted the failure of successive South Vietnamese governments to undertake significant land reform. The report, written by Dr. Roy L. Prosterman, a consultant on land law at the Stanford Research Institute and a member of a six-man team that had recently investigated the land policies of the Thieu government, pointed to the Tet attacks as a vivid demonstration of "the near bankruptcy of the Saigon regime's efforts to win the loyalty of the masses."

Nothing had proven so fatal to the relationship between the South Vietnamese people and their government as the failure of ARVN to provide real security from Vietcong at-

tack, a situation the government was unable to remedy in the aftermath of the Tet offensive. Their serious losses notwithstanding, both VC and NVA Main Force units continued to threaten most South Vietnamese cities. To many senior U.S. officers the enemy's willingness to operate in populated areas where they could be located and attacked constituted a golden tactical opportunity. Instead of taking advantage of the situation, however, government forces initially remained inside the cities displaying what many Americans felt was "a greater defensive-mindedness" than ever before. As VC propaganda continued to promise a second wave of attacks, night patrolling was largely curtailed and draft call-ups for eighteen-year-olds were delayed.

Under relatively little pressure from ARVN, battered VC units struggled to make up their losses with stepped-up recruitment and the addition of North Vietnamese regulars. While government troops and militia forces continued to operate with outmoded weapons, the Communists received a steady supply of new arms, including Chinese

7.62MM automatic weapons and Soviet 122MM rockets. The 122, with its seven-mile range, 41-pound warhead, and total weight of only 200 pounds, gave the enemy what amounted to mobile long-range artillery. With Communist mortar shells and rockets continuing to fall on Saigon and at least twenty other cities and military installations, enemy units accelerated their attacks in the countryside, keeping marines south of Hue restricted to daytime patrols within 180 meters of Highway 1, and forcing the chief of Kien Hoa Province to ring his headquarters with armored cars each night.

Meanwhile, the Communists launched a new political offensive featuring the formation of a countrywide Alliance of National, Democratic and Peace Forces of Vietnam. Like the revolutionary government of the same name that had ruled Hue in February, the new organization was designed to operate separately from the National Liberation Front, in order to attract support from opponents of the Saigon regime unwilling to associate themselves with the NLF and because of Hanoi's fears that the Vietcong might prove politically unreliable in any future coalition government. Saigon's concern over the new Communist organization was exemplified in July when a five-man military court convicted the ten-member leadership of the alliance of treason and sentenced them to death *in absentia*.

Symbolic prosecution of yet another Communist front, however, could neither rebuild cities nor win South Vietnamese peasants to the government's cause. While the offensive had plunged the Saigon regime into the most serious crisis of the war, it had also provided Thieu with an opportunity to assert his leadership. Instead, the president had in general allowed strong words to take the place of vigorous action. "If ever there was a need for a single national leader, it is now," wrote an American journalist in March, "but President Thieu, who is by nature a cautious man, given to withdrawing in a crisis and then trying to pick up the pieces, has been reluctant to take

charge." One American embassy official concluded: "The greatest casualty in this whole affair has been the South Vietnamese Government. Why don't we get moving?"

With reconstruction efforts lagging and serious reform nowhere in sight, with his capital still in a state of psychological siege and his government's control of the countryside shattered, some observers expected a quick end to Thieu's presidency. Yet the former general was a survivor. If many Vietnamese saw in the Tet offensive an opportunity for the government to bolster its sagging reputation with decisive action, Thieu saw in the crisis an unprecedented opportunity to secure his personal position. In the months after Tet he would step by step eliminate his opponents and consolidate his power, transforming his nation's tragedy into his own political triumph.

The new dictatorship

The most formidable obstacle in Thieu's path was his own vice president, Nguyen Cao Ky. Eight years younger than the forty-five-year-old president, the former commander of the South Vietnamese air force had shared power with Thieu from 1965 to 1967, only to be outmaneuvered by his fellow general before the 1967 presidential elections. But if Thieu was now the elected head of state, his government was riddled with Ky partisans waiting only for an opportunity to return the former prime minister to power.

In the intense bargaining between the two rivals following the elections, Ky had persuaded Thieu to name a Saigon lawyer and Ky confederate, Nguyen Van Loc, as South Vietnam's first premier. Lacking administrative experience and with no political base of his own, Loc came under mounting criticism for his hesitant response to the Communist offensive. Unwilling to let the National Assembly force his hand, Thieu had adroitly fought off a motion of no confidence against Loc in the House in March. Two months later, with Ky and his wife absent from Saigon, Thieu abruptly fired Loc, naming in his place the former mayor of Saigon and current secretary general, Nguyen Van Huong.

The president then began systematically removing Ky supporters from positions of power, including the mayor of Saigon, the commander of the Capital Military District, the heads of the Central Intelligence Office and the Military Security Department, and fourteen province chiefs with close ties to the vice president. National Police Chief Loan, wounded in Saigon street fighting, was replaced by Colonel Tran Van Hai who promptly dismissed eight Saigon police commissioners. Two weeks later, six of Ky's closest political allies were killed when a U.S. pilot accidentally bombed their Cholon headquarters; their posts were taken by Thieu loyalists who carried out a wholesale purge of their predecessors' appointments. By the end of June the president had stripped Ky of major influence within the government.

Mobilization

RVNAF Year-End Force Strength

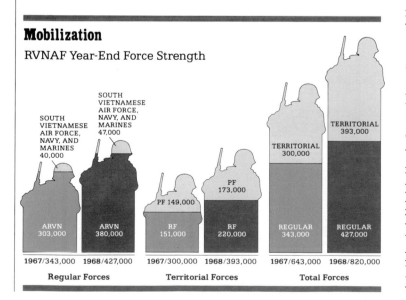

| SOUTH VIETNAMESE AIR FORCE, NAVY, AND MARINES 40,000 | SOUTH VIETNAMESE AIR FORCE, NAVY, AND MARINES 47,000 | PF 149,000 | PF 173,000 | TERRITORIAL 300,000 | TERRITORIAL 393,000 |
| ARVN 303,000 | ARVN 380,000 | RF 151,000 | RF 220,000 | REGULAR 343,000 | REGULAR 427,000 |

| 1967/343,000 | 1968/427,000 | 1967/300,000 | 1968/393,000 | 1967/643,000 | 1968/820,000 |
| **Regular Forces** | | **Territorial Forces** | | **Total Forces** | |

Over the next several months the vice president trimmed his mustache, abandoned his dashing flight suits in favor of Mao jackets, and attempted to fashion a nationalist image designed to appeal to the younger generation. The new look was unveiled in a series of speeches attacking both the United States and the Saigon regime. "If the Americans want to withdraw, they can go ahead," he told ARVN soldiers in Saigon. "We only want people who want to stay." Praising Ho Chi Minh and Vo Nguyen Giap, he denounced Thieu's government as "a bunch of servile and corrupt officials" and dismissed the previous year's presidential elections as "a loss of time and money. . . . They have served to install a regime that has nothing in common with the people—a useless, corrupt regime."

But Ky soon discovered that Thieu had effectively silenced most of the vice president's potential allies. Ho Thong Minh, one of the February detainees released on April 11, was immediately deported to France. Truong Dinh Dzu, also freed in April, was rearrested on May 1, tried by a military court, and sentenced to five years' hard labor at the infamous prison island of Poulo Condore. The Buddhist monk Thich Tri Quang was finally released from

prison on June 30. Any inclination he may have had to speak out against the arrest of his followers, however, was forestalled by a government campaign aimed at linking militant Buddhist leaders with the Vietcong.

What gains had been made as a result of the assembly's press reforms were also soon lost. On July 25 the government sentenced the editor of a student newspaper to five years' hard labor for publishing news that "leant toward false peace in favor of the Communists." Although the liberalized press laws stayed on the books, the Thieu government maintained an effective indirect censorship by "requesting" the omission of certain news items on the grounds that they were false.

Equally damaging to Ky's hopes for a political comeback was the attitude of the Americans. While they admired his energy and charm, they valued stability in Saigon more. Thieu already had the backing of senior American generals, and with the Tet offensive Washington threw its support squarely behind the president. Any doubts about the American position were dispelled in March at a meeting between Deputy U.S. Ambassador Samuel Berger and a group of senior American and Viet-

A captured VC weapon and a heroic mural of ARVN soldiers are featured at a Saigon exhibit sponsored by the GVN in an attempt to restore shaken civilian morale.

Catholics demonstrate in front of the American Embassy to protest the partial bombing halt. The banner reads: "To Johnson we strongly protest the betrayal of the sacrifices made with the blood and bones of the VN people and the VN Army."

namese military commanders. As they discussed the pace of recovery from the Tet offensive, one Vietnamese officer volunteered that the Communists were bound to take advantage of any political crisis to launch another attack on Saigon. With that Berger leaped to his feet to inquire precisely what kind of "political crisis" the general had in mind. "I want you to understand that the United States is against coups," insisted Berger. "We are backing General Thieu now. We will not tolerate a coup."

The emasculation of Ky, the ongoing arrests, a return to press censorship—all were commented upon bitterly by the president's critics. Yet nothing drew as much attention, or provoked as much anxiety, as the return of followers of Ngo Dinh Diem to positions of power. Thieu's chief ally in his purge of Ky supporters had been General Tran Thien Khiem, the new minister of the interior and a former member of Ngo Dinh Nhu's notorious secret police, the Can Lao. And although Thieu declared he had no intention of restoring "the old regime," he appointed large numbers of former Can Lao members and Diemist officials to high government and military positions.

To some critics the Thieu regime looked "more and

more like Ngo Dinh Diem's in structure if not yet in action." Others claimed that the former Diemists were already being organized into political cells at key points in the civil and military administration. "The restoration is all set," said one Diemist senator confidently. "We lack only a pretender to the throne." By the summer of 1968 Nguyen Van Thieu, second president of the republic, had earned a new and less exalted title: At the cafés along Saigon's Tu Do Street, they began to call him "the little dictator."

The fear of peace

Whatever success Thieu may have had in neutralizing political opposition within South Vietnam, there remained a far more formidable adversary with which he had to contend: the government of the United States of America. Mistrust of Washington had been growing steadily since the first moments of the Tet offensive. A discouraging number of South Vietnamese believed that the Americans had collaborated with the Vietcong in the January attacks. Some thought that the United States had agreed to allow the offensive in hopes that a weakened GVN would have no choice but to negotiate. Others speculated that the Americans had agreed to stand aside for twenty-four hours to see whether the people would respond to the call for a General Uprising, in which case the United States would have recognized the VC as South Vietnam's legitimate government. The rumors became so widespread that Ambassador Bunker requested time on South Vietnamese television to deny the "ridiculous" claims.

Groundless as the rumors were, they seemed all too credible to some Vietnamese. If the rumors weren't true, they asked, why hadn't the Americans fought with the ARVN during the first several days of Tet? Why had the Communists made the vast majority of their assaults against ARVN bases or government installations, while it seemed that only token attacks were directed against the Americans? And most unanswerable of all, how could plans for such a major military campaign have eluded the sophisticated American intelligence net? Even President Thieu was plagued with doubts. At the end of February he voiced his suspicions to a visiting Washington official. "Now that it's all over," said Thieu, "you really knew it was coming, didn't you?" The official demurred, but Thieu was not persuaded. "Don't kid me, you had to know," he insisted. "You're just not willing to level with me. Why don't you tell me the truth?"

Lyndon Johnson's decision on March 31 to curtail the bombing of the North only deepened the mood of apprehension in Saigon. Resentful of Washington's unilateral initiative and fearful that American impatience would lead to a premature settlement, Vietnamese politicians and civil servants, generals whose power resided in the divisions they commanded, and businessmen grown wealthy on the profits of war, shared a common anxiety. They believed that the United States was preparing to abandon them to the Communists. For many South Vietnamese the bombing halt and the promise of negotiations brought with them not the hope of a quick end to the bloody conflict, but an abiding fear of peace.

Throughout the spring, the GVN fought a bitter rear-guard action to restrain Washington and to protect Saigon's identity in the peace process. As Thieu and Ky proclaimed their opposition to a coalition government, to

Thieu got what he wanted from President Johnson at their July meeting in Honolulu: full participation in negotiations with the Communists and no imposition of a coalition government.

any policy short of military victory, the National Assembly condemned the American initiative as "a surrender concession." The South Vietnamese Senate declared that the bombing halt should be the final allied gesture of good will toward the North, and in June the House voted seventy-two to two against any NLF role in negotiations.

Official hostility to American peace efforts reflected a rising wave of defensive Vietnamese nationalism. "While the Americans may be utterly unable to adjust themselves to the terms of this strange war," wrote a Saigon newspaper columnist, "it is by no means too late for the South Vietnamese armed forces to de-Americanize themselves and start fighting the simple way and beating the Communists at their own game with as little American tactical support as possible." "If we have to accept coalition under American pressure," thundered Vice President Ky, "that means we are going to die in the next five or six months, or at least lose the country. So it is better to lose it fighting. At least we would die with a clear conscience." With political and religious groups hardening their public posture toward negotiations, with much of the nation's press warning of an American sellout, the situation reminded many South Vietnamese of an earlier debacle. "Washington," said the Saigon daily *Cong Chung*, "is following in the tracks of the French."

President Thieu joined the chorus of disaffection, suggesting that if the United States were no longer able to help, he would appeal to other allied nations. He soon made good his pledge, establishing a coordinating committee of representatives from South Korea, Thailand, Australia, New Zealand, and the Philippines to prevent unilateral American action during the negotiations. At home he compiled a "black list" of officials and public figures considered unreliable because of their close connection with the Americans and formed a youth brigade called the Movement of Anti-Communist Students as a counterweight to U.S.-backed youth groups within the country. Although Thieu publicly supported the bombing restrictions, he privately warned Ambassador Bunker that South Vietnam reserved the right to repudiate any agreement made between Hanoi and Washington.

Honolulu

More than any other American in Saigon, it was Ellsworth Bunker who felt the heat of South Vietnamese anger. Seventy-three years old, a tall, white-haired diplomat who had won high marks for his work in Brazil, Indonesia, and the Dominican Republic, he came to Vietnam in the spring of 1967 with a reputation for sensitivity and candor. He could be aloof—the Vietnamese referred to him as "Mr. Refrigerator"—but to William Westmoreland he was a "warm and personable" man, "something of a raconteur and a wit." Thieu also liked the gentle New Englander. "He is very quiet, very clever," he told an American re-

porter, "but," said the president laughing, "very frank. When I met President Johnson in Guam, he told me he was sending his number one man, and Bunker has turned out to be the best Ambassador we have ever had."

Although some Vietnamese generals worried that Bunker had been dispatched to preside over the liquidation of South Vietnamese sovereignty, he became a ready advocate for their cause. A staunch supporter of the American military command, the ambassador stood behind Thieu during Tet when others were ready to write him off, reassuring the president of continued American commitment, even as he pushed for serious reforms. But after March 31 Thieu could no longer rely on vague promises of support from an American representative, even so distinguished and sympathetic a man as Bunker. With his country battered and fearful, the future of his own government uncertain, he had to speak directly to the one man whose reassurances might count, Lyndon Johnson.

On his departure from Saigon on July 18 to meet with the American president in Honolulu, Thieu told reporters he was not going to Hawaii "to surrender to Communists, to sell out the nation, to concede territory or to accept a solution involving coalition with Communists imposed by the United States such as Communists and a number of unscrupulous politicians have charged." His fears proved unfounded. With a specificity that delighted Thieu, the communiqué issued at the close of the conference affirmed in unequivocal language that Saigon would be "a full participant playing a leading role in discussions concerning the substance of a final settlement," that the two governments "would act in full consultation with each other," and that the United States "will not support the imposition of a 'coalition government,' or any other form of government, on the people of South Vietnam."

The results of the Honolulu conference, reported the *New York Times*, "left Mr. Thieu smiling." His country had survived the Tet offensive, he had used the crisis to solidify his own position, and now he had assurances that his government would not be left out in the cold during the peace negotiations.

Yet for all his political success, Thieu could not arrest the momentum of events that continued to shift the focus of decision making away from Saigon. In this regard the Honolulu conference obscured a fundamental reality of the post-Tet situation. The United States wanted out. With six months remaining in office Lyndon Johnson was determined that neither North Vietnamese belligerence nor South Vietnamese recalcitrance would stand in the way of what he hoped would be his final political legacy: putting all parties to the bitter conflict at last on the road to peace. Toward that goal Johnson would admit no impediment from Saigon. In the gilded halls of Paris and on the battlefield of South Vietnam, the Americans would call the shots.

Although he had successfully consolidated his authority within South Vietnam, President Thieu found himself increasingly isolated between Communist military pressure and American efforts to negotiate an end to the war.

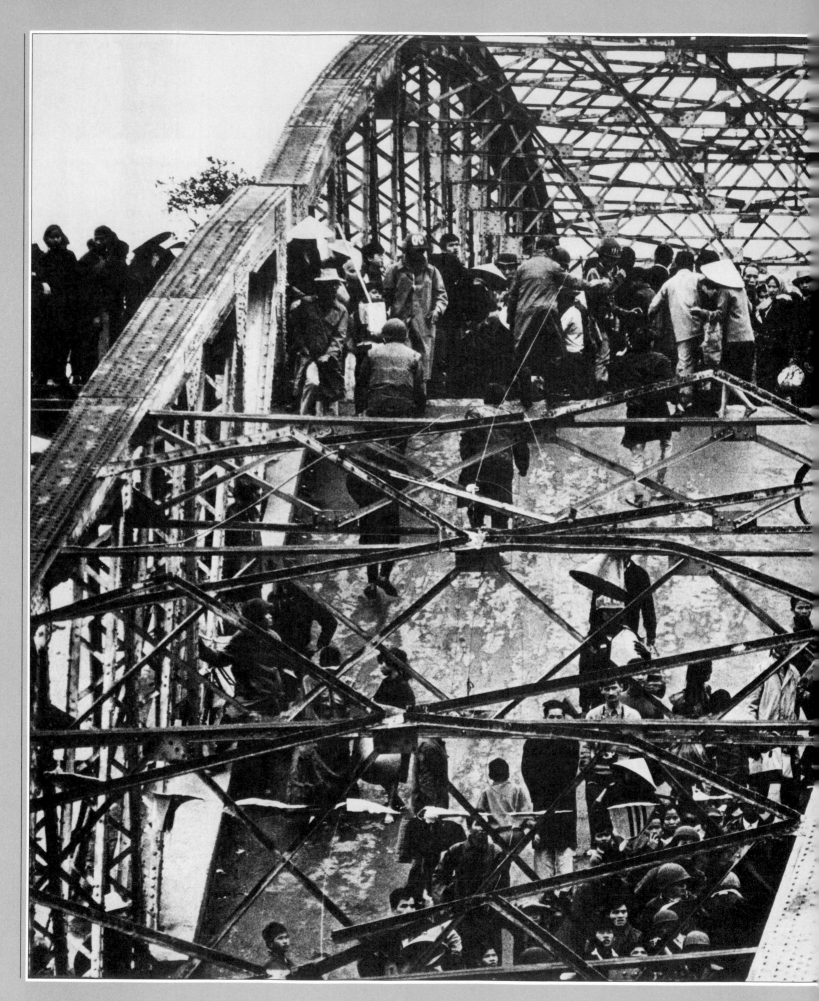

"If Only There is No More War"

Refugees fleeing the fighting in Hue stream south across the Perfume River.

With much of the city in ruins, what remained of Hue became a giant refugee center. Here families seek shelter in a Catholic church.

They filled the coastal towns of Phan Thiet and Tuy Hoa, crowded into the highland capitals of Ban Me Thuot and Da Lat, poured into Vinh Long in the delta. Eighty thousand of them huddled in schools and churches in Hue; nearly 250,000 besieged Saigon. Peasant farmers and urban clerks, Buddhist priests and grieving widows, the very young and the very old were all the same: they were the refugees.

How many there were no one could really say. By March 1968 GVN officials calculated that between 1 and 2 million people—as many as one out of eight South Vietnamese—were refugees. Some Americans thought the totals were much higher, as great as 4 million.

Whatever the figures, the Saigon government was scarcely prepared for the tidal wave of displaced persons generated by the Tet offensive. Camps sprang up everywhere, with and without official sanction. While some were reasonably hygienic, many others were squalid slums without adequate water supplies or sanitation facilities. And while the government endeavored to distribute rice, bread, and tins of fish, too often promised food and medicine simply failed to arrive.

In other wars the refugee camp, for all its misery and filth, had at least been a place of safety. No longer in Vietnam. Even as the fighting convulsed the cities a quieter, more insidious war was being waged over control of the camps. There had always been some Vietcong activity among the battered victims of the war. Now as the refugee population swelled beyond the government's capacity to respond, VC influence—and in some places domination—became more open. Camp residents began to ask Americans to leave for fear of Vietcong reprisal, and the government officially declared numerous camps unsafe.

The shock of the attack, the loss of their homes, the sporadic response of the GVN all produced in the refugees a profound demoralization. Peasants driven from their farms into the chaos of the cities were particularly shaken. But the crisis was all-encompassing. During two days among the refugees sheltered at the University of Hue, American photographer Carl Mydans did not see "a single instance of leadership."

Family groups fended for themselves, tending and protecting their own injured, cooking on

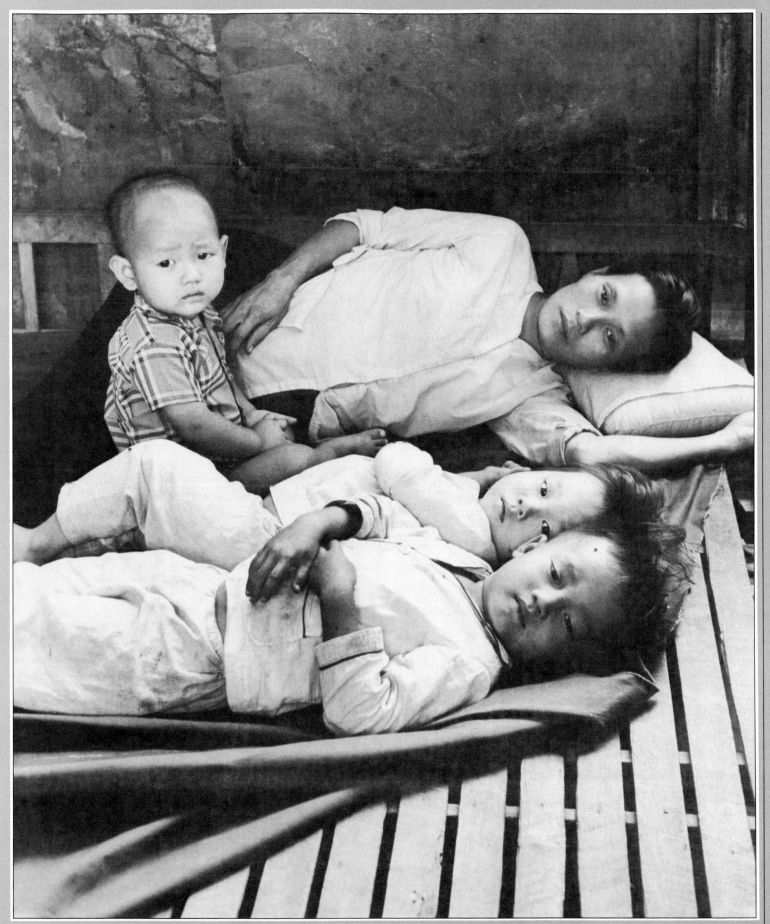

Former residents of Ben Tre. In many places nervous authorities prohibited men from accompanying their families to refugee centers for fear that some of the men might be infiltrators.

Although faced with unprecedented numbers of homeless people, the government managed to ward off starvation by distributing rice and other foodstuffs.

One of the luckier refugees returns to her house in Hue; most had nothing to return to.

individual wood fires, many of them kindled right in the classrooms and lecture halls. . . . There was no sharing. Nor did they display a semblance of community order by lining up at the single well, nor by digging latrines. The tracked mud of the university grounds was widely spread with feces, and the halls and rooms stank of urine.

"Government subsidy has brushed starvation aside, and government shacks have given them shelter," concluded Mydans. "But for many, dignity and hope have vanished."

Apathetic, disoriented, frightened, and bewildered, they clung to the meager belongings they had carried from their homes and to a desperate wish for peace. "We will go anywhere and live anywhere," pleaded Nguyen Duc Ngai, a Saigon gardener whose house burned down in the fighting, "if only there is no more war."

Some refugees were resettled in housing projects like this one at Nha Trang, but most remained in the makeshift camps that ringed the cities.

Talking Peace, Making War

For all the horror that had been, for all the difficulties that lay ahead, the spring of 1968 brought the first whisper of hope that the long, painful conflict in South Vietnam might at last be brought to an end. The willingness of the North Vietnamese to begin negotiations raised expectations of an imminent cease-fire, while heavy Communist losses at Tet held out the possibility of a respite in the fighting. Yet neither was to be. The months that followed witnessed instead an agonizing counterpoint of diplomatic futility and military impasse. It was a time of confusion and despair, of new leadership and old dilemmas, a time ambassadors spent talking peace and soldiers spent making war.

The president's announcement of a partial bombing halt and a renewed call for negotiations had taken the world by surprise. Hanoi's acceptance of the American offer three days later may have been just as great a shock to Washington. In assessing the reasons for the Communist turn-

around, officials postulated a number of alternatives. Some suggested that the huge casualties suffered during Tet and the failure of the General Uprising had forced Hanoi to the negotiating table to save a deteriorating situation, while they regrouped their forces and prepared for a new offensive. North Vietnamese leaders obviously wanted to limit the cost of the war and may have begun to doubt their capacity to achieve military victory.

Others maintained that Tet was designed to precipitate the "talk-fight" stage of revolutionary warfare. Hanoi's ultimate goal of a unified Vietnam under its control remained the same, and what evidence was available suggested that the North Vietnamese command firmly believed that they could persist long enough to obtain a favorable negotiated settlement. Paris afforded them the opportunity to undermine U.S.-GVN relations, to set the stage for a withdrawal of U.S. forces, and to create a better chance for a coalition government in the South.

But perhaps the simplest explanation was the best. The limitation of air attacks north of the twentieth parallel suggested that Washington was ready to halt the bombing entirely. If that could be obtained at the negotiating table rather than on the field of battle, so much the better. Hanoi, in short, had nothing to lose.

Although there had been indications that the North Vietnamese might react positively, an "Eyes Only for Ambassador" cable sent to U.S. embassies throughout Southeast Asia, Australia, and New Zealand on the night of March 30 expressed little American optimism. "You should make clear," instructed the cable, "that Hanoi is most likely to denounce the project and thus free our hand after a short period." The North Vietnamese did, in fact, condemn the partial bombing halt as a "perfidious trick" to appease public opinion and agreed to sit down with American representatives only "to decide with the U.S. side the unconditional cessation of bombing and all other war acts against the DRV so that talks could begin." It was hardly an auspicious beginning.

As if to emphasize the fragility of the agreement, what followed was a month of wrangling over the site for the talks. Johnson proposed Geneva. Hanoi countered with Phnom Penh, a suggestion the president took to mean that "the Communists were going to use these talks for every propaganda advantage and we had to protect ourselves." The U.S. named some alternatives—Vientiane, Rangoon, New Delhi. North Vietnam came back with Warsaw. When the Americans turned that down Hanoi accused Johnson of going back on his word to meet anywhere, anytime. Indonesia sought to break the deadlock with the offer of a ship floating in international waters, but this too was rejected.

Preceding page. A U.S. 9th Division soldier radios his command post as fighting erupts in Saigon in the first week of May.

By April 30 Johnson was worried. "We are going into our fifth week. We have counseled patience, but you have to look at the calendar." Even as discussions began of potential bombing targets north of the twentieth parallel, Hanoi on May 3 proposed Paris as the conference site. Although some U.S. diplomats regarded the French capital as an unfortunate setting—"the whole effort [giving] the appearance of one defeated colonial power arranging for a defeated imperialist power to extricate itself from Vietnam"—Johnson accepted the North Vietnamese offer on the following day. But he also warned that "this is only the first step and there are many hazards and difficulties ahead."

Talking peace

Johnson entrusted the American side of the peace talks to a veteran team of negotiators headed by seventy-six-year-old ambassador-at-large W. Averell Harriman. Other key members of the delegation included Cyrus Vance as Harriman's second-in-command, press spokesman William Jorden, State Department officials Philip Habib and Daniel Davidson, and General Andrew Goodpaster, commandant of the National War College. Hanoi was represented by an equally professional contingent under the direction of Xuan Thuy, a fifty-five-year-old veteran propagandist and secretary of the Central Committee of the North Vietnamese Communist party. On June 3 an important addition was made to the North Vietnamese delegation when Le Duc Tho arrived in Paris. Although he was officially classified as an "adviser" to the delegation, Tho's standing in the party—the seventh-ranking member and, next to Ho Chi Minh, chief theoretician of the North Vietnamese Politburo—suggested a more central role in the talks.

Of the two parties not represented in Paris—the South Vietnamese government and the NLF—it was Saigon that had the most to lose from the bilateral discussions. On the eve of the opening session President Thieu vowed that his country "will not yield even a centimeter of land to the Communists, will not form a coalition government with the NLF, and will firmly not acknowledge the NLF as an equal political entity to negotiate with us," a position that seemed to doom the talks even before they began. To soothe his anxious ally, Johnson went out of his way to reassure Saigon that the Americans had no intention of signing an agreement that did not provide the means to a genuine peace. The GVN, Johnson promised, would be a "full participant in any negotiations designed to bring about a settlement of the conflict."

The president had also called for close consultations between the U.S. and its allies during the peace process. But his offer to negotiate with Hanoi had provoked anger and apprehension among many Southeast Asian leaders who resented Washington's unilateral initiative and who feared that the Americans were simply seeking a face-saving means of withdrawal. Although officials in Australia and New Zealand gave public support for the U.S. move, one prominent Australian politician expressed a more candid opinion. "If you heard that Ho Chi Minh was resigning office at the end of the year, that General Vo Nguyen Giap had been booted upstairs, that North Vietnamese troops in South Vietnam were being cast in a 'less active' role, and that Hanoi was virtually begging us to come to the conference table—well, what would you think?" The Laotians worried that they would soon become "a battlefield between Thais and North Vietnamese," while Thai interior minister Prapus Charusthien warned that if the Americans negotiated their way out of South Vietnam only to turn to Thailand as the "new line of defense," Washington should shed its illusions. "No one will believe you."

Whatever suspicions the allies harbored, the negotiating process was finally underway. The first formal session took place on May 13 at the Majestic Hotel, the site of the 1946 talks between France and Vietnamese nationalists led by Ho Chi Minh. Graced with a crystalline spring morning, surrounded by more than 1,300 reporters from thirty-nine countries, Harriman and Xuan Thuy shook hands in the hotel's rococo Grande Salle and went to work.

For Harriman the American objective could be suc-cinctly stated—"to preserve the right of the South Vietnamese people to determine their own future without outside interference or coercion." In order to accomplish this he called for a true demilitarization of the DMZ, the neutralization of Laos and Cambodia, and a strengthening of the International Control Commission overseeing the Geneva agreements. Alluding to the president's decision to restrict air attacks over North Vietnam, Harriman asserted that "even this limited bombing could come to an early end—if our restraint is matched by restraint on the other side," and reiterated an offer made by the U.S. at the Manila Conference in 1966 to withdraw American forces from South Vietnam "as the other side withdraws its forces to the North, stops the infiltration, and the level of violence thus subsides."

All of this meant nothing to the North Vietnamese. Indicting the United States for "monstrous crimes," Xuan Thuy charged that Johnson had ordered the partial bombing halt only under the strongest pressure from world opinion and because of defeat on the battlefield. He condemned American involvement in Vietnam, accusing the United States of preventing the Geneva accords from being carried out, placing a "puppet" regime in Saigon, and launching a "war of destruction" against the Vietnamese people. The American demand for "mutual de-escalation" as a prerequisite for peace was simply unac-

The American and North Vietnamese delegations open the peace talks on May 13. Averell Harriman, head U.S. negotiator, is seated third from left; his counterpart, Xuan Thuy, is in the center of the North Vietnamese team.

At the Paris Peace Talks

Daniel I. Davidson

To the American public, the peace talks going on in Paris during the summer of 1968 were a strange affair: half tragedy, half farce. But even those more intimately acquainted with what was taking place behind the scenes found themselves caught up in an intricate game of public posturing and secret discussions. One of the participants at the talks was Daniel I. Davidson, a member of the United States delegation and one of two Americans who first met with North Vietnamese representatives outside the regular weekly sessions at the Hotel Majestic.

Unquestionably the most important figure in the early negotiations was the chief of the American delegation. Averell Harriman brought to the Paris peace talks an unexcelled experience in diplomacy at the highest levels, which began during World War II when he served as President Roosevelt's lend-lease representative to Great Britain and as his ambassador to the Soviet Union. A former assistant secretary of state for Far Eastern affairs, he had extensive exposure to Indochina. In addition, he was a dogged worker concentrating almost excessively on his task, immersing himself in every detail and pursuing his goals both during the working day and during ostensibly social events.

Harriman recognized that his role in Paris was not only that of negotiating with the North Vietnamese but also seeking desirable shifts in the American position. In that role, his personal prestige and his ability to maneuver through the bureaucracy proved invaluable. His reputation for integrity, his standing, his ability to see the other party's position, his treatment of the North Vietnamese as responsible human beings also served his country.

Even before the United States delegation arrived in France, we were very aware that while we would pursue peace in the overcivilized setting of Paris other Americans would die in Vietnam. I was particularly conscious of this contrast during the tedium of the weekly talks at the Hotel Majestic, when each side made its formal statement, almost entirely repetitive of previous public positions, and then sat while the lengthy speeches were translated twice—first into French and then into either Vietnamese or English.

There were occasional translation problems. After General Westmoreland was replaced by General Abrams, the North Vietnamese referred to Westmoreland as "limoges." It took some effort before we discovered that the word referred to the French practice of appointing a general who was a failure in combat as head of the garrison of Limoges—a city located almost equidistant from the French frontiers and therefore unlikely to involve him in further fighting. On another occasion, the Vietnamese asked us for the meaning of a phrase used by President Johnson when he exhorted troops in Vietnam to "nail the coonskin to the wall."

The only immediate utility of the weekly talks was that during breaks pairs of Americans and Vietnamese would have tea. The tea breaks eventually led to the very secret private talks conducted away from the glaring publicity of the weekly meetings, and it was those talks that finally led to results.

Arranging the locale of the secret meetings, when it was our turn to be host, and providing transportation was a task assisted by the CIA. Whatever his other abilities, the CIA officer was not particularly attentive to vehicular laws. Once, when driving Vance to a secret meeting, he was nearly picked up by a French policeman. This could well have threatened the secrecy of the whole activity.

President Johnson was determined that there would be no leaks to the press. At the onset, Vance informed all members of the delegation and the staff that the first person to talk to a reporter would be on the next plane to Washington and that this prohibition was not to be made known.

At our hotel, a note from an American journalist inviting me to dinner at a three-star restaurant awaited me. I ignored it. The next day a second note arrived from her with boxes to be checked. The final box was "No. I am out of my mind and do not wish to have dinner with you." With time, the prohibition was gradually relaxed. It is true, however, and it is a source of pride, that there were no leaks from the American delegation.

The president's determination to preserve secrecy was demonstrated to an extraordinary degree in the handling of the cables concerning the meetings. Ordinary communications from the American delegation to Washington bore the heading HARVAN for Harriman-Vance. More sensitive material distributed only to selected officials had the heading HARVAN PLUS. The cables that reported on the secret meetings bore the heading HARVAN DOUBLE PLUS and were personally restricted by the president to an extremely small number of officials. As a result, senior officials of the government who thought they had access to the most sensitive material because they were recipients of the HARVAN PLUS cables remained ignorant of the fact that they had been cut off from the most important reports. One member of the Paris staff complained to Undersecretary of State Nicholas Katzenbach that he was not seeing reports of the secret meetings. Katzenbach asked him if he would feel any better knowing that the director of the CIA had also had his access cut off.

To the best of my knowledge, no report to the president from Paris mentioned any electoral considerations. Once, at a secret meeting in October, when the North Vietnamese hinted broadly that they hoped to reach an agreement before the presidential election, I prepared the draft of the reporting cable. Vance deleted that comment because of concern that its mention would make it less likely that the president would accept an understanding reached before the election.

This is not to say that for tactical reasons the Americans did not mention the election in the talks. At one tea break I briefly reviewed Hubert Humphrey's record in a low key attempt to suggest that the North Vietnamese might consider whether the chances of an agreement might not be improved by speeding things up and by doing so assisting Humphrey's chances of becoming president. As the break ended I hastily said, "I am sure you are familiar with Richard Nixon's history." My counterpart, speaking in English for the first and last time, replied, "I wouldn't buy a used car from that man."

ceptable. "Since the USA has unleashed the war of aggression," declared Thuy, "the USA must stop it. Since the USA has continually escalated the war, the USA must de-escalate it." Hanoi's position at the outset of the talks, as it had been since the first Rolling Thunder sorties three years earlier, was the same: There could be no substantive discussions until the bombing stopped and all other acts of war against its territory came to an end.

Hanoi would offer no gesture of reciprocity until the bombing stopped. Washington would not stop the bombing without evidence of North Vietnamese reciprocity. Virtually as soon as they began, the talks descended into a sterile repetition of irreconcilable positions. "Never," remarked one hardened U.S. diplomat, "have I heard two nations call each other sons of bitches so politely." But the stalemate in Paris reflected more than an unwillingness to compromise. The prospect of peace had always depended on the bloody course of the war. And just as the negotiators who faced one another across the green baize table at the Majestic Hotel had reached an impasse, so for the opposing armies struggling across the green land of South Vietnam in the late spring of 1968, there was no end in sight.

Counteroffensive

If the allied command had been shaken by the suddenness and magnitude of the Tet offensive, it had also been presented with an unprecedented opportunity. General Westmoreland had argued from the beginning that the enemy's "desperate gamble" had decimated his ranks and left him open for punishing counterblows that could transform initial allied reverses into a major victory. Even

as officials in Washington debated the wisdom of continued American military involvement in Vietnam, the allies struck back.

They turned their attention first to the countryside surrounding Saigon where three Communist divisions threatened a renewed attack on the capital. On March 11 some 50,000 U.S. and ARVN troops fanned out across a six-province belt in the largest operation of the war to date. Code-named Quyet Thang (Resolve To Win), the month-long campaign netted over 2,600 enemy killed. Although the operation failed to provoke a major fight or destroy a sizable Communist unit, the constant patrolling and night ambushes prevented enemy forces from concentrating for another attack. Quyet Thang was immediately followed by an even larger operation optimistically called Toan Thang, or Complete Victory. Employing seventy-nine maneuver battalions, the allied command sent over 100,000 men into Gia Dinh Province on small unit patrols, daylight search missions, night ambushes, and cordons. By the time the operation ended on May 31, some 7,600 enemy soldiers had been killed.

Eighty-five miles to the south in the Mekong Delta, the allies capitalized on a series of dry-weather fires in the U Minh Forest to drive Communist forces from one of their most formidable bases. U.S. jets roared over the 1,550-square-mile jungle feeding the fire with napalm and white-phosphorous rockets, while U.S. Navy cruisers in the Gulf of Thailand sent hundreds of rockets into suspected enemy positions. As the VC frantically dug fire-breaks and attempted to haul tons of supplies to safer ground, the onrushing fire tore through their camps setting off explosions of ammunition and fuel. By the middle of April, 85 percent of the U Minh was a smoking ruin. The

SPOT THE BALL!

The long debate over a site for the peace talks provoked ironic comment on both sides of the Atlantic, as this British cartoon testifies.

A paratrooper of the 101st Airborne Division guides a medevac helicopter into a gap in the heavy foliage as wounded soldiers await evacuation from the A Shau Valley.

Communist refuge would not be habitable for at least a year.

As smoke darkened the sky over the southern delta, U.S. aircraft pounded the North Vietnamese "panhandle" south of the nineteenth parallel in some of the most intensive bombing of the war. Taking advantage of the end of the spring monsoon, U.S. fighter-bombers executed over 7,000 sorties during April against targets ranging from staging areas along the DMZ to the rail and highway center of Vinh 150 miles north. Guided by aerial photographs from droopnosed RF–4C Phantoms based in northern Thailand, U.S. airmen struck repeatedly at truck convoys, radar sites, gun emplacement rail links, and bridges. American commanders estimated that by concentrating their attacks on the area just north of the DMZ, they were destroying more men and materiel heading into South Vietnam than before the bombing restrictions had gone into place.

A Shau

The most spectacular operation of the allied counter-offensive was the raid into the A Shau Valley. Located in the southwestern corner of Thua Thien Province along the Laotian border, the A Shau had been held by the North Vietnamese since they overran a Special Forces camp at the southern end of the valley in March 1966. By the beginning of 1968 the A Shau was the strongest enemy base in South Vietnam, an enormous storehouse of supplies and a key infiltration route from Laos and the Ho Chi Minh Trail. Garrisoned by 5,000 to 6,000 troops, ringed by a sophisticated complex of interlocked antiaircraft batteries, it had been from the A Shau that the enemy had launched his Tet attacks on the northern provinces. And it was from the A Shau, many American commanders feared, that he was preparing to unleash a second offensive.

Planning for the operation, code-named Delaware/Lam Son 216, had begun in early April, even as the relief of Khe Sanh was underway. As conceived by Lieutenant General William B. Rosson, commander of the newly designated Provisional Corps, Vietnam, the operation called for a multipronged drive into the valley, led by heliborne assault troops and supported by a punishing application of aerial firepower.

For six days prior to the first attack, waves of B–52s blasted enemy weapons sites, troop concentrations, and bunkers. Despite the tons of explosives rained down on the valley, the first helicopter assault on April 19 came under withering fire from antiaircraft batteries hidden in the surrounding hills. "There were white puffs of smoke everywhere," recalled a pilot who flew one of the earliest missions. "I mean, when I came in the ground *erupted* right

at me." On the first day of battle Communist gunners brought down ten helicopters, including the first giant Flying Crane to be lost in the war. "I'll tell you this," said Major Charles Gilmer, executive officer of the 1st Air Cavalry's helicopter reconnaissance unit, "if you fly over that valley you have a good chance of getting killed."

Making matters worse was the weather, which one senior officer called "almost unbelievably bad." Although the operation had been carefully timed to avoid the heavy downpours that inundated the valley much of the year, helicopters and air force supply planes continually battled heavy clouds, fog, and thunderstorms. Cloud cover also blanketed departure sites at Camp Evans and along the coast, forcing helicopters to climb through the overcast on instruments to more than 9,000 feet, reassemble in formation, fly to the target area, then search for a break in the clouds to make their descent. "What should have been a simple twenty-minute flight," said Lieutenant General John J. Tolson, "was usually an hour and twenty minutes of stark terror."

After establishing LZs Tiger and Vicki at the northern end of the valley, units of the 1st Air Cav cut Route 548 and moved southeast to secure an old French landing strip at A Luoi. To the east, one battalion of the 101st Airborne began clearing operations along Route 547, while another established an LZ at the junction of Routes 547 and 547A.

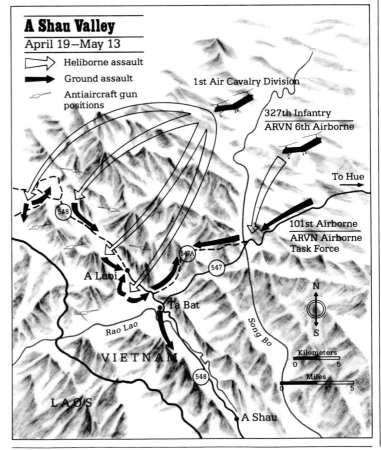

A Shau Valley
April 19–May 13

▷ Heliborne assault
➤ Ground assault
↝ Antiaircraft gun positions

1st Air Cavalry Division
327th Infantry
ARVN 6th Airborne
To Hue
101st Airborne
ARVN Airborne Task Force
548
547A
547
A Luoi
Ta Bat
Rao Lao
Song Bo
N
S
VIETNAM
Kilometers
0   5
Miles
0   5
548
LAOS
A Shau

When the cloud cover finally broke on April 22, CH-47 Chinook helicopters thundered over the jungle hauling 105 MM and 155MM howitzers to positions overlooking the valley floor, providing protective fire for ground units conducting reconnaissance patrols to the south and west. By the twenty-ninth an LZ had been opened at Ta Bat airfield, enabling the ARVN 3d Regiment to initiate attacks along the Rao Lao River toward the abandoned Special Forces camp. Two days later C-123 Providers began regular supply runs into the refurbished A Luoi airstrip.

Except for the murderous antiaircraft fire—which cost allied forces some sixty helicopters destroyed or damaged and one C-130 aircraft—the A Shau proved to be lightly defended on the ground. NVA units avoided contact and retreated into the hills from which they harassed allied patrols with heavy barrages of 122MM rockets and artillery. What they left behind, however, was a treasure trove of war materiel. Although the operation accounted for no more than 850 enemy killed (compared to 139 Americans) by the time Delaware/Lam Son came to a close on May 13—a figure even General Rosson admitted was disappointing—allied forces had uncovered a huge quantity of enemy supplies, including 2,300 small arms, 36 machine guns, 13 antiaircraft guns, 10 recoilless rifles, 11 rocket launchers, 31 flame throwers, 2,200 pounds of explosives, 135,000 rounds of small arms ammunition, 800 rounds of recoilless rifle ammunition, 35 mines, 25,000 grenades, 2 bulldozers, 75 wheeled vehicles, 3 tracked vehicles, 1 tank, 76,000 rounds of miscellaneous ammunition, 72,000 pounds of food, and 90,000 pages of documents.

While General Rosson would call the A Shau campaign technically "one of the most audacious, skillfully executed, and successful combat undertakings of the Vietnam War," perhaps more important was its psychological impact. Almost from the beginning of the American build-up the Communists had considered the A Shau, like the U Minh Forest, their personal territory, a symbol of their relative invulnerability. In the aftermath of the Tet offensive and the siege of Khe Sanh, Operation Delaware was ample demonstration that the allied command was not prepared to cede military victory by default.

Fight-talk

Although they found themselves on the defensive in various parts of South Vietnam, it was imperative for the Communists to maintain military pressure on the allies. To the American public the opening of negotiations suggested the beginning of the end of the long conflict. To Hanoi it signaled a new phase of the war: the "fight-talk" stage in which negotiation became a tactic of warfare and warfare a tactic of negotiations. By continuing and even increasing

The partial bombing halt meant no relaxation for this worker at a Hanoi factory. His rifle remains close at hand as he continues to turn out bicycles, thousands of which were used to transport men and equipment down the Ho Chi Minh Trail.

the intensity of fighting while the talks went on, the Communists hoped to demonstrate their capacity to wage a protracted war, capture territory that could later be given up as part of a face-saving American withdrawal, and convince the South Vietnamese and American people that however long it took, they could not be defeated.

With the breathing space provided by the partial bombing halt, North Vietnamese authorities initiated a furious program of rebuilding, resupply, and refitting of its armed forces both north and south of the DMZ. The North used the pause to reconstruct roads, railroads, and bridges heavily damaged by U.S. air raids, to put several large factories back into operation, and to strengthen the capital's air defenses. Meanwhile, huge convoys of Russian trucks bearing rocket launchers, rifles, and soldiers rolled at high speed along the now-resurfaced roads toward the South. The infiltration of NVA regulars down the Ho Chi Minh Trail increased to nearly 12,000 men a month in the early spring, double the usual rate. U.S. intelligence officials estimated that from February to May some 50,000 fresh soldiers made the journey south to reinforce depleted units and to prepare for a new onslaught.

South Vietnamese guerrilla forces were also active. Although badly battered, the VC had far from disappeared. The CIA estimated that at worst the Vietcong would be able to replace their losses within six months, and a JCS report found "no evidence" that Vietcong guerrillas had become dormant, pointing to a continuing high level of terrorism and harassment. The southern Communists also retained sufficient resources to create a host of political associations, revolutionary councils, and regional fronts, and to overhaul party administration in NLF-controlled areas.

Nonetheless, Vietcong losses at Tet had been severe. Secret urban cadres had revealed their true identities, only to find themselves forced to flee when the General Uprising never materialized. In areas where the NLF infrastructure had been compromised, the party was left with little or no organization. The arrest of numerous district-level cadres, who formed a crucial "bridge" between policy makers and action units, placed a critical strain on the Communists' urban apparatus. Equally serious was the loss of highly trained specialty units such as sappers and political cadres whose replacement would not be easy. By the end of February decimated Vietcong units were being withdrawn to outlying bases, reducing their level of attack to small-unit forays or harassment by fire. Guerrilla and local forces were diverted to logistical missions as the Communist command trained new recruits.

Some of the replacements had not come willingly, exacerbating morale problems within VC ranks. When the promise of the General Uprising had turned instead into bloody losses and retreat, a wave of frustration and disappointment swept the guerrilla camps. Attempts to upgrade guerrilla and local-force units into Main Force battalions led to desertions and declining confidence.

Captured documents revealed widespread resentment toward the northerners whom many felt had "used" the southern soldiers for their own purposes.

"The truth was that Tet cost us half of our forces," recalled Truong Nhu Tang, a founder of the NLF. "Our losses were so immense that we were simply unable to replace them with new recruits. One consequence was that the Hanoi leadership began to move unprecedented numbers of troops into the South, giving them a new and much more dominant position in NLF deliberations." By May, some 15,000 NVA troops had been placed in Vietcong units. U.S. intelligence estimated in June that fully 70 percent of all Communist forces in South Vietnam were soldiers of the DRV.

Yet for all their difficulties, the Vietcong remained a potent weapon in the Communist arsenal. During March and April VC cadres smuggled arms and ammunition into Saigon, making contact with underground cells still intact after the February battles. Storing tons of new supplies in caches ringing the city, they built and resurfaced a dozen new roads, including one within thirty miles of the capital. By the first week of May, three months after they had suffered, in General Westmoreland's words, "a striking military defeat," the Communists were ready to attack again.

"Tet II"

As the conferees in Paris prepared for the opening session of negotiations, Communist troops launched 119 attacks against provincial and district capitals, allied military installations, and major cities. Most of their efforts were limited to mortar and rocket fire. "It was exactly the kind of attack we expected," said a senior American officer, "a lot of smoke and not much fire." But in several places the fighting was savage and costly. At Dong Ha, a U.S. Marine supply base in northeastern Quang Tri Province, 8,000 men of the NVA 320th Division fought a three-day battle with 5,000 marines and South Vietnamese troops before retreating across the DMZ, leaving 856 Communists and 68 Americans dead. Two hundred kilometers away on the northern edge of the central highlands, two regiments of the NVA 2d Division trapped 1,800 allied soldiers inside the Special Forces camp at Kham Duc. With the isolated garrison under intense attack, army and marine helicopters and air force C-130s flew through ferocious ground fire to evacuate the base as allied fighters hurled rockets, cluster bombs, and napalm into enemy positions as close as twenty meters from the camp's perimeter. Most of Kham Duc's defenders were rescued but not without the loss of two C-130s, an A-1 Skyraider, and five helicopters. One of the C-130s went down with a full load of Vietnamese CIDG troops and their dependents—150 men, women, and children.

Unlike the Tet offensive, when Vietcong units bore the brunt of the fighting, the May attacks were conducted in most areas almost exclusively by North Vietnamese troops. Once again there was evidence of careful planning. But this time the Communists lacked the advantage of surprise. They had warned repeatedly of a renewed round of attacks, and in late April the highest-ranking defector yet to fall into allied hands, a North Vietnamese colonel and political commissar attached to the Vietcong 9th Division, surrendered with detailed plans for a "second wave" of attacks. Allied units intercepted the majority of Communist forces heading for Saigon before they reached the outskirts of the city. The thirteen enemy battalions that did penetrate the city's outer defenses, however, were more than enough to once more plunge the capital into chaos (see picture essay, page 154).

At 4:00 A.M. on May 5, the 150th anniversary of the birth of Karl Marx, a barrage of rockets and mortars slammed into the heart of Saigon signaling the start of the attack. The battle began on the northeast edge of the city where Communist troops seized the Saigon–Bien Hoa Highway bridge, then swirled around to the west and southwest engulfing Tan Son Nhut Airport. Elements of the U.S. 25th Infantry Division and air cavalry units repelled the advance on the air base, and for a time it appeared that the attack was over. But two days later intense fighting broke out in Cholon and around the nearby Phu Tho racetrack.

The tenacity of the enemy surprised allied commanders. At Phu Lam, Communist troops equipped with 75MM recoilless rifles and antiaircraft weapons were so well entrenched that it took the ARVN 38th Ranger Battalion, supported by armor, artillery, and tactical air strikes, two days to drive them out. One of the stubbornest pockets of resistance was a shantytown near Saigon's "Y" Bridge. "We've had it," said an American officer on the seventh day of fighting. "We're going to level the whole damn place. We've been in there twelve times and we've been thrown out each time. If we don't get them out soon, we'll spend our lives here."

By May 13 Communist forces had been driven from the city, only to reappear two weeks later in a second surge of attacks. Two NVA regiments reached the densely populated northern suburbs, transforming numerous pagodas into fortified positions, while local-force battalions reoccupied Cholon where they raised a Vietcong flag over the Central Post Office. ARVN brigades using tactical air support and tear gas cleared enemy units from the northern sector by June 3. But small groups of Communist troops occupied high-rise buildings in Cholon and dug in for a bitter defense. Only after a series of painful and drawn-out assaults supported by helicopter gunships firing repeatedly into enemy nests on the top floors of several buildings were they finally dislodged.

Their departure brought little relief to the residents of Saigon as enemy ground assaults gave way to a daily barrage of 122MM rockets. Firing from distances as great as seven miles from downtown Saigon, Communist gunners sent a steady rain of random death into the battered city. Their only warning a high-pitched whistle, the warheads tore into shops and houses, exploding in quiet residential sections and crowded squares. Twenty-five times in 38 days rockets pounded the capital killing hundreds of civilians and wounding nearly 1,000 more. Raising the terror to an almost unbearable level, Communist radio broadcasts threatened 100 days of shelling, 100 rockets a day. If to General Westmoreland the rocket attacks had no "real military significance," their psychological impact was incalculable.

Although the city was never in danger of being captured, the May offensive wrought new havoc and devastation on Saigon: 4,800 civilians wounded; 160,000 new refugees; whole districts in ruin. American officers vehemently defended the allied reliance on helicopter gunships and napalm strikes in populated areas. "There is no clean way of fighting a city war," argued one American general. "If you try to fight with gloves on, the casualty rate is going to be so high that you can't stomach it, and you don't get the enemy out anyway." But for the residents of Saigon's 8th district, where 8,000 homes were destroyed in five days of fighting, it was a logic impossible to comprehend.

Young Vietnamese referred sarcastically to the "liberation" of their neighborhoods and suggested that in place of the swastikas and Rising Suns of an earlier war, U.S. pilots now adorned their aircraft with rows of houses. Said

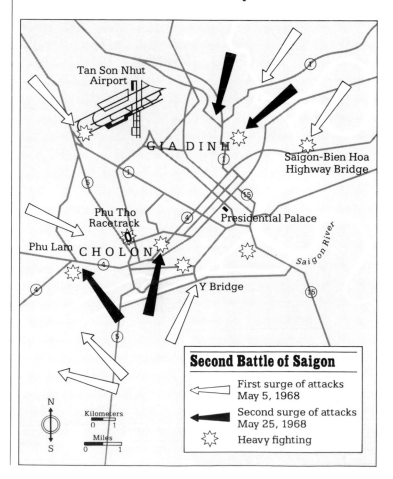

Second Battle of Saigon

First surge of attacks
May 5, 1968

Second surge of attacks
May 25, 1968

Heavy fighting

one ARVN officer bitterly, "We cannot go on destroying entire blocks everytime a Vietcong steps into a house." They failed to rouse the people to their cause or bring down the Thieu government, but the Communists had demonstrated anew their capacity to attack the seat of South Vietnamese power and bring destruction down upon the heads of its inhabitants. "The Vietcong offensive is like the tide lapping at a beach," said one refugee from the Cholon fighting "It comes and it goes. But each time, a little bit of the government's authority is swept away."

The longest war

Even as fighting subsided in Saigon, new clashes broke out across the northern provinces where American forces found themselves fighting a conventional war against regular NVA divisions that had largely abandoned their earlier hit-and-run tactics to stand and fight. Citing the enemy's increased use of artillery, the frequency of counterattacks, and the use of maneuver elements, American commanders marveled at the "beautiful equipment, first-line weapons, helmets, clean uniforms, and high morale" of the Communist troops.

There were no spectacular victories or defeats for either side but rather an endless series of bloody clashes. The cost of these countless skirmishes was painfully evident in the growing casualty lists. According to U.S. intelligence, American troops in I Corps alone had killed an average of more than 1,500 enemy soldiers a week since the outbreak of the Tet offensive five months earlier. But U.S. casualties had also grown. During May, 2,000 Americans perished in the fighting—the highest monthly death toll of the war.

The military contest in Vietnam was rapidly falling into the pattern set in Korea where the worst fighting, and highest casualty rates, took place after both sides had sat down to talk peace. As if to underline this grim prospect, Hanoi directed a return to the policy of "protracted war." In a speech in June, Truong Chinh, third-ranking member of the North Vietnamese Politburo, warned party workers to "overcome pacifist ideas." "We must attack the enemy with determination," Chinh urged. "But at times, under certain circumstances, we must shift to the defensive to gain time, dishearten the enemy, and build up our forces for a new offensive." In the aftermath of the February and May offensives, it was time again to "grasp the motto of long-drawn-out fight."

How long, no one could say. By the end of the month, U.S. military personnel in South Vietnam had reached a new milestone. Since December 22, 1961, when Vietcong bullets killed an army private in a delta ambush, Americans had been fighting for more than six-and-a-half years: longer than they had in Korea, in World War I or II, the Civil War, or the War for Independence. At midnight, June 13, 1968, the 2,376th day of conflict, Vietnam became America's longest war.

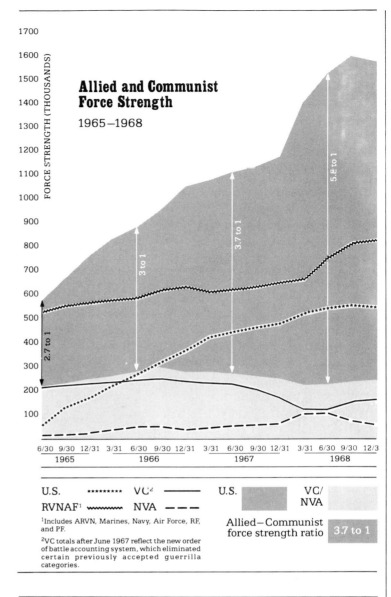

Allied and Communist Force Strength
1965–1968

FORCE STRENGTH (THOUSANDS)

6/30 9/30 12/31 / 1965 — 3/31 6/30 9/30 12/31 / 1966 — 3/31 6/30 9/30 12/31 / 1967 — 3/31 6/30 9/30 12/3 / 1968

| U.S. | ••••••••• | VC[2] | ——— | U.S. | | VC/ NVA |
| RVNAF[1] | ∿∿∿∿ | NVA | – – – | | | |

[1]Includes ARVN, Marines, Navy, Air Force, RF, and PF.

[2]VC totals after June 1967 reflect the new order of battle accounting system, which eliminated certain previously accepted guerrilla categories.

Allied–Communist force strength ratio   3.7 to 1

Hard-line

The reverberations of the explosions that rocked Saigon in late May and early June were felt as far away as Paris where chief U.S. delegate Averell Harriman cautioned the North Vietnamese that continued attacks "could have the most serious consequences for the talks. If our restraint continues to be met with escalation," the ambassador warned, there would be no progress toward peace. In Washington, where the May attacks had ignited a new debate over the wisdom of the bombing halt, the talk was even tougher. Led by the Joint Chiefs, General Maxwell Taylor, and National Security Adviser Walt Rostow, some of the president's closest aides argued that the continuing high level of enemy military activity proved that Hanoi had no interest in peace, that the Communists had agreed to negotiate only because they found themselves on the verge of defeat. If Johnson took the occasion of the May offensive to rescind the partial bombing halt and renew full-scale military operations, they suggested, the U.S. would soon find itself in the dominant bargaining position.

The president was susceptible to the hard-line arguments, but he felt trapped. "Any move we made that we had not made the week before would be regarded by our critics as 'escalation,'" he complained in his memoirs. "But Hanoi could send men by the thousands down the Ho Chi Minh Trail, could carry out regimental attacks and could hit Saigon, yet no one would mention 'escalation.'" Conscious that he would have little public support for a resumption of the bombing, yet receptive to the idea that the enemy could still be made to "cry uncle," Johnson's ambivalence made Harriman's task in Paris doubly difficult.

Since the beginning of the formal negotiating sessions, Harriman had pushed for secret talks with the North Vietnamese. By early June they were underway and quickly produced a compromise formula. The Americans would stop the bombing, and the North Vietnamese would restore the demilitarized character of the buffer zone. The United States would maintain the cessation of bombing if the Communists refrained from indiscriminate attacks on urban areas and joined in substantive talks with the Saigon government. The American delegation also made a proposal to solve the seating problem at the expanded talks: There would be two "sides," within which each group could work out its own composition.

As diplomats in Paris hammered out the framework for an intermediate settlement, there was a curious lull in the fighting in South Vietnam. Through July and early August, Communist attacks decreased sharply. The rocketing of Saigon ended, a number of Main Force units pulled back into Cambodia, Laos, and across the DMZ, and in a gesture of good will Hanoi released three captured American pilots. Compared with the period from February to June, U.S. casualties dropped dramatically. Some suggested

that the enemy's new restraint was the long-sought "reciprocity" the Americans had been demanding. But Johnson was dubious, citing infiltration estimates of some 30,000 men during July and captured documents pointing to a "third wave offensive" in August. At the close of the Honolulu talks on July 21, the president stressed that there had been "no solid evidence of de-escalation."

Harriman, to the contrary, was encouraged. The ambassador suggested to Johnson that he treat the lull as a deliberate act of restraint and halt the bombing, while informing Hanoi of certain "assumptions" the U.S. would make about subsequent Communist military activity. The Harriman plan received influential support from Secretary of Defense Clark Clifford and Vice President Hubert Humphrey. Then on July 29 the *New York Times* published an editorial advocating a similar strategy. But the president, sensing a conspiracy to put pressure on him through the media, and resenting Harriman's suggestion that the North Vietnamese might be waiting to see who won the November elections before responding to any formal proposal, sharply rejected the plan.

For the remainder of the summer numerous officials within the administration continued to push for a complete bombing halt, but Johnson was adamant. His resistance was stiffened by Ambassador Ellsworth Bunker, who in early June had recommended bombing Hanoi in retaliation for the rocketing of Saigon, and by senior American generals who cited the impact of the bombing on the flow of enemy supplies and the "intolerable menace" of Communist forces along the DMZ. On August 19 Johnson reiterated his hard-line stance in a speech to the Veterans of Foreign Wars, declaring forcefully that there would be no bombing halt until the U.S. "has reason to believe that the

Three American pilots released from captivity by Hanoi manage to smile as they tell reporters, "It's great to be home." Left to right: Major James F. Low, Captain Joe Carpenter, Major Fred M. Thompson.

other side intends seriously to join with us in de-escalating."

Change of command

Of all those who urged President Johnson to maintain a tough military posture in South Vietnam, few were as emphatic in their optimism as outgoing MACV commander General William Westmoreland. After four and a half years, the principal architect of American military strategy in Vietnam was leaving to become army chief of staff. The change of command had been planned since December 1967 and publicly announced by the president in late March.

Westmoreland spent his final week out in the field with his troops on a nostalgic farewell tour. Everywhere he went he told his men that they were winning the war. "The quality of men coming down from the North is obviously deteriorating," the general asserted. "The quality of the enemy's battlefield performance is—well, it approaches the pathetic in some cases." Admitting that the war could not be won "in the classic sense, because of our national policy of not expanding the war," Westmoreland flatly rejected the notion of a stalemate. U.S. forces had "denied to the enemy a battlefield victory" and "arrested the spread of communism" to South Vietnam. "Resolve," he declared, "is still the key to success."

Creighton W. "Abe" Abrams, the fifty-three-year-old general who took over Westmoreland's job on the third of July, was a good deal less sanguine about American prospects. While Westmoreland staunchly refused to admit that Tet had been anything but a disaster for the enemy,

Abrams was known to believe that the allies had taken a military and psychological thrashing during the February offensive. In other ways as well the two men could hardly have been more different. Unlike his tall, blue-eyed predecessor with the starched good looks, who rarely drank or smoked and only occasionally muttered a mild oath under his breath, Abe Abrams was a short, tough, cigar-chomping ex-tank commander renowned for his profanity and a distinctive combat style: "careful planning and violent execution."

Where Westmoreland was known for the lavishness of his operations, Abrams took a more bare-bones approach. During the siege of Khe Sanh, when as Westmoreland's deputy he served as the U.S. commander for the northern provinces, his slogan was simple and direct: "If you can't wear it, eat it, or shoot it, don't bring it." Fellow officers who admired both men contrasted their different styles. "Westmoreland believes in striking at the enemy, killing as many as possible, and getting the hell out," said one general. "Abrams likes to hit the enemy, hit them again, and stay with them until he has killed every one of them."

Moreover, the military and political realities that faced the new MACV commander in July 1968 were far different than those with which William Westmoreland had had to deal. Abrams took charge after a major shift in American policy, with no expectation of further manpower and with instructions to turn the war over to the Vietnamese as quickly as possible. President Johnson's decision to authorize only 24,500 more troops for Vietnam and Secretary of Defense Clark Clifford's flat assertion that there was "no plan to ask for any more American troops" signaled

the end of American escalation. Abrams's overriding responsibility was to prepare the military framework for a negotiated settlement and the withdrawal of American troops. Throughout the summer the new MACV commander received repeated messages from CINCPAC and the Joint Chiefs of Staff urging a new approach to the war. Abrams would have to find a way to do more with less. As one senior U.S. officer put it: "Abe knows damn well that he wasn't sent here to win the war, but to hold the fort until the Indians make peace."

For all their differences, however, Abrams shared with Westmoreland the task of containing an elusive and deadly enemy. And if he had the benefit of the summer lull to contemplate the job ahead, the relative quiet on the battlefield was accompanied by signs of new Communist activity. All across the delta Vietcong cadres raided villages in a stepped-up "recruitment" drive bolstered by the continuing heavy infiltration from the North. In the jungle near Cambodia the Communists finished a new steel bridge linking the Ho Chi Minh Trail with an expanding network of roads radiating east from the border. With remarkable speed, North Vietnamese units had reasserted their control over the A Shau Valley, opening new roads into the central highlands. Some Communist divisions had for the moment disappeared, but others were gathering around Saigon, stockpiling arms, infiltrating Special Action Command troops into the capital, and reconnoitering potential targets. By mid-July, allied intelligence placed fifty to fifty-two enemy battalions within striking distance of the city.

The Abrams approach

The first order of business was to reestablish the security of Saigon and diminish the threat of rocket attacks. "We have to stop them," said Abrams, "and we have the means to stop them." He began by shifting thousands of men from the countryside, ringing the capital with a U.S.–South Vietnamese blocking force of some 100,000 troops. He ordered the construction of sixty-foot-high lookout towers, used pinpoint B–52 strikes to destroy firing positions and arms caches, and sent U.S. soldiers on repeated sweeps across the "rocket belt."

Shielding the capital reflected a change in tactical priorities. Arguing that the "key strategic thrust" was "to provide meaningful, continuing security for the Vietnamese people," Abrams moved elements of the 1st Air Cavalry from I Corps to the areas around Tay Ninh and Quan Loi, collected the entire 1st Marine Division at Da Nang, and deployed the 7th Squadron of the 1st Air Cav to Vinh Long in the Mekong Delta, an area heretofore left largely to ARVN. The emphasis on population security also led to a larger role for the pacification program and a renewed drive to destroy the Vietcong infrastructure (VCI). Allied operations "must succeed in neutralizing the VCI and separating the enemy from the population," the general maintained. "The enemy Main Forces and NVA are blind without the VCI. They cannot obtain intelligence, cannot obtain food, cannot prepare the battlefield, and cannot move unseen." The American military effort, said Abrams, simply could not "recognize a separate war of big battalions, war of pacification or war of territorial security."

Changes in tactical priorities were accompanied by changes in tactics. Instead of distributing B–52 strikes to various units weeks in advance, Abrams looked for targets of opportunity, sending massed flights of the giant Stratofortresses against enemy troop concentrations and employing the "strategic" bombers as a close-support weapon. What made this possible in part was an increasing sophistication of electronic sensors and the steady improvement of allied intelligence. There was also more emphasis on the "cordon-and-pile-on" technique, a tactic used extensively by the commander of the 101st Airborne Division, Major General O. M. Barsanti. "I'd send out maybe fifty little patrols and just let them wiggle around," explained General Barsanti. "Then, if the enemy shot at some of those guys, I'd grab every soldier I could lay my

hands on—cooks, clerks, and everybody—and throw me a tight cordon around the area. . . . We wouldn't try to kill or capture just part of the unit, we wanted to get every single man in there."

The new approach was in part a response to a shift in enemy tactics from massed assaults against urban and military targets to economy-of-force, stand-off rocket attacks. The increased use of B–52s and techniques such as the cordon-and-pile-on also husbanded human resources that Abrams knew were at a premium, while maximizing the firepower available to the Americans. For the same reason Abrams displayed little enthusiasm for the large-scale search and destroy operations of the past. In their place he sent small-unit patrols searching for enemy bases and supply caches, in effect preempting enemy initiatives by preventing him from "seeding" the battlefield long in advance with ammunition, rations, medical supplies, and headquarters installations necessary to mount a major attack.

If the Communists could be kept off balance and the military situation stabilized, Abrams told the president in

One of the chief areas of renewed fighting in the late summer was I Corps, where these South Vietnamese and American Special Forces soldiers defend a hilltop outpost in Quang Ngai Province.

October, it would be possible to begin withdrawal of some American troops in 1969. A significant disengagement of American forces, however, depended upon the ability of the South Vietnamese to take over a greater share of the fighting. During a tour of South Vietnam in July, Secretary of Defense Clark Clifford had left no doubt that Vietnamization of the war had become Washington's top priority. It was up to Abrams to make it work.

As Westmoreland's deputy commander, Abrams had already spent more than a year working with ARVN to improve its performance. The ability of the South Vietnamese army to withstand the Tet attacks suggested that he had had some success, but much more needed to be done. Poor leadership had afflicted ARVN from its inception. Now some of the better senior officers were gaining front-line commands. In March Washington initiated a major effort to provide all regular ARVN forces with M16 rifles. Along with them came thousands of machine guns, grenade launchers, mortars, howitzers, and APCs. South Vietnamese Regional and Popular Forces also began to receive M16s as part of a plan to turn pacification over to the "Ruff-Puffs," thereby freeing some fifty-four ARVN battalions for combat. A new emphasis was placed on getting the South Vietnamese army to go it alone in selected areas. The Americans turned over four Special Forces camps to local forces, U.S. advisers to some ARVN units were sharply reduced, and plans were made to gradually turn over the defense of the vital area just south of the DMZ to the ARVN 1st Division.

Some American commanders were skeptical of ARVN's capacity to defend South Vietnam on its own. But others argued that they were already doing more and better fighting. "Their kill ratio is high, the number of captured enemy weapons is increasing, and there are lower casualties," said one American officer. "For the first time since 1961 I feel there is great improvement to be seen."

"Third wave"

Vietnamization would take time, but Abrams's new tactics and manpower deployments were soon put to the test. During the third week of August Communist forces broke their silence, shelling dozens of towns and military outposts and launching a series of coordinated assaults throughout South Vietnam. The capital itself was subjected to the first serious rocket attack since late June, a barrage that killed eighteen civilians, wounded sixty-nine more, and partially damaged the National Assembly building. Hoping to forestall a ground assault against the city, B-52 bombers pummeled Communist base areas and infiltration routes with close to one million pounds of high explosives a day. The attack never materialized, but whether this was the result of the bombing raids or not was uncertain.

In fact, there was little hard evidence of what the Com-

munists were up to. The fighting in August hardly matched the intensity of the earlier drives, and some American officers were convinced that the attacks were no more than a prelude to a "third wave" offensive yet to come. Others argued that this *was* the beginning of the long-awaited third offensive but that U.S. spoiling actions during the previous months had blunted its effectiveness. Some observers speculated that the enemy hoped to demonstrate his control over large areas of the countryside and, with an eye toward the peace talks in Paris, proclaim a provisional government. U.S. intelligence had another theory, suggesting that attacks along the Cambodian and Laotian frontiers were designed to lure American and South Vietnamese forces away from Saigon, the real target of the new fighting.

If that was their intention, the Communists had little hope of success. Abrams continued to pound suspected enemy concentrations near the capital with massive B-52 raids, and despite the temptation to strike back at the enemy where he opened himself up, the ring of allied troops around Saigon remained in place. But the defense of the cities had the disadvantage of allowing the VC to rebuild their strength in the countryside where a campaign of assassinations took the lives of more than 120 local officials, policemen, and pacification workers. Third wave or not, the Communists had put an end to the lull that had prevailed for nearly eight weeks. U.S. estimates put enemy casualties during the first weeks of renewed fighting at a stunning 10,000 men. During the same period, more than 700 Americans died in action, the highest rate in three months.

For all the upheaval of the first six months of the year, not much had changed on the ground in South Vietnam. For both sides, there could be no letup. The Communists still faced the necessity of keeping the pressure on the allies while consolidating their control over as much of the countryside as possible. The Americans still sought to punish Hanoi for its intransigence by destroying as many of the enemy as they could. If American tactics and tactical priorities had changed, if the task now was not victory but accommodation, the basic strategy remained the same.

Since 1965 American soldiers had struggled through force of arms to compel Hanoi to yield; now they struggled to compel the Communists to negotiate seriously. As it had been at the end of 1967, so the war remained in the fall of 1968, a question of time: for the Communists—once again committed to protracted war—to prolong the fighting until the Americans tired of the endless sacrifice of men and resources 10,000 miles from home; for the Americans—now committed to withdrawal—to prolong the fighting until the South Vietnamese could assume the burden of defending their country. But after Tet, the enemy had at least one advantage. As protracted negotiations gave way once more to protracted war, many Americans had already had enough.

In the wake of the Tet offensive, the beginning of peace talks, and a major change of command, not much had changed for these soldiers of the U.S. 9th Infantry Division on patrol in the Mekong Delta.

The Second Battle of Saigon

As fighting erupts in Saigon for the second time in three months, an ARVN Ranger tends a wounded civilian.

During the early days of the Tet offensive an "absolutely secret" memorandum signed by COSVN leader Pham Hung circulated among the Communist hierarchy in South Vietnam. While many of the Tet attacks had fallen short of their marks, the document said, such failures were to be expected. "Ours is a strategic offensive of long duration. We must attack the enemy repeatedly three or four times if need be, in those areas under contest, and we must not withdraw just because we fail in our first effort."

In the last weeks of April—despite the loss of more than 75,000 men since the beginning of the year and into the teeth of alerted allied defenses—Communist troops once more moved into range of South Vietnamese cities and military bases. By May 4, as Communist mortar crews slipped into Saigon's suburban precincts, VC sappers had established command centers in the slum housing ringing the central business district. They waited only for the signal to attack.

The second battle of Saigon was the first great test of ARVN after the Tet offen-

sive. This time most units were ready. South Vietnamese marines repelled multibattalion Communist attacks on several bridges over the Saigon River. With support from RVNAF aircraft and U.S. helicopters, ARVN and American troops pinned down two enemy battalions near the Phu Tho racetrack as South Vietnamese fighter-bombers roared across the sky bombing enemy positions throughout the city. During the days that followed ARVN soldiers engaged in some of the heaviest street fighting of the war.

Twice in four weeks allied forces drove Communist attackers from the capital, with heavy enemy losses. But defending Saigon proved costly as well to the South Vietnamese military leadership. Tan Son Nhut commander Colonel Luu Kim Cuong was killed by an enemy B40 rocket while directing a counterattack. Another casualty was Colonel Dao Ba Phuoc, commander of the 5th Ranger Group. Brigadier General Nguyen Ngoc Loan was wounded leading a charge on a sniper position in a Saigon alley. His second-in-command, Colonel Dan Van

Quy, fell to another sniper's bullet two days later.

The enemy attacks left the crowded city in a shambles and refugee camps bursting with a new influx of terrified civilians. Many of those who had moved to Saigon to escape the war in rural areas now thought of returning to the countryside. In at least one district of the capital three times the number of houses destroyed during Tet lay in ruins. At least 100 civilians had been killed and over 40,000 were left homeless.

Disillusionment was widespread. "It's hard to say," reported an American journalist, "whether Cholon's residents were most bitter at the Vietcong who had started the fighting, the South Vietnamese troops who went on a rampage of looting in the midst of the battle, or the American planes and tanks that had blasted their homes." Of one thing, though, all Saigon's residents were sure: The illusion of the security of the capital had been dispelled forever. The war had come again to Saigon; this time, it seemed, for good.

Above left. Brilliant flares illuminate Saigon Cathedral as the battle rages into the night.

Above. Firemen foam down flames during the attack on Tan Son Nhut air base.

Left. An M60 machine gunner and two other men of the 7th Battalion, ARVN Airborne Division, advance on Communist positions in the village of Tan Son Nhut, near the air base.

Left. ARVN bore the brunt of the second battle of Saigon, but U.S. soldiers also joined the fray. Here troops of the U.S. 9th Infantry Division take cover during fighting south of Cholon.

Right. Linking Saigon with its southern suburbs and the Mekong Delta, the "Y" Bridge was the scene of some of the heaviest fighting in the city.

Below. A VC soldier with a three-day-old stomach wound receives water from members of the U.S. 9th Division. "Any soldier who can fight for three days with his insides out can drink from my canteen anytime," said one of the GIs.

Left. Carrying his belongings, a Buddhist monk crosses the Bien Hoa Highway Bridge only hours after ARVN troops had fought off an enemy attack.

Right. Fearing their homes will be looted, refugees abandon embattled areas of the city with everything they can carry.

Below. Despite frantic efforts to save them, thousands of Saigon homes, like this one, were destroyed during the May offensive. Fire trucks donated by the U.S. were too wide to travel the city's narrow streets.

Not Yet Peace

Sunday, August 25, 1968. Never before in the history of the Republic had the electoral process of the world's oldest democracy been surrounded by such an arsenal of naked force. On the eve of the thirty-fifth Democratic National Convention, Mayor Richard Daley had transformed the city of Chicago into an armed camp.

There had been threats of massive demonstrations, fears that the huge black ghetto on the city's South Side might erupt in violence, warnings that black militants would lay siege to white neighborhoods, and alleged plans for the assassination of Democratic candidates and the poisoning of the city's water supply. Lacking any mechanism for distinguishing the serious from the absurd, police and city officials took every rumor in grim earnest.

The entire metropolitan police department of 12,000 was placed on week-long, twelve-hour duty, their plans already drawn up complete with bivouacs, command posts, and mobile

tactical forces. Some of the 5,650 men of the Illinois National Guard deployed to the city waited in armories, while others set up machine-gun emplacements along the city's most luxurious thoroughfare, Michigan Avenue. School buildings and parks were set aside to house 5,000 extra guardsmen, and the 7,500 regular army troops at Fort Hood, Texas, ready to be airlifted to Chicago on twenty-four hours' notice. Not to be outdone, the sheriff of Cook County purchased two armored trucks, outfitting them with heavy weapons, tear gas, and Mace.

Over 1,000 Secret Service agents swarmed around town, bumping into federal narcotics investigators, military intelligence agents, and private cops. FBI agents established security positions in the corridors of the Conrad Hilton Hotel, headquarters of the convention, manned rooftop lookout perches, and checked passengers getting off the elevators. In fact, arriving delegates found the downtown Loop blanketed in law enforcement: police stationed on every corner and in the middle of every block.

The convention site itself—the old International Amphitheater—had been turned into a veritable fortress surrounded by a one-square-mile security area into which no one was admitted without proper credentials. Barricaded with barbed wire and a chain-link fence, the main entrance had been hidden behind a mockup of the north face of the White House to protect candidates from possible snipers. Helicopters patrolled overhead, while manhole covers on the approaches to the building were sealed shut to prevent attack from below. Two thousand police guarded the surface, 200 fire fighters stood ready to deal with bomb throwers and arsonists, and police and Secret Service agents equipped with binoculars, walkie-talkies, and rifles hovered on a catwalk ninety-five feet above the convention floor. Four days earlier Soviet troops had crossed the Czech border and put an end to a seven-month experiment in Socialist freedom. Delegates driving into Chicago from O'Hare Airport on the Sunday before the convention saw fresh paint on the city's fire hydrants and a crude, hand-lettered sign: "Welcome to Prague."

"Kill the pigs!"

The bristling security precautions reflected the mayor's concern that hordes of antiwar protesters would stream into Chicago to disrupt the city and paralyze the convention. The army of violent demonstrators never appeared, but Daley's fears were not wholly groundless. In a series of meetings following the October 1967 March on the Pentagon, the National Mobilization Committee To End the War in Vietnam laid the groundwork for what some

hoped would be the largest antiwar protest to date. Led by chairman David Dellinger, with organizational cooperation from SDS veterans Tom Hayden and Rennie Davis, "Mobe" charted strategy and logistics, planned radio communications and mobile command posts, and sent out a call for a half million demonstrators to converge on Chicago for a series of symbolic confrontations with the political system.

The youthful protesters who eventually did come to Chicago never numbered more than 10,000, and while some were clearly intent on provoking violence, most were there to express by peaceful protest their indignation at the administration's war policy. A much larger number of potential demonstrators had been frightened away by Daley's well-publicized security measures or dissuaded from coming by the mayor's refusal to grant permits enabling the protesters to parade near the Amphitheater or pitch tents in the city's parks. Convinced that the Chicago police were ready to answer provocation with force, Senator Eugene McCarthy vetoed plans to bring hundreds of thousands of young supporters to the convention city.

Yet Daley's attempts to keep them out of town altogether only strengthened the resolve of the most committed. "To remain passive in the face of escalating police brutality is foolish and degrading," said a young activist leading self-defense classes on the eve of the convention. Some mobilization leaders played down the possibility of violent confrontations with the police, but others saw it as inevitable. "We're going to march and they're going to stop us," said a young Californian. "How can you avoid violence?"

Even before the convention began, demonstrators defied the mayor's ban and set up camp in Lincoln Park, a mile north of the Loop. The police ordered them to disperse, then drove them from the park with truncheons and Mace. The young men and women reassembled the following evening behind a barricade of trash cans and picnic tables, taunting the "pigs" with shouts of "oink, oink," "shitheads," and "motherfuckers." Someone threw a lighted cigarette on a policeman's arm. Others set rocks bouncing off the officers' riot helmets. When a squad car was surrounded by demonstrators and battered with rocks and bottles, the elite police Task Force Unit charged the barricade behind a shower of tear gas. They beat scores of youths to the ground, pursuing others into the city's Old Town section, clubbing fleeing demonstrators, reporters, and spectators alike amid crashing bottles and shouts of "Kill the pigs!" "Fuck the pigs!" Many of the protesters ended up in hospitals, others in jail. When angry demonstrators returned to the park the following night only to be driven out once more by clouds of stinging tear gas, they moved downtown to Grant Park in front of the Hilton Hotel. National Guard troops relieved the police, and delegates returning from Convention Hall got their first good look at the crisis brewing in the streets.

The Democrats

The Democrats also expected trouble, not on Michigan Avenue but on the convention floor. On the surface there seemed little opening for the dissidents to mount an assault. Although he had avoided the primaries, Hubert Humphrey arrived in Chicago with 1,400 to 1,500 delegates, comfortably more than the 1,312 needed to nominate, his convention strategy well in hand, his opponents in disarray. Yet everywhere he looked there was growing disaffection and the threat of last-minute repudiation.

Labor leaders and party regulars who had delivered the delegates to Humphrey had been disappointed by his lackluster campaign and the small, often hostile crowds that greeted the stumping vice president. Many wondered aloud whether he could climb out of the president's shadow and overtake Richard Nixon's sizable lead in the polls. Once the darling of the Democratic left, he had been vilified by the liberals for his association with Johnson and

his support of the administration's war policies. Nor was there peace from the right where Texas governor John Connally warned Humphrey that his 527 southern delegates would not remain firm if the vice president yielded too much to northern liberals. Waiting in the wings was South Dakota senator George McGovern and the threat of a convention draft for Ted Kennedy. And hovering like a grim puppeteer over Humphrey's march to the nomination was the unseen presence of Lyndon Johnson, spending the week on his Texas ranch, but pulling the strings on the speaker's podium and in the critical southern delegations.

If Humphrey was harassed, Eugene McCarthy was despondent. Robert Kennedy's death had vaulted the Minnesotan back into the race just when it seemed his quixotic crusade had begun to unravel, propelling him to surprising success in the New York primary on June 18. Crowds thronged to hear him speak, money flowed into his campaign, and polls showed him beating Humphrey in one state after another. Yet he reached Chicago with only 500 delegates and no hint of a strategy to stop the vice presi-

Voices for peace. Although consigned by convention managers to the back of the hall, the New York delegation provided some of the most vocal support for the minority plank on the war.

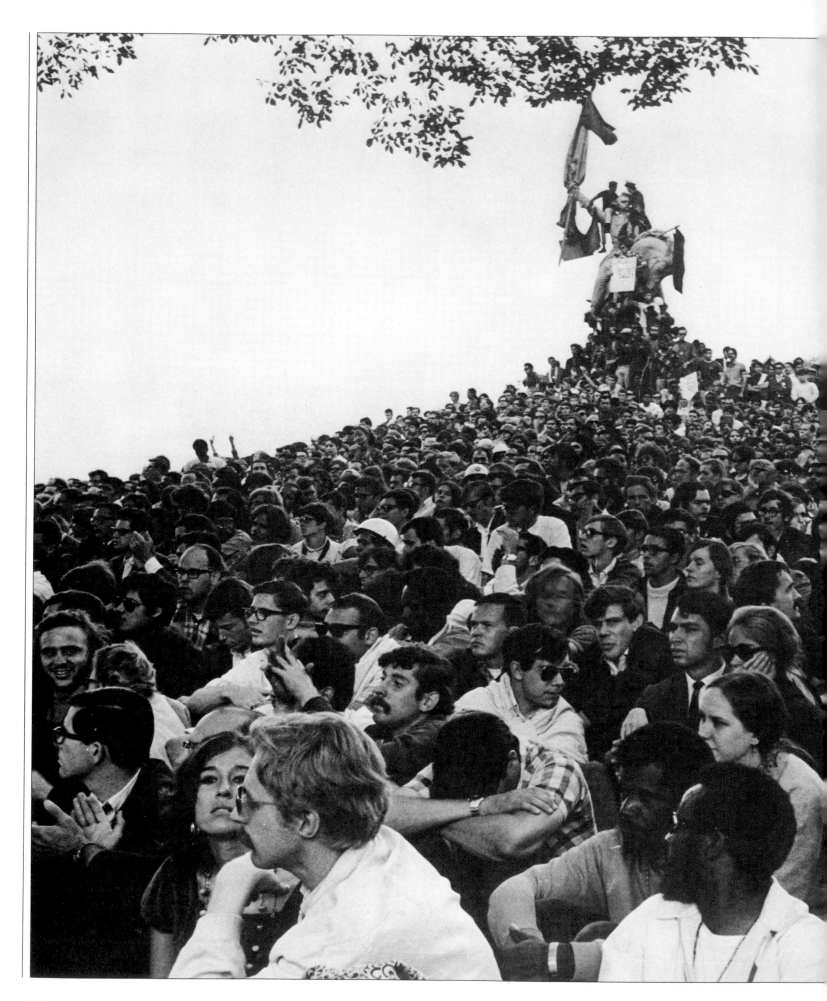

Their numbers diminished by arrest and injury, the demonstrators remain defiant as they gather in Grant Park on August 28 and prepare to march on the convention.

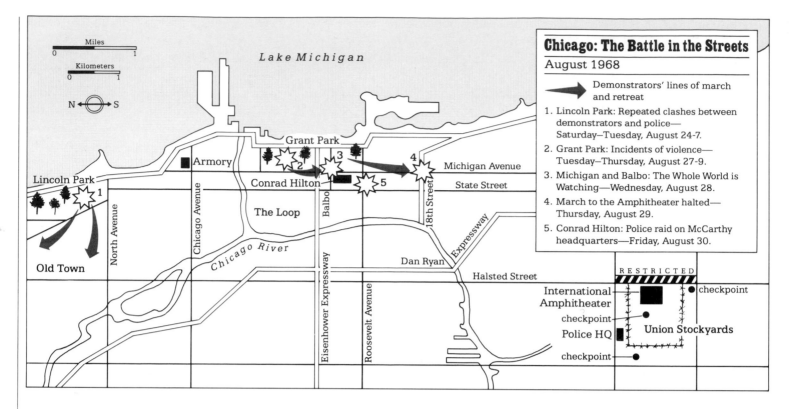

dent. While Humphrey darted from delegation to delegation shoring up his margin of victory and preaching Democratic unity, McCarthy brooded. Contemptuous of political rituals and bored by conferences and strategies, he told a group of newspaper editors that Humphrey had the nomination wrapped up.

Without a leader ready to do battle, lacking the delegate strength to defeat Humphrey directly, the dissidents chose to fight a guerrilla war on the floor of the convention. They focused their energies on a series of contests over democratization of the party's rules, the seating of biracial southern delegations, and, most important, the Vietnam plank in the party's platform.

The issue of the war lay at the very heart of the convention. It had turned to ashes the Democratic triumph of 1964, driven two Democratic senators into the primaries against a Democratic president, and threatened to hand the White House to the Republicans in November. No question had so tested the party since the Dixiecrat revolt twenty years earlier, and none provoked such passionate disagreement in 1968.

At the platform committee hearings in Washington the week before the convention, antiwar Democrats marshaled some of the party's leading doves and quickly began moving the committee away from an outright defense of the administration's war policies. But just at the moment of apparent success for the peace forces, the Russian invasion of Czechoslovakia stiffened presidential supporters who denounced the doves for advocating "appeasement" and called for a plank condemning "not our actions but . . . Communist aggression in South Vietnam, Czechoslovakia, and anywhere else in the world."

The result was two reports and the certainty of a floor fight. The majority plank bluntly rejected "unilateral withdrawal" and praised the president for bringing the North Vietnamese to the negotiating table. Calling for a reduction of U.S. military involvement "as the South Vietnamese forces are able to take over their larger responsibilities," the majority offered a conditional cessation of bombing, but only "when the action would not endanger the lives of our troops," and taking into account "the response from Hanoi." The minority plank demanded instead "an unconditional end to all bombing in North Vietnam," the negotiation of a mutual withdrawal of all U.S. and North Vietnamese forces, and a "political reconciliation" between the Saigon government and the NLF leading to a coalition government. "Now the lines are clearly drawn," proclaimed McCarthy, "between those who want more of the same and those who think it necessary to change our course in Vietnam. The convention as a whole will decide."

The debate, which took place on Wednesday, August 28, began on a conciliatory note. Senator Edmund Muskie of Maine suggested that between the two sides "the dividing line is not the desire for peace or war, the dividing line is limited to means, not ends." But as speaker after speaker rose to address the convention, the atmosphere quickly turned acrimonious. Theodore Sorensen charged that the majority plank was "a call to affirm and continue past Vietnam policies," offering "no way out of the present mess." To Kenneth O'Donnell, like Sorensen, a former aide to John Kennedy, the majority position was "the height of irresponsibility." Governor Warren F. Hearnes of Missouri argued to the contrary that the minority proposal would "jeopardize the lives of American servicemen in Vietnam" and warned the doves not to "play God with their lives." But to Tennessee senator Albert Gore the real issue was one of credibility. "The American people think overwhelmingly we made a mistake," declared Gore, "and yet in the platform we are called upon not only to approve this unconscionably disastrous policy but to applaud it."

As delegates chanted and jeered, the doves made their case that to approve the majority plank would be to "rubber stamp" policies that had utterly failed at the cost of thousands of men's lives, the emasculation of desperately needed domestic programs, and the embitterment of an entire generation. Administration supporters replied that the majority position represented a commitment to peace, that the antiwar plank would imperil American troops and undermine the Paris negotiations. The debate finally came to a close when Louisiana representative Hale Boggs divulged the contents of a cable to the president in which General Abrams predicted a 500 percent increase in enemy strength near the DMZ if the bombing were halted.

It was impossible to tell whether Abrams's warning had any effect on wavering delegates. The vote of 1,567 to 1,041 for the majority plank was a substantial victory for the administration, ending any hope of stopping Humphrey. Yet it also meant that fully 40 percent of the Democratic delegates had refused to endorse their own president. Even before the final tally was read, members of the New York delegation began singing "We Shall Overcome." Standing on chairs, pounding their feet, delegates from California, New Hampshire, Wisconsin, and Oregon donned black armbands and joined in the singing as the gallery erupted in chants of "Stop the War! Stop the War!" But the war went on; in Vietnam, where 408 Americans died during the week of the convention, and in the streets of Chi-

Denounced by antiwar delegates, condemned by demonstrators, an angry Chicago mayor Richard Daley was determined to remain in control—of his city and the convention.

cago, where a harried police force—reviled, spat upon, pelted with rocks, bottles, and sticks—had abandoned all restraint.

"The whole world is watching"

They had already been beaten and gassed at Lincoln Park. Many had been hurt. Some had been arrested. Others had been too frightened to stick around. But they had vowed to march to the Amphitheater on the night of the presidential balloting—permit or no permit—and by mid-afternoon on Wednesday the twenty-eighth some 3,000 demonstrators had assembled in Grant Park. Furious at the convention's defeat of the peace plank, some members of the crowd tore down an American flag, getting a new cloud of tear gas from the police for their trouble. As darkness began to fall, police backed up by guardsmen and army troops barricaded one of the bridges leading east toward Lake Michigan, then lined up in triple ranks across Michigan Avenue, the harsh television lights at the hotel's entrance painting menacing shadows across the broad boulevard.

Packed into a confused mass by the surrounding police, the demonstrators halted at the intersection of Michigan

Right. A demonstrator hurls a tear gas canister back at police during the confrontation at the Grant Park flagpole on the afternoon of August 28.

170

and Balbo, their chants bounding off the massive face of the hotel: "Peace Now! Peace Now!" "Stop the War! Stop the War!" Rolls of toilet paper, wads of paper, and some bottles fell to the ground from hotel windows as the police ordered the marchers to clear the street. But the mob of protesters had nowhere to go, breaking instead into a new chant: "Fuck you LBJ! Fuck you LBJ!" Five minutes later, after several bus loads of reinforcements had arrived, the police attacked.

Their nightsticks raised, a wedge of helmeted police tore into the intersection, clubbing at random. Screams, whistles, people running, blood flowing down their faces. "We'll kill all you bastards," raged a cop as he grabbed one long-haired demonstrator and jammed a billy club into his groin. Panicked demonstrators tried to escape, only to fall in heaps, the police pounding them to the pavement with their clubs. Pushed up against a wall by a trio of policemen prodding her in the stomach with their batons, a young girl dropped to her knees, screaming "Help me. Please God, help me." When a neatly dressed young man came to her aid the police beat him over the head, leaving boy and girl blood-drenched, wrapped in each other's arms. "You murderers! You murderers!" screamed

"These were our children in the streets," wrote columnist Tom Wicker in the New York Times, *"and the Chicago police beat them up."*

171

a youth, until a cop silenced him with a blow to the face.

When their first charge had cleared the intersection, police began ranging along the sidewalks, beating demonstrators and bystanders, anyone who crossed their path. Without warning, or apparent cause, a squad of police suddenly charged several dozen hotel guests standing quietly behind wooden barriers. They crushed the spectators against the window of a hotel restaurant until it gave way, sending screaming women and children backward through the broken shards of glass. Crashing through the debris the police leaped in after them, beating some of the victims, hauling others off under arrest.

For more than a week, reporters had suffered at the hands of the police some of the same mistreatment the demonstrators had endured. Now they gained a measure of revenge. For the police had made their stand only a few feet away from a battery of network television cameras that recorded the bloody confrontation in shocking detail, sending unforgettable images of rampant violence into the homes of a stunned and disbelieving nation.

After ten minutes there was a momentary halt. Those in the front rank of the crowd knelt, their arms folded across their chests singing "America the Beautiful." More police arrived and violence erupted again. But even as they cringed from the blows, the demonstrators remained defiant. "The whole world is watching!" they shouted. "The whole world is watching! The whole world is watching!"

No peace

As taped scenes of flailing police nightsticks appeared on television sets throughout the convention hall, the nominating process became an outpouring of accumulated grievance: over the defeat of the minority Vietnam plank, over the way the party regulars had run roughshod over the convention, over the manhandling of delegates and reporters on the convention floor, and over the brutal manner in which Richard Daley had pacified his city.

Speaker after speaker referred to the scene at the Hilton, denouncing the violence to a rising chorus of angry boos directed at the Illinois delegation. "Is there any way to get Mayor Daley to suspend the police-state tactics that are being perpetrated at this very moment?" demanded an angry Colorado delegate. "Thousands of young people are being beaten on the streets of Chicago!" shouted Wisconsin delegation chief Donald Peterson. "I move this convention be adjourned for two weeks and moved to another city." Convention chairman Carl Albert overruled the motion for adjournment, but he could not halt Connecticut senator Abraham Ribicoff who excoriated the "Gestapo

Confrontation. An angry demonstrator and a phalanx of National Guardsmen face off on Michigan Avenue at the beginning of the long night of conflict.

Left. Later that night, violence reigns.

A campaign worker readies a Humphrey display in a Chicago hotel lobby. The Democratic presidential candidate faced an uphill battle after the convention.

tactics in the streets of Chicago." Shaking with rage, Daley leaped to his feet screaming obscenities that were unmistakable even though his voice was drowned out in the tumult that engulfed the hall. "How hard it is to accept the truth," replied Ribicoff staring down at the mayor from the podium. "How hard it is."

The balloting that followed was almost anticlimactic, Humphrey outdistancing McCarthy by more than a thousand votes. In his acceptance speech the following day the vice president lamented "the violence which has erupted, regrettably and tragically, in the streets of this great city." But the violence continued: another attempted march on the Amphitheater halted with tear gas and truncheons; an early morning police raid on McCarthy headquarters at the Hilton, the police breaking into rooms, beating heads, forcing people to leave, dragging anyone who resisted out of their rooms and into the elevators. By the time the convention was gavelled to a close, more than 800 civilians and 150 police had been injured, one demonstrator killed, and 668 people thrown in jail. "I didn't believe it could happen here," said a bystander describing himself as ultraconservative. "I am shocked."

So was Stewart Alsop, a long-time supporter of the administration's Vietnam policy. "In Chicago," he wrote in his nationally syndicated column, "for the first time in my life it began to seem to me possible that some form of American fascism may really happen here." Other journalists joined in the chorus of outrage, labeling the police actions a "sustained rampage," a verdict endorsed two months later by the Johnson-appointed Walker Commission, which characterized what had taken place as a "police riot."

For many of the young, including those with little or no connection to radical politics, the lessons of Chicago seemed inescapable. Said one Indiana youth: "The Nazis in the blue uniforms were pretty well exposed for what they are." Others, however, saw it differently. Letters poured into Chicago City Hall commending the police for giving the demonstrators what they deserved. But wherever the blame might lie for the confrontations in Chicago, the events that surrounded the Democratic National Convention had made one thing clear. There could be no peace in America until there was peace in Vietnam.

The "New Nixon"

The war had dominated the convention, and although other issues would appear before election day, it would be the question of war and peace that would have the most decisive impact on the fall campaign. It had already left the Democrats in shambles. "Here was our situation right after Chicago," remembered one Humphrey campaign manager. "We had no money. We had no organization. We were fifteen points behind in the polls." The party's liberals had all but abandoned the vice president, taking

with them many of the fund raisers, publicists, and precinct workers without whom no Democrat is likely to become president. McCarthy refused to appear on the convention podium with Humphrey in the traditional gesture of unity and withheld his endorsement from the party's nominee. For Humphrey, the nomination had become a bitter prize indeed. "I felt when we left that convention we were in an impossible situation," he said after the election. "Chicago was a catastrophe. My wife and I went home heartbroken, battered and beaten. I told her I felt just like we had been in a shipwreck."

The Republicans, by contrast, were in excellent shape. Richard Nixon had stormed through one primary victory after another. The loser image that had followed him since 1960 was gone. In its place emerged a seemingly stronger, more self-assured candidate—what his public relations

An exuberant Richard Nixon on the eve of receiving the Republican nomination for president.

people liked to call the "New Nixon." Potential opponents fell by the wayside or never got on track. The only credible threat to the former vice president was California governor Ronald Reagan, whose homespun delivery and hard-line philosophy—"It is time to tell friend and foe alike that we are in Vietnam because it is in our national interest to be there"; and "It's very difficult to disagree with most of the things that Mr. Wallace is saying"—delighted southern delegates crucial to Nixon's winning margin. But the Republicans had sacrificed enough in 1964 for the sake of ideological purity. "We have no choice, if we want to win, except to vote for Nixon," North Carolina's Strom Thurmond told southern party leaders. "Believe me, I love Reagan, but Nixon's the one."

Unlike the Democrats' turbulent convocation in Chicago, the Republican gathering in Miami two weeks earlier was a smoothly controlled coronation. His margin of victory was not overwhelming—692 votes with 667 needed to nominate. But the party belonged to Richard Nixon, whose acceptance speech neatly struck the themes he would pursue in the weeks ahead: the need for unity, the demand for "law and order," the grievances of a "silent majority," and the urgency of peace.

When the strongest nation in the world can be tied down for four years in a war in Vietnam with no end in sight, when the richest nation in the world can't manage its own economy, when the nation with the greatest tradition of the rule of law is plagued by unprecedented racial violence, when the President of the United States cannot [safely] travel abroad or to any major city at home, then it's time for new leadership for the United States of America.

Throughout September, Nixon appeared invincible. He saturated the airwaves with commercials showing looted buildings at home and dejected American GIs in Vietnam, barnstormed the country giving standard speeches to outdoor audiences in Republican strongholds, and held carefully orchestrated live panel discussions to impress television viewers with his willingness to face the issues. One issue he declined to comment upon, however, was Vietnam.

Nixon promised to "end the war and win the peace," an objective almost all Americans shared, but he preferred not to provide details of his "secret plan" for fear of upsetting the administration's negotiations with the North Vietnamese. On rare occasions he did provide some hints of what he had in mind, citing his opposition to "military escalation," "precipitate withdrawal," or an unconditional bombing halt, the importance of "Vietnamization," and the necessity of talks with the Soviet leadership. Perhaps Nixon's most revealing remarks came at a meeting with the Florida delegation at the Republican convention. "How do you bring a war to a conclusion?" he asked. "I'll tell you how Korea ended. We got in there and had this messy war on our hands. Eisenhower let the word go out—

let the word go out diplomatically to the Chinese and the North Koreans that we would not tolerate this continual ground war of attrition. And within a matter of months, they negotiated. . . . What we've got to do is walk softly and carry a big stick." Even such general prescriptions, however, were few and far between. Nixon was shrewd enough—and lucky enough—to avoid having to make concrete proposals, capitalizing simultaneously on American voters' dissatisfaction with events in Southeast Asia and their unwillingness to face up to the painful specifics of "an honorable end to the war in Vietnam."

Back on the track

Humphrey, too, usually restricted himself to vague generalities, but while the Nixon campaign sailed along, the vice president foundered time and again on the issue of the war. Trying to put some distance between himself and the president, he declared that "negotiations or no negotiations we could start to remove some of the American forces in early 1969 or late 1968," a comment that drew an immediate rebuke from both Secretary of State Rusk and Johnson himself. Then Humphrey stated he could have run on the minority plank, forgetting that it demanded an unconditional bombing halt. All the while, antiwar demonstrators plagued his campaign appearances, heckling the candidate and perpetuating memories of the terrible week in Chicago. But Vietnam wasn't his only problem: Capitalizing on the Democratic debacle, George Wallace was steadily eating away at the Humphrey constituency. By mid-September, public opinion polls gave the feisty Alabaman 21 percent of the vote.

The Humphrey campaign hit rock bottom on September 27, when polls showed him trailing Nixon 43 to 28 percent with five weeks to go. When he arrived in Portland, Oregon, that day, the crowds were small, and during the evening demonstrators chanted antiwar slogans outside his hotel. Seattle was no better. Student protesters interrupted him repeatedly with shouts of "fascist, fascist, dump the Hump." There was little money and less support. The destitute Democratic National Committee had been unable to purchase even a single advertising spot on national radio or television, and party leaders, wrote veteran political reporter Theodore White, "fled him as if he were bearer of contagion."

By the time he reached Salt Lake City on September 29, he had decided he had nothing to lose. He desperately wanted to shed the label of Johnson's boy, to campaign as he saw fit, to win back, at least, his own self-respect. The following day he went on national television to deliver his own declaration of independence, a three-point program calling for a UN-supervised cease-fire and withdrawal of all foreign forces from South Vietnam, a turnover of the fighting to the South Vietnamese, and a bombing halt. Before taking any such action, Humphrey required "evidence of Communist willingness to restore the demilitarized zone between North and South Vietnam," and he reserved the right to resume the bombing "if the government of North Vietnam were to show bad faith." But he was convinced that a bombing halt was the best chance to bring the war to an end, "the best protection of our troops."

It was scarcely a radical departure from the administration's position, but for millions of Democrats with no place else to go it was an offer of reconciliation they had no choice but to accept. All at once money poured into the campaign treasury. Allard Lowenstein pledged his support, so did Abraham Ribicoff. The liberal Americans for Democratic Action endorsed Humphrey by a vote of seventy-one to sixteen of its executive board. Just as important, John Connally was back in line, stumping Texas with the vice president and promising his full support. Where a week before there had been few interested in hearing him, now there were huge crowds. "Thank you, Mr. Humphrey," read a sign at a Nashville rally, "if you mean it, we're with you." The Democrats were coming home.

Humphrey's resurgence was matched by Wallace's collapse. In part he was the victim of organized labor, in part of his own disastrous selection of a running mate. The AFL-CIO's Committee on Political Education churned out 20 million pieces of anti-Wallace literature, registered 4.6 million voters, and sent union representatives around the country to convince the rank and file to vote Democratic. If labor had pointed the gun at Wallace's head, General Curtis LeMay—World War II hero, former air force chief of staff—pulled the trigger.

On October 3 the governor introduced his newly selected running mate, and without further ado the general began speaking about the unspeakable. "We seem to have a phobia about nuclear weapons," LeMay observed. "The smart thing to do when you're in a war . . . [is] get in it with both feet and get it over with as soon as you can." Wallace, stunned, tried to intervene, but the man who had boasted that the United States could "bomb the North Vietnamese back into the Stone Age" was in his element. "Use the force that's necessary," he continued to the increasing disbelief of the assembled reporters. "Maybe use a little more to make sure it's enough to stop the fighting as soon as possible. . . . I think there are many times when it would be most efficient to use nuclear weapons." Before Wallace could reclaim the dais, Curtis LeMay had reduced his campaign to ground zero.

By the middle of October, Humphrey was in high gear. In the Gallup poll at the end of September, Nixon led by a comfortable fifteen points. Two weeks later the lead was down to twelve. On October 21 the difference was only eight. An election victory that had appeared beyond reach a fortnight earlier now seemed a real possibility. But the issue of the war had a momentum of its own. It had cast Humphrey down in Chicago only to raise him up again in Salt Lake City, and now it would consume the final two weeks of the campaign. Although neither candidate knew it, the ice had already begun to melt in Paris.

Breakthrough

After President Johnson had rejected his initiative in late July, Harriman persuaded the North Vietnamese to resume secret talks, stressing that what the United States wanted was not a humiliating public act of reciprocity but concrete steps that would insure the safety of American and allied troops following a complete bombing halt. When Cyrus Vance met with the president in Washington on October 3, he was "basically optimistic." But Johnson was still skeptical of Hanoi's intentions. He insisted that the North Vietnamese be made to understand precisely the three basic requirements of an agreement: respect for the demilitarized zone, de-escalation of violence against South Vietnamese cities, and participation by the Saigon government in the Paris talks.

Vance met secretly with North Vietnamese Colonel Ha Van Lau twelve times, drilling him on the American formula. Again and again he would read a part of the draft text, then ask Lau to repeat it in translation. At one point Vance left an informal "talking paper" on a table for Lau to pick up, the two men thus maintaining the diplomatic fiction that no formal messages had passed between their governments. Then, at the regular weekly session on October 9, Le Duc Tho quietly asked whether he understood correctly that the U.S. would stop the bombing if Hanoi agreed to meet with South Vietnamese representatives. With Tho's question, a White House staff member later recalled, the "lights went on throughout the government."

Harriman relayed news of the breakthrough to the president, who immediately began to round up a consensus. He cabled Ellsworth Bunker and Creighton Abrams. Would a bombing halt be an "unwarranted gamble with the safety of our men?" Bunker replied that both he and the general believed the North Vietnamese response a "fairly clear indication that Hanoi is ready for a tactical shift from the battlefield to the conference table." Since the middle of September a sizable number of NVA units had begun to pull out of South Vietnam, and they now saw no impediment to an early cessation of attacks against the North. The following day Johnson gathered together his senior advisers to ask each man what he thought. They told the president to go ahead. So did the Joint Chiefs of Staff. At the end of the day Johnson met once more with Rusk, Clifford, Rostow, and Wheeler. Again he asked them if they agreed with the proposal to announce a complete bombing halt. Each man answered "yes." "All right," said the president. "I don't want to have it said of me that one man died tomorrow who could have been saved by this plan. I don't think it [peace] will happen, but there is a chance. We'll try it."

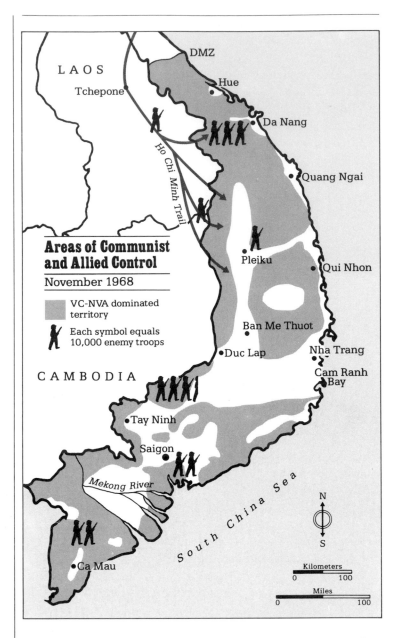

Areas of Communist and Allied Control

November 1968

VC-NVA dominated territory

Each symbol equals 10,000 enemy troops

LAOS
DMZ
Tchepone
Hue
Da Nang
Ho Chi Minh Trail
Quang Ngai
Pleiku
Qui Nhon
Ban Me Thuot
Duc Lap
Nha Trang
CAMBODIA
Cam Ranh Bay
Tay Ninh
Saigon
Mekong River
South China Sea
Ca Mau

Kilometers
0 — 100

Miles
0 — 100

N
S

can proposals. Although they would give no written guarantees on maintaining the demilitarized zone or restraining attacks against the cities, Harriman assured the president that the Communists understood that violations of the terms would risk resumption of the bombing. "To make doubly sure that there was no misunderstanding of our basic requirements," Johnson decided "to restate our position to the Soviet Union." Within hours of receipt of word from Hanoi, Soviet ambassador Anatoly Dobrynin was given a detailed written explanation of the American terms. The Russians reported back the next day that the North Vietnamese understood what the United States wanted. Any doubts regarding their willingness to accept the American proposals were "groundless."

For the president, there was one more thing to do. "I wanted to look the field commander of our troops in the eye and have him tell me candidly . . . would we, or would we not, be endangering the lives of our fighting force." So Creighton Abrams flew to Washington, arriving just past midnight on October 29. After reviewing the events of recent weeks, Johnson asked Abrams if the agreement would be a military advantage for the allies. "Yes sir," he answered. He was confident that the North Vietnamese would honor the DMZ, especially in light of their reduced strength in that area. A major attack on Saigon, though still a possibility, could not succeed. "What will this do to the morale of our men and of the South Vietnamese army?" inquired the president. "I don't believe it will have a measurable effect," Abrams replied. After further discussion Johnson turned to Abrams "and looked hard at him for a few moments." This was a critical period, the president began, did the general have "any reluctance or hesitancy" about stopping the bombing. "No sir." If he were president, would he do it? "I have no reservations," said Abrams. "I know it is stepping into a cesspool of comment. But I do think it's the right thing to do. It is the proper thing to do."

Going it alone

Even as the Abrams meeting was drawing to a close, word reached the White House that Bunker was having problems with the South Vietnamese. First, Thieu insisted that Vice President Ky needed more time to organize the delegation to the Paris talks, scheduled to begin on November 2. Second, the South Vietnamese president claimed that no major foreign policy decision could be formalized without the approval of the National Assembly. That would also take time. Third, Thieu had received a message from Pham Dang Lam, his chief observer in Paris, that the Americans were "tricking" the South Vietnamese by allowing Hanoi to seat the NLF as a separate delegation. Fourth, Thieu wanted guarantees that Hanoi would join the allies in a de-escalation of military activities. Finally, Saigon demanded that all procedural

In the early hours of October 16 a message arrived in Saigon instructing Ambassador Bunker to get President Thieu's agreement to issue a joint communiqué once Hanoi formally accepted the American proposals. Bunker called on Thieu at 6:45 that morning and later cabled Johnson that the two men had worked out a statement. It was time to get back to the North Vietnamese.

But Hanoi balked. They had said earlier that once the bombing stopped a meeting could be held "the next day." Now they wanted a delay of several weeks to consult with the National Liberation Front. It had been made clear to them that a bombing halt was dependent upon their willingness to exercise military restraint. Now they wanted a communiqué describing the bombing halt as "unconditional." They had apparently agreed in July to the "two sides" arrangement for the negotiations. Now they wanted a "four party" conference.

For two weeks the haggling went on behind the scenes. Finally on October 27, Hanoi accepted the original Ameri-

arrangements for the expanded talks be worked out in advance.

For President Johnson, the South Vietnamese position was "a grave disappointment." To Secretary of Defense Clark Clifford, Saigon's last-minute protests were "reprehensible and utterly without merit." The president and his advisers knew that Saigon's conditions were "impossible"; the embassy would have to attempt to bring the South Vietnamese president around. Bunker and Deputy Ambassador Samuel Berger met with Thieu on the evening of October 30. Agreeing that a rift with Washington could only be of benefit to the Communists, Thieu suggested that the president restrict his announcement to the bombing halt, leaving the other details of the package for further discussion. The Americans told him that could not be done. Tempers flared, Thieu muttering at Berger in Vietnamese, "Are you representing Hanoi or Washington?" Bunker informed the White House of his failure to persuade Thieu to go along only hours before Johnson was scheduled to deliver a nationally televised speech on the war. The language of his address was changed to read that South Vietnam would be "free to participate" in the expanded talks. If necessary the United States would act alone.

The two-and-a-half days since the Abrams meeting had been for the president "a blur of meetings and phone calls, of cables and conferences." As Johnson faced the American people at 8:00 P.M. on Thursday, October 31, his face was lined with fatigue, his voice hoarse, but he spoke firmly of the course he had determined to follow.

I have now ordered that all air, naval, and artillery bombardment of North Vietnam cease as of 8:00 A.M. Washington time, Friday morning. I have reached this decision on the basis of the

LBJ and his weary secretary of defense, Clark Clifford, ponder South Vietnam's latest demands only two days before Johnson's announcement of a bombing halt.

developments in the Paris talks. And I have reached it in the belief that this action can lead to progress toward a peaceful settlement of the Vietnamese war.

Johnson indicated that South Vietnamese representatives would be welcome to join the expanded talks, emphasizing that the participation of the NLF "in no way involves recognition" of the Vietcong's political front. Without revealing the specific understanding the American negotiators had reached with Hanoi, he made it clear that if the North Vietnamese took military advantage of the bombing halt, the United States would not hesitate to resume the air attacks. "There may well be very hard fighting ahead," he warned the nation. But what he now expected, "what we have a right to expect, are prompt, productive, serious, and intensive negotiations."

Nixon's the one

As the rumors of an imminent breakthrough in the negotiations mounted, Richard Nixon saw the presidency slip-

ping from his grasp. Now, in the wake of the president's announcement, his margin in the polls crumbled overnight. Both the Harris and Gallup surveys released Saturday, November 2, revealed that the Republican's lead had dwindled to insignificance—42 to 40 percent. The shift in momentum was so overwhelming that had voters gone to the polls on Saturday or Sunday it appeared likely that Humphrey would have emerged the victor. The final Harris poll of the campaign, released on Monday morning, showed Humphrey ahead 43 to 40.

But the issue of the war wouldn't go away, wouldn't remain quite the same for two days at a time. On Thursday night when Johnson announced the bombing halt and the beginning of four-party negotiations, peace, to many voters, did seem to be at hand. But on Friday Thieu announced tersely that the United States had acted unilaterally. His government did not support the bombing halt, which was not justified by concessions from Hanoi. On Saturday, after Thieu told the National Assembly that his government would not attend the talks as long as the North Vietnamese treated the NLF as a separate delega-

Along with the rest of the nation, President and Mrs. Johnson watch the broadcast of his taped announcement on October 31 of a complete bombing halt and the start of four-party negotiations.

The Shape of Things to Come

The South Vietnamese were satisfied. "All our demands and conditions have been met," said Foreign Minister Tran Chanh Thanh. "This is a big victory for the South Vietnamese people." The boycott of the Paris peace talks had ended a month after it began. By December 8 all four delegations were at last in Paris—the Americans, the North Vietnamese, the National Liberation Front, and the South Vietnamese. Only the "modalities," or physical arrangements, of the expanded negotiations remained to be determined.

Of all the procedural details to be solved—the size of the delegations, the order in which they would speak, the site of the meetings—one issue came to dominate, even overwhelm the preliminary discussions: the shape of the conference table. The North Vietnamese sought a seating arrangement that would enhance the political "legitimacy" of the NLF as an independent party to the talks. The South Vietnamese wanted a conference table that would reflect their contention that the NLF was simply a creature of Hanoi. For its part the United States was willing to entertain any compromise that would finally get the talks underway without unduly antagonizing Saigon.

The initial designs for the table reflected these concerns. The Americans suggested two rectangular tables, one for each "side." The North Vietnamese proposed a square table, with each delegation having its own side. The South Vietnamese offered no plans or designs of their own but announced they would reject any proposal that seemed to support the NLF's claims to independent status. It

quickly became clear that the shape of the negotiating table was the major obstacle to the beginning of official sessions. "We may put the French furniture industry to a real test before we're through," observed an American diplomat. After a while the joke didn't seem so funny.

The topic of the table preoccupied news reports on the peace talks and played like a kind of daily diplomatic soap opera. Would they decide on a shape today? Were there new shapes to consider? Would they ever find an answer?

On December 10 the North Vietnamese suggested four tables arranged in a square, rectangular, or diamond pattern. The next day came various proposals for square, oblong, elliptical, and circular tables. The French suggested, unofficially, a "split diamond." The diplomats talked on, exchanged diagrams, but reached no agreement. On December 14, after five allied and four Communist proposals had been submitted, each side produced a new design. The United States called for two half-circles, separated by rectangular tables for the secretaries, a proposal that maintained the "our side, your side" concept. The North Vietnamese countered with a round table, symbolizing the equality of the four parties. Both proposals were said to be demonstrations of "good will" and a willingness to compromise.

And there it stood, stalemated by what *Time* magazine called "Those Maddening Modalities." Meanwhile, the internal strains between the allies began to show. Washington and Saigon issued contradictory statements on various proposals, and each seemed, as one reporter said, to be conducting its own set of negotiations. Declaring the United States "ready to sit at any kind of table," Secretary of Defense Clark Clifford accused the South Vietnamese of delaying a compromise. Vice President Ky couldn't understand "what Mr. Clifford is talking about. It isn't we who raised procedural questions. ... My problem is, I have to fight not only my enemies but also my so-called friends."

To some the deadlock was a source of ironic amusement. *Le Canard Enchaîné*, a French newspaper specializing in political satire, drew a table of labyrinthian design that permitted each of the four

parties to be seated with their backs to one another. One American thought it likely "that the next winner of the Nobel Peace Prize will be a furniture designer."

If the endless wrangling over the shape of the table seemed absurd to many observers, it was a deadly serious business to the participants and not without diplomatic precedent. At the Congress of Vienna in 1814, a fourth door was cut to enable the Austrian, French, Russian, and British representatives to enter the conference room simultaneously and thus avoid any insult to their rank.

But as days became weeks of impasse, Americans both in and out of the government began to lose patience. The *New York Times* called the procedural talks a "charade." Democratic senator George McGovern accused Ky of "playing around in the plush spots of Paris and haggling over whether he is going to sit at a round table or a rectangular table," while "American men are dying to prop up his corrupt regime." Joining a growing number of other citizens expressing their frustration in letters to the editor columns, a Brooklyn couple echoed the senator's outrage, noting grimly that "nobody seems to argue over the shape of artificial limbs or pine boxes."

By year's end the futility of what was taking place in Paris was apparent to all. On December 30 a South Vietnamese pacifist proposed that the talks be held around an eight-sided table on his "island retreat" in the Mekong Delta. The same day American negotiator Cyrus Vance called off a previously scheduled meeting with his South Vietnamese counterpart Pham Dang Lam. There was, explained allied sources, "nothing new to talk about."

It would not be until January 25, 1969, that all four parties sat down at a table everyone agreed upon: to satisfy the Communist demand for equal representation of the NLF, a circular table at which all four parties would be seated; and to satisfy the allied wish for negotiations between "two sides," a pair of rectangular tables for secretaries and support personnel, placed eighteen inches from the circular table at opposite sides. Now all that remained were the comparatively simple questions of war and peace.

tion, the legislators adopted by acclamation a resolution condemning President Johnson for "betrayal of an ally," then marched to the U.S. Embassy to protest the American action. The South Vietnamese could "trust the Americans no longer," declared Vice President Ky, adding more fuel to the fire, "they are just a band of crooks." It had quickly become apparent that the bombing halt would not soon bring an end to the killing in South Vietnam, and the tide of public opinion now returned to Richard Nixon. In his own private poll the day before the election, Harris found the Republican marginally ahead.

On November 5, as Ambassador Bunker went on U.S. armed forces radio to appeal to the Saigon government to end its boycott of the Paris negotiations, and Thieu in reply reaffirmed that "we will never attend the Paris talks if we have to talk to the NLF as an independent delegation," America went to the polls and narrowly elected Richard Nixon the thirty-seventh president of the United States. Out of nearly 73 million ballots cast, Nixon's winning margin was fewer than 500,000 votes, only seven-tenths of 1 percent. In a tumultuous year of constantly shifting military and diplomatic fortunes, a year of torment at home and confusion abroad, a fragmented nation had rendered a divided verdict. Now Richard Nixon, the one man who had so deftly avoided the agonizing question of Vietnam, would have to assume the burden of the war and the burden of the peace the American people so urgently desired.

Not yet peace

Fifteen days after the election, a ceremony was held at the White House to award the Medal of Honor to five veterans of the Vietnam fighting. "Other bitter days and other battles still lie ahead," the president told the small group that had gathered in the East Room. "I cannot emphasize strongly enough that we have not attained peace—only the possibility of peace."

In the first weeks after the bombing halt, military activity in South Vietnam dropped significantly. The Communists seemed to be avoiding big-unit encounters, U.S. cas-

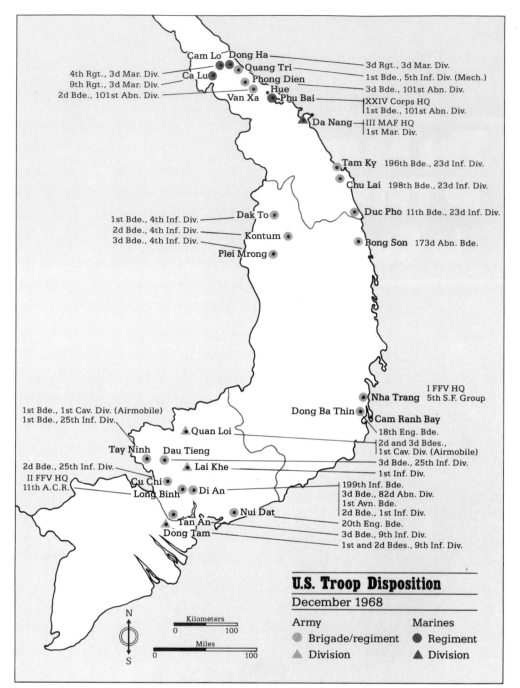

U.S. Troop Disposition

December 1968

Army
- Brigade/regiment
- Division

Marines
- Regiment
- Division

ualty figures fell to the lowest rate of the year, and the pullback of enemy forces continued. Altogether allied intelligence estimated that one-third of the Communists' 120,000 Main Force troops had retreated into North Vietnam and the Cambodian and Laotian sanctuaries. Citing the heavy toll of year-long VC and NVA losses, the growing number of enemy defections, and the withdrawal of a substantial portion of Communist forces, American commanders asserted that the allies had regained the military initiative. President Johnson agreed, urging General Abrams to make a "maximum effort" to keep the enemy on the run.

But if for the moment the military advantage appeared to be swinging firmly in the allied direction, observed American correspondent Robert Shaplen, "the political indicator remains on dead center—or if anything, is still pointing toward the Vietcong." Aiming to build up their party apparatus in areas they already held and secure control over as much additional territory as possible in the event of a quick cease-fire, the Communists stepped up their campaign of propaganda and terror in the countryside and established some 1,800 "liberation committees" among the nation's 12,000 rural hamlets. They continued to feed political operatives and sapper teams into their underground urban cells and set up a series of new coalition fronts that demanded the creation of a "peace Cabinet" in hopes of driving a wedge between the Thieu government and those Vietnamese more willing to enter into the Paris negotiations. The allies fought back, launching the Accelerated Pacification Campaign (APC) on November 1, with the goal of extending at least token government control into 1,200 previously contested or VC-dominated hamlets within three months, and put into operation the Phoenix Program, an attempt to neutralize the Vietcong infrastructure through improved intelligence gathering and the selective arrest of key party cadres.

The success of these countermeasures remained open to question. Phoenix was plagued by parallel American-South Vietnamese commands and a lack of "aggressiveness" on the part of the local officials, while the great majority of those arrested occupied only minor roles in the Vietcong hierarchy. Similarly, APC program director William Colby would admit to no more than "moderately positive" results during the first months of the new pacification effort. MACV reported at the end of the year that 73 percent of South Vietnam's population now lived under GVN control, but other statistics revealed that most hamlets remained no more than "relatively secure."

And while the fighting had diminished, it had far from disappeared. The Communists shelled ninety-eight civil-

Accompanied by his wife, Vice President Nguyen Cao Ky arrives in Paris to head the South Vietnamese delegation to the four-sided peace talks.

ian areas in the first two weeks of the bombing halt, raked allied bases in Da Nang with rocket and mortar fire, and fought a sharp battle with the ARVN 51st Regiment twelve miles south of the city.

There were other indications that the optimistic assessments of some American commanders might well be premature. As it had in the spring, Hanoi took quick advantage of the cessation of bombing to rebuild bridges and rail lines, stockpile supplies north of the demilitarized zone, and begin construction of a petroleum pipeline from the area around the nineteenth parallel to bases above the DMZ. Their willingness to press on with the war was all too evident in a sharp upsurge of military contacts in I Corps during the first week of December. But the area of greatest concern was III Corps, where Communist strength had risen to seventy Main- and local-force battalions. Two weeks before Christmas, as four enemy divisions moved back into South Vietnam from their Cambodian sanctuaries and heavy fighting broke out west of Saigon, allied forces were placed on alert in anticipation of a new enemy offensive.

Only the dead

A National Security Memorandum prepared for the incoming administration concluded that despite the reverses they had suffered during 1968, the Communists continued to pursue the objective of a unified Vietnam under their control. During the previous four years the enemy had been able to "double his combat forces, double the level of infiltration, and increase the scale and intensity of the main force war even while bearing heavy casualties." Although MACV placed Communist strength at approximately 330,000 men, both the CIA and the State Department considered 435,000 to 595,000 a more realistic estimate. But whatever the actual enemy order of battle, and even should casualty rates continue at the high level of 1968, reported the JCS, the North Vietnamese and VC had sufficient manpower to replenish understrength units for "at least the next several years." The Communists still controlled the tempo of the war, still had the capacity to launch major offensives, and still retained significant influence over at least 50 percent of the rural population. At the current rate of pacification, it would take eight to thirteen years to bring the whole of South Vietnam under Saigon's control.

Alongside this bleak picture was the hope of Vietnamization and the promise of political stability. There could be little doubt that the armed forces of South Vietnam were larger, better equipped, and somewhat more effective than a year earlier. But the RVNAF still faced severe problems of motivation and leadership—difficulties reflected in a net desertion rate equivalent to losing one ARVN division per month. Similarly, while there had been some progress made toward political mobilization of the

Saigon government, factionalized interest groups continued to wage a perpetual struggle for power, with growing acceptance of the NLF as a partner to an eventual political settlement. The plain facts were these: ARVN "could not now, or in the foreseeable future handle both the VC and sizable NVA forces without US combat support"; nor was there any certainty that the GVN "will be able to survive a peaceful competition with the NLF for political power in South Vietnam."

Equally discouraging to the Americans was the continuing refusal of Saigon to join the Paris negotiations, leading to postponement of the opening sessions and deepening the strains that had developed between the two governments. Part of the problem lay in Saigon's resentment of what it took to be U.S. bullying—forcing the GVN into negotiations before it was politically or militarily ready. "South Vietnam," declared Thieu, "is not a railroad car that can be attached to a locomotive and led anywhere the locomotive wishes to take it." Partly it rested on fears that Washington was prepared to sacrifice the Vietnamese for the sake of an early disengagement.

But the disagreement between Saigon and Washington was also the result of a certain ambiguity in their discussions over the "our side, your side" formula. To the United States, it was an ingenious device to enable talks to go forward while avoiding the issue of recognition of the NLF. But once it became clear that the arrangement would mean in reality four separate, and presumably equal, delegations, it seemed to the South Vietnamese that they had been maneuvered that much closer to a coalition government—the first step, many felt, toward Communist domination of their country. While the United States claimed that Saigon had backed out of the deal at the last moment, the South Vietnamese maintained that they had never agreed to the deal in the first place.

Making matters worse, Saigon now insisted on speaking for the entire allied delegation once the talks began, a proposal the United States regarded as offensive and unrealistic. Only after three-and-a-half more weeks of further negotiations, punctuated by charges of bad faith from both sides and American threats to proceed on their own, did Washington and Saigon agree. The U.S. restated its formal nonrecognition of the NLF and declared it would oppose any imposition of a coalition government. Saigon would speak for the allied delegation on all matters of an internal political nature; the U.S. would take the lead on such military questions as the withdrawal of foreign troops.

On November 26 the Thieu government ended its boycott of the expanded negotiations. But when Ky arrived in Paris on December 8 he raised immediate objections to any seating plan that would place the NLF on an equal footing with Saigon. The year would end with the four parties arguing over the shape of the conference table, as the South Vietnamese waited for the inauguration of a man they hoped would be a more tractable partner than Lyndon Johnson. "Perhaps the talks will be able to begin by mid-December," a GVN official suggested archly at the beginning of the month. "But then you have Christmas and the New Year. No, I doubt whether any serious talks will start before well into January, and the real crunch won't come until March, or April."

But for some young men there would be no January, or March, or April. For them there would only be a violent death in a savage war, in a place far from home. On a day just before Christmas, thirty-one Americans died in the fighting. Among them were a group of marines "mopping up" a trapped enemy unit near Da Nang and an infantryman caught in an ambush forty miles north of Saigon. No one would ever be able to single him out, but one of those who fell that day died a very special death. From 1961 to 1967, 16,022 U.S. serviceman had been killed in action in Vietnam. During the year of the Tet offensive, a year that began with six North Vietnamese officers standing outside the wire at Khe Sanh combat base, that witnessed the most massive urban engagements of the war, that brought a change of Communist strategy and a change of U.S. command, 14,521 more Americans lost their lives. On a day just before Christmas, the 30,000th name was added to the mounting toll of a war that seemed to go on forever. In South Vietnam, at the end of 1968, only the dead were at peace.

Christmas in South Vietnam, 1968.

Bibliography

I. Books and Articles

Agence France Presse. *Vietnam: L'Heure Décisive. (L'Offensive du Tet)*. R. Laffont, 1968.

Allen, Robert L. *Dialectics of Black Power*. Weekly Guardian Associates, 1968.

Anderson, Patrick. "The New Defense Secretary Thinks Like the President." *New York Times Magazine*, January 28, 1968.

Arlen, Michael J. *Living-Room War*. Viking Pr., 1969.

Arnett, Peter. "Tet Coverage: A Debate Renewed." *Columbia Journalism Review* (January/February 1978): 44–7.

Ashmore, Harry, and William Baggs. *Mission to Hanoi*. Putnam, 1968.

Bailey, George. "Television War: Trends in Network Coverage of Vietnam 1965–1970." *Journal of Broadcasting* 20, no. 2 (Spring 1976): 147–58.

Bailey, George, and Lawrence W. Lichty. "Rough Justice on a Saigon Street: A Gatekeeper Study of NBC's Tet Execution Film." *Journalism Quarterly* 19 (Summer 1972): 221–9, 238.

Ball, George. *The Past Has Another Pattern*. Norton, 1982.

Baskir, Lawrence M., and William A. Strauss. *Chance and Circumstance: The Draft, the War, and the Vietnam Generation*. Knopf, 1978.

BDM Corporation. *A Study of the Strategic Lessons Learned in Vietnam*. 8 vols. National Technical Information Service, 1980.

Berman, Larry. *Planning a Tragedy: The Americanization of the War in Vietnam*. Norton, 1982.

Bishop, Jim. *The Days of Martin Luther King, Jr.* Putnam, 1971.

Blaufarb, Douglas S. *The Counterinsurgency Era*. Free Pr., 1977.

Bonds, Ray, ed. *The Vietnam War*. Crown, 1979.

Braestrup, Peter. "The Abrams Strategy in Vietnam." *The New Leader*, June 9, 1969.

——————. *Big Story*. 2 vols. Westview, 1977.

Brandon, Henry. *Anatomy of Error*. Gambit, 1969.

——————. "Enter Clark Clifford." *Saturday Review*, February 24, 1968.

Brooks, Thomas R. "Voice of the New Campus 'Underclass.'" *New York Times Magazine*, November 7, 1965.

Brown, Ens. F.C. "The Phoenix Program: A Postmortem." *Military Intelligence* (April/June 1977): 8–12.

Buckley, Kevin P. "General Abrams Deserves a Better War." *New York Times Magazine*, October 5, 1969.

——————. "No One Can Be Sure What Thieu is Thinking." *New York Times Magazine*, March 2, 1969.

Bullington, James R. "And Here, See Hue!" *Foreign Service Journal* (November 1968): 18–21, 48–9.

Cagan, Phillip et al., eds. *Economic Policy and Inflation in the Sixties*. Am. Enterprise, 1972.

CBS News. "The Uncounted Enemy: A Vietnam Deception." Broadcast January 23, 1982. Transcript.

Chester, Lewis, Godfrey Hodgson, and Bruce Page. *An American Melodrama: The Presidential Campaign of 1968*. Viking Pr., 1969.

Clifford, Clark M. "A Viet Nam Reappraisal." *Foreign Affairs* (July 1969): 601–22.

Cohen, Mitchell, and Dennis Hale, eds. *The New Student Left: An Anthology*. NAL, 1966.

Converse, Philip E., and Howard Schuman. "'Silent Majorities' and the Vietnam War." *Scientific American* 222, no. 6 (June 1970): 17–25.

Cooper, Chester. "The Complexities of Negotiations." *Foreign Affairs* (April 1968): 454–66.

——————. *The Lost Crusade: America in Vietnam*. Fawcett, 1972.

Cowan, Paul. "Wallace in Yankeeland: The Invisible Revolution." *The Village Voice*, July 18, 1968.

Cox Commission. *Crisis at Columbia: Report of the Fact-Finding Commission Appointed to Investigate the Disturbances at Columbia University in April and May 1968*. Vintage, 1968.

David, Jay, and Elaine Crane, eds. *The Black Soldier: From the American Revolution to Vietnam*. Morrow, 1971.

Davis, Maj. Gen. R.G., and 1st Lt. S.W. Bell, III. "Combined Operations with ARVN." *Marine Corps Gazette* 53, no. 10 (October 1969): 18–29.

Davis, Maj. Gen. R.G., and 1st Lt. H.W. Brazie. "Defeat of the 320th." *Marine Corps Gazette* 54, no. 3 (March 1969): 22–30.

Dickinson, William B., Jr. "Protest Movements in Time of War." *Editorial Research Reports* (February 24, 1966): 143–49.

D'Orcival, François, and J.R. Chaunac. *Les Marines A Khe Sanh: Vietnam 1968*. Presses de la Cité, 1979.

Duiker, William J. *The Communist Road to Power in Vietnam*. Westview, 1981.

Eisenhower, Dwight D. "Let's Close Ranks on the Home Front." *Reader's Digest*, April 1968.

Ellsberg, Daniel. *Papers on the War*. Simon & Schuster, 1972.

Epstein, Edward Jay. *News from Nowhere*. Vintage, 1974.

——————. "The War in Vietnam, What Happened vs. What We Saw." *TV Guide*, September 29, 1973.

——————. "We Lose Our Innocence." *TV Guide*, October 6, 1973.

Eszterhaz, Joseph et al. "The Massacre at My Lai." *Life*, December 5, 1969.

Fallaci, Oriana. *Interview with History*. Trans. by John Shepley. Liveright, 1976.

——————. *Nothing and So Be It*. Doubleday, 1972.

Ferber, Michael, and Staughton Lynd. *The Resistance*. Beacon Pr., 1971.

FitzGerald, Frances. *Fire in the Lake: The Vietnamese and the Americans in Vietnam*. Atlantic-Little, Brown, 1972.

——————. "The Vietnam Numbers Game." *The Nation*, June 26, 1982.

Frady, Marshall. *Wallace*. World Publishing Co., 1968.

Gallucci, Robert L. *Neither Peace Nor Honor: The Politics of American Military Policy in Vietnam*. Johns Hopkins Pr., 1975.

Gallup, George, ed. *The Gallup Poll: Public Opinion 1935 to 1971*. Vol. 3, *1959–1971*. Random, 1972.

Gans, Herbert J. *Deciding What's News*. Pantheon, 1979.

Gitlin, Todd. *The Whole World is Watching*. Univ. of California Pr., 1980.

Goldstein, Joseph, Burke Marshall, and Jack Schwartz. *The My Lai Massacre and its Cover-up: Beyond the Reach of the Law?* Free Pr., 1976.

Goodman, Allan E. *The Lost Peace: America's Search for a Negotiated Settlement of the Vietnam War*. Hoover Inst. Pr., 1978.

Goodman, Walter. "War in the Peace Camp." *New York Times Magazine*, December 3, 1967.

Goulden, Joseph C. *The Superlawyers*. Weybright & Talley, 1972.

Graff, Henry F. *The Tuesday Cabinet*. Prentice-Hall, 1970.

Gravel, Sen. Mike, ed. *The Pentagon Papers*. 5 vols. Beacon Press, 1971.

Gurtov, Melvin. *Hanoi on War and Peace*. Rand Corporation P-3696, December 1967.

Hahn, Harlan. "Correlates of Public Sentiments About War: Local Referenda on the Vietnam Issue." *The American Political Science Review* 64 (1970): 1186–98.

——————. "Dove Sentiments Among Blue-Collar Workers." *Dissent* (May/June 1970): 202–5.

Halberstam, David. *The Best and the Brightest*. Random, 1972.

——————. "The Man Who Ran Against Lyndon Johnson." *Harper's*, December 1968.

Harriman, W. Averell. *America and Russia in a Changing World: A Half Century of Personal Observation*. Doubleday, 1971.

Harris, Louis. *The Anguish of Change*. Norton, 1973.

Hastings, Max. *The Fire This Time: America's Year of Crisis*. Taplinger, 1969.

Herr, Michael. *Dispatches*. Avon, 1978.

Herring, George C. *America's Longest War*. Wiley, 1979.

Hersh, Seymour. *My Lai 4*. Random, 1970.

Hodgson, Godfrey. *America in Our Time*. Doubleday, 1976.

Hoopes, Townsend. "LBJ's Account of March 1968." *New Republic*, March 14, 1970.

——————. *The Limits of Intervention*. Rev. ed. David McKay Co., 1973.

Hosmer, Stephen T. *Viet Cong Repression and its Implications for the Future*. Heath, 1970.

Irving, Frederick F. "The Battle of Hue." *Military Review* (January 1969): 56–63.

Jacobs, Paul, and Saul Landau, eds. *The New Radicals*. Random, 1966.

Jenkins, Brian M. *The Unchangeable War*. Rand Corporation RM-6278-2 ARPA, September 1972.

Johnson, Gen. Harold K. "The Enclave Concept: A 'License to Hunt.'" *Army* (April 1968): 16–7.

Johnson, Lyndon B. *The Vantage Point: Perspectives of the Presidency 1963–1969*. Holt, Rinehart & Winston, 1971.

Joiner, Charles A. *The Politics of Massacre*. Temple Univ. Pr., 1974.

Kahin, George McTurnan, and John W. Lewis. *The United States in Vietnam*. Rev. ed. Dell, 1969.

Kalb, Marvin, and Elie Abel. *Roots of Involvement*. Norton, 1971.

Kann, Peter. "That Long Night at the U.S. Embassy." *Wall Street Journal*, February 19, 1969.

Kearns, Doris. *Lyndon Johnson and the American Dream*. Harper & Row, 1976.

Keesing's Research Report. *South Vietnam: A Political History, 1954–1970*. Scribner, 1970.

Kellen, Konrad. *Conversations with Enemy Soldiers in Late 1968/Early 1969: A Study of Motivation and Morale*. Rand Corporation RM-6131-1-ISA/ARPA, September 1970.

Kendrick, Alexander. *The Wound Within: America in the Vietnam Years, 1945–1974*. Little, Brown, 1974.

Keniston, Kenneth. *Young Radicals*. Harcourt, Brace & World, 1968.

Kerner, Otto et al. *Report of the National Advisory Commission on Civil Disorders*. Bantam, 1968.

Kissinger, Henry A. "The Viet Nam Negotiations." *Foreign Affairs* (January 1969): 211–34.

Klein, Alexander, ed. *Natural Enemies? Youth and the Clash of Generations*. Lippincott, 1970.

Komer, Robert W. "Clear, Hold and Rebuild." *Army* (May 1970): 16–24.

——————. "Pacification: A Look Back." *Army* (June 1970): 20–9.

Kopkind, Andrew. "Of, By, and For the Poor: The New Generation of Student Organizers." *New Republic*, June 19, 1965.

Kraslow, David, and Stuart H. Loory. *The Secret Search for Peace in Vietnam*. Vintage, 1968.

Laird, Melvin R. "Unforgettable Creighton Abrams." *Reader's Digest*, July 1976.

Langguth, A.J. "Our Policy-Making Men in Saigon." *New York Times Magazine*, April 28, 1968.

——————. "Thieu and Ky Think About the Unthinkable." *New York Times Magazine*, April 14, 1968.

Larner, Jeremy. *Nobody Knows: Reflections on the McCarthy Campaign of 1968*. Macmillan, 1970.

Leinster, Colin. "One Day They Will Go It Alone." *Life*, April 25, 1969.

LeMasters, E.E. *Blue Collar Aristocrats: Lifestyles at a Working Class Tavern*. Univ. of Wisconsin Pr., 1975.

Lewy, Guenter. *America in Vietnam*. Oxford Univ. Pr., 1978.

Little, Roger W., ed. *Selective Service and American Society*. Russell Sage, 1969.

Loory, Stuart H. "Secret Bomb Halt Sessions Revealed." *Los Angeles Times*, March 9, 1969.

Lubell, Samuel. *The Hidden Crisis in American Politics*. Norton, 1970.

Lynd, Staughton. "The New Radicals and 'Participatory Democracy.'" *Dissent* (Summer 1965): 324–33.

McCarthy, Eugene. *The Year of the People*. Doubleday, 1969.

McCarthy, Mary. *The Seventeenth Degree*. Harcourt Brace Jovanovich, 1974.

McCulloch, Frank. "The Young Generals Who Run the Country." *Life*, February 25, 1966.

McEnery, Lt. Col. John W. " 'Mainstreet': A Successful Cordon and Search." *Armor* (January/February 1969): 36–9.

McGarvey, Patrick J. *Visions of Victory: Selected Vietnamese Communist Military Writings, 1964–1968.* Hoover Inst. Pr., 1969.

McGinnis, Joe. *The Selling of the President.* Trident Pr., 1969.

Maclear, Michael. *The Ten Thousand Day War.* St. Martin, 1981.

McMahon, Lt. Col. Richard A. "The Indirect Approach." *Army* (August 1969): 56–63.

Mailer, Norman. *The Armies of the Night.* NAL, 1968.

_____. *Miami and the Siege of Chicago.* NAL, 1968.

Martin, Bruce. "House to House." *Leatherneck*, (May 1968): 54–7, 88.

Meissner, Capt. Joseph P. "The Battle of Duc Lap." *Army* (May 1969): 50–6.

Menashe, Louis, and Ronald Radosh. *Teach-ins: U.S.A.* Praeger, 1967.

Meyers, Col. Bruce F. "Jungle Canopy Operations." *Marine Corps Gazette* (July 1969): 20–6.

Meyerson, Harvey. *Vinh Long.* Houghton Mifflin, 1970.

Mildren, Lt. Gen. Frank T. "From Mekong to DMZ: A Fighting Year for the U.S. Army's Best." *Army* (November 1968): 82–95.

Miller, Merle. *Lyndon: An Oral Biography.* Ballantine, 1980.

Millet, Allan R. *Semper Fidelis: The History of the United States Marine Corps.* Macmillan, 1980.

Millet, Stanley, ed. *South Vietnam. U.S.–Communist Confrontation in Southeast Asia.* Vol. 3, *1968.* Facts on File, 1974.

Mitford, Jessica. "The Indignant Generation." *The Nation*, May 27, 1961.

Mueller, John E. "Reflections on the Vietnam Anti-War Movement." Paper presented at the Conference on the History of the Vietnam War, Woodrow Wilson International Center for Scholars, Washington, D.C., December 21, 1982.

_____. *War, Presidents and Public Opinion.* Wiley, 1973.

Mydans, Carl. "Refugees on a Bridge to Nowhere." *Life*, April 26, 1968.

Newfield, Jack. *A Prophetic Minority.* NAL, 1966.

Nixon, Richard. *RN: The Memoirs of Richard Nixon.* Grosset & Dunlap, 1978.

Norman, Lloyd. "The '206,000 Plan'—The Inside Story." *Army* (April 1971): 30–5.

Oberdorfer, Don. *Tet!* Doubleday, 1971.

_____. "Tet: The Turning Point." *Washington Post Magazine*, January 29, 1978.

O'Brien, James P. "The New Left's Early Years." *Radical America* 2, no. 3 (1968): 1–25; 2, no. 5 (1968): 1–22; 2, no. 7 (1968): 28–43.

Oglesby, Carl, ed. *The New Left Reader.* Grove Pr., 1969.

_____. "On Draft Resistance." *New Left Notes*, (March 27, 1967): 1–12.

O'Neill, Robert J. *The Strategy of General Giap Since 1964.* Australian National Univ. Pr., 1969.

O'Neill, William L. *Coming Apart: An Informal History of America in the 1960s.* Quadrangle, 1971.

Page, Benjamin I., and Richard A. Brody. "Policy Voting and the Electoral Process: The Vietnam War Issue." *The American Political Science Review* 66 (September 1972): 979–95.

Palmer, David R. *Summons of the Trumpet: U.S.–Vietnam in Perspective.* Presidio Pr., 1978.

Peers, Lt. Gen. W.R. *The My Lai Inquiry.* Norton, 1979.

Pham Van Dong. *Forward! Final Victory Will Be Ours!* Foreign Languages Publishing House, 1968.

Pike, Douglas. *The Viet-Cong Strategy of Terror.* U.S. Mission, South Vietnam, 1971.

_____. *War, Peace and the Viet Cong.* MIT Pr., 1969.

Pisor, Robert. *The End of the Line: The Siege of Khe Sanh.* Norton, 1982.

Pohle, Victoria. *The Viet Cong in Saigon: Tactics and Objectives During the Tet Offensive.* Rand Corporation RM–5799–ISA/ARPA, January 1969.

Polenberg, Richard. *One Nation Divisible.* Penguin, 1980.

Porter, Gareth. "The 1968 'Hue Massacre.' " *Indochina Chronicle* 33 (June 24, 1974): 2–13.

_____. *A Peace Denied.* Indiana Univ. Pr., 1975.

Powers, Thomas. *The War at Home: Vietnam and the American People.* Grossman, 1973.

Race, Jeffrey. *War Comes to Long An: Revolutionary Conflict in a Vietnamese Province.* Univ. of California Pr., 1972.

Reeves, Richard. "Peace, Man, Says Baby Doctor Spock." *New York Times Magazine*, July 16, 1967.

Robinson, John P. "Public Reaction to Political Protest: Chicago 1968." *The Public Opinion Quarterly* (Spring 1970): 1–9.

Rosenberg, Milton J., Sidney Verba, and Philip E. Converse. *Vietnam and the Silent Majority.* Harper & Row, 1970.

Rostow, Walt W. *The Diffusion of Power: 1957–1972.* Macmillan, 1972.

Rothstein, Richard. "ERAP: Evolution of the Organizers." *Radical America* (March/April 1968): 1–18.

Sale, Kirkpatrick. *SDS.* Random, 1973.

Schandler, Herbert Y. *The Unmaking of a President: Lyndon Johnson and Vietnam.* Princeton Univ. Pr., 1977.

Schlesinger, Arthur M., Jr. *Robert Kennedy and His Times.* Houghton Mifflin, 1978.

Schuman, Howard. "Two Sources of Antiwar Sentiment in America." *American Journal of Sociology* 78, no. 3 (November 1972): 513–35.

Sexton, Patricia C., and Brendan Sexton. *Blue Collars and Hard Hats: The Working Class and the Future of American Politics.* Random, 1971.

Shaplen, Robert. "A Reporter at Large: Seats at the Table." *New Yorker*, November 16, 1968.

_____. *The Road from War: Vietnam 1965–1970.* Harper & Row, 1970.

Shulimson, Jack, and Maj. Ed Wells. "First In, First Out: The Marine Experience in Vietnam 1965–1971." Paper presented at the 1982 International Military History Symposium, Carlisle Barracks, Pa., August 1982.

Skolnick, Jerome H. et al. *The Politics of Protest.* Ballantine, 1969.

Smith, Col. R.B. "Leatherneck Square." *Marine Corps Gazette* (August 1969): 34–42.

Staff of the Columbia *Daily Spectator.* *Up Against the Ivy Wall: A History of the Columbia Crisis.* Atheneum, 1969.

Staff of the *Infantry* Magazine, ed. *A Distant Challenge: The U.S. Infantryman in Vietnam, 1967–1970.* Birmingham Publishing, 1971.

Stanton, Shelby L. *Vietnam Order of Battle.* U.S. News Books, 1981.

Stern, Sol. "When the Black GI Comes Back From Vietnam." *New York Times Magazine*, March 24, 1968.

Summers, Col. Harry G., Jr. *On Strategy: A Critical Analysis of the Vietnam War.* Presidio Pr., 1982.

Tang, Truong Nhu. "The Myth of a Liberation." *The New York Review of Books*, October 21, 1982, 31–5.

Taylor, Clyde, ed. *Vietnam and Black America: An Anthology of Protest and Resistance.* Anchor Bks., 1973.

Taylor, Maxwell D. *Swords and Plowshares.* Norton, 1972.

Thompson, W. Scott, and Donaldson D. Frizzell, eds. *The Lessons of Vietnam.* Crane, Russak & Co., 1977.

Trullinger, James Walker. *Village at War: An Account of Revolution in Vietnam.* Longman, 1980.

Turner, Robert F. *Vietnamese Communism: Its Origins and Development.* Hoover Inst. Pr., 1975.

Van Dyke, Jon M. *North Vietnam's Strategy for Survival.* Pacific Bks., 1972.

Vaughn, Roger. "The Defiant Voices of SDS." *Life*, October 18, 1968.

"Viet Nam War Spurs 'Peace' Movement in United States." *Congressional Quarterly* (July 1, 1966): 1398–1405.

Viorst, Milton. *Fire in the Streets.* Simon & Schuster, 1979.

Vo Nguyen Giap. *Big Victory, Great Task.* Praeger, 1968.

Walker, Daniel et al. *Rights in Conflict.* Bantam, 1968.

Westmoreland, William C. *A Soldier Reports.* Doubleday, 1976.

White, Theodore. *The Making of the President, 1968.* Atheneum, 1969.

Witcover, Jules. *45 Days: The Last Campaign of Robert Kennedy.* Putnam, 1969.

Zimmerman, Gereon. "What Makes Dr. Spock March?" *Look*, February 20, 1968.

II. Government Publications

Albright, John, John A. Cash, and Allan W. Sandstrum. *Seven Firefights in Vietnam.* Office of the Chief of Military History, U.S. Army, 1970.

Berger, Carl, ed. *The United States Air Force in Southeast Asia, 1961–1973.* Office of Air Force History, 1977.

Collins, Brig. Gen. James Lawton, Jr. *The Development and Training of the South Vietnamese Army, 1950–1972.* Department of the Army, Vietnam Studies Series, 1975.

Dees, Joseph L. "The Viet Cong Attack that Failed." *Department of State Newsletter*, May 1968.

Fleet Marine Force–Pacific. *U.S. Marine Corps Operations in Vietnam, January–February–March 1968.* GPO, 1968.

Foreign Affairs Division, Congressional Research Service. *Impact of the Vietnam War.* GPO, 1971.

Fulton, Maj. Gen. William B. *Riverine Operations 1966–1969.* Department of the Army, Vietnam Studies Series, 1973.

Futrell, R. Frank et al. *Aces and Aerial Victories: The United States Air Force in Southeast Asia 1965–1973.* Office of Air Force History, 1976.

Gropman, Lt. Col. Alan. *Airpower and the Airlift Evacuation of Kham Duc.* United States Air Force, 1979.

Hinh, Maj. Gen. Nguyen Duy. *Vietnamization and the Cease-Fire.* U.S. Army Center of Military History, Indochina Monograph Series, n.d.

Lung, Col. Hoang Ngoc. *The General Offensives of 1968–1969.* U.S. Army Center of Military History, Indochina Monograph Series, 1981.

Momyer, Gen. William W. *Air Power in Three Wars.* United States Air Force, 1978.

Nalty, Bernard C. *Air Power and the Fight for Khe Sanh.* Office of Air Force History, 1973.

Ott, David Ewing. *Field Artillery, 1954–1973.* Department of the Army, Vietnam Studies Series, 1973.

Pearson, Willard. *The War in the Northern Provinces, 1966–1968.* Department of the Army, Vietnam Studies Series, 1975.

Pham Van Son, and Le Van Duong, eds. *The Viet Cong Tet Offensive 1968.* Military History Division, RVNAF, 1969.

Sharp, Adm. U.S. Grant, and Gen. William C. Westmoreland. *Report on the War in Vietnam.* GPO, 1969.

Shore, Capt. Moyers S., II. *The Battle for Khe Sanh.* Historical Branch, United States Marine Corps, 1969.

Shulimson, Jack. *The U.S. Marines in Vietnam, 1966: An Expanding War.* History and Museums Division, Headquarters, United States Marine Corps, 1982.

Starry, Gen. Donn A. *Mounted Combat in Vietnam.* Department of the Army, Vietnam Studies Series, 1979.

Tolson, Lt. Gen. John J. *Airmobility 1961–1971.* Department of the Army, Vietnam Studies Series, 1973.

U.S. Congress. House Select Committee on Intelligence. *U.S. Intelligence Agencies and Activities: Risks and Control of Foreign Intelligence.* September 11, 18, 1975.

_____. *National Security Study Memorandum–1* (February 21, 1969). Congressional Record. GPO, May 10, 1972.

_____. U.S. Senate. *Civilian Casualty and Refugee Problems in South Vietnam.* 90th Cong. 2d sess., 1968.

_____. U.S. Senate Armed Services Committee. *Hearings on Investigation into the Electronic Battlefield Program.* Electronic Battlefield Subcommittee of the Preparedness Investigating Subcommittee. 91st Cong., 2d sess., 1970.

_____. *Stalemate in Vietnam.* 90th Cong., 2d sess., 1968.

U.S. Department of Defense. *Statistics on Southeast Asia.* GPO, 1972.

_____. *United States-Vietnam Relations 1945-1967* (Pentagon Papers). GPO, 1971.

U.S. Department of State. *Vietnam Documents and Research Notes*, nos. 2-3, 12, 19-22, 26-32, 43-44. GPO, 1961-68.

U.S. Marine Corps. History and Museums Division. *The Marines in Vietnam 1954-1973: An Anthology and Annotated Bibliography*. U.S. Marine Corps, 1974.

III. Unpublished Government and Military Reports

Adams, Samuel A. "Intelligence Failures in Vietnam: Suggestions for Reform." Central Intelligence Agency, Carrollton Pr., January 24, 1969. Microfiche.

Combat Operations After-Action Reports:

Operation Hue City
1st Cavalry Division (Airmobile) February 2-26, 1968.
1st Brigade, 101st Airborne Division, February 22-March 2, 1968.
1st Marines, 1st Marine Division (REIN), February 1-March 2, 1968.
Task Force X-Ray, 1st Marine Divison (REIN), January 31-March 2, 1968.
1st Battalion, 5th Marines, 1st Marine Division (REIN), January 31-March 2, 1968.

Operation Scotland
26th Marines, November 1, 1967-April 1, 1968.
1st Battalion, 9th Marines, 3d Marine Division (REIN), January 22-March 31, 1968.

U.S. Army Special Forces Detachment A-101, Lang Vei Special Forces Camp, February 6-7, 1968.

MACCORDS. Province Reports: Vinh Long Province, Dinh Tuong Province, Kontum Province. Periods Ending January 31, 1968; February 29, 1968; March 31, 1968.

_____. Province Report: Darlac Province. Periods Ending December 31, 1967; January 31, 1968; February 29, 1968; March 31, 1968.

Operational Reports—Lessons Learned:
1st Cavalry Division (Airmobile), Period Ending April 30, 1968.
9th Infantry Division, Periods Ending January 31, 1968; April 30, 1968.

U.S. Military Assistance Command, Vietnam. *Command History, 1968*. USMACV, 1969.

_____. *Commander's Summary of the MACV Objectives Plan*. USMACV, 1969.

_____. *Enemy Order of Battle Report*. USMACV, 1970.

_____. *MACV Strategic Objectives Plan*. USMACV, 1969.

_____. *Study of the Comparisons Between the Battle of Dienbienphu and the Analogous Khe Sanh Situation*. USMACV, 1968.

IV. The authors consulted the following newspapers and periodicals:

Chicago Tribune, 1968; *Far Eastern Economic Review*, 1968-69; *Le Monde*, 1968; *Newsweek*, 1967-69; *The New York Times*, 1967-69; *Time*, 1967-69; *U.S. News and World Report*, 1967-69; *Washington Post*, 1967-69.

V. Archival Sources

Lyndon Baines Johnson Library, Austin, Texas:
Presidential Papers of Lyndon Baines Johnson
White House Central File
Countries 312 (Vietnam)
National Defense 19 (Wars)/CO 312
Confidential File, ND 19/CO 312
National Security File
Country File, Vietnam
NSC History of the March 31, 1968 Speech
NSC Meetings File
Intelligence File
White House Aides File
Meeting Notes File
Declassified and Sanitized Documents
Oral History Interviews: William P. Bundy, George Christian, Clark M. Clifford, Chester L. Cooper, Alain C. Enthoven, W. Averell Harriman, Richard M. Helms, Lyndon B. Johnson, Nicholas deB. Katzenbach, Harry McPherson, Cyrus Vance, Paul C. Warnke, Gen. William C. Westmoreland.
Rostow, Walt W. "Memorandum for the Record," January 25, 1982.

U.S. Army Center of Military History, Washington, D.C.

U.S. Army Military History Institute, Carlisle Barracks, Pa.
Senior Officer Oral History Program:
Ambassador Samuel Berger, Gen. Donn A. Starry, Lt. Gen. Phillip B. Davidson, Jr., Adm. Thomas H. Moorer.

U.S. Marine Corps, History and Museums Division, Headquarters USMC, Washington, D.C.

Yale University Archives, New Haven, Conn.: Movement Protest Collection.

VI. Interviews

Samuel A. Adams, former intelligence analyst, Central Intelligence Agency.
Gar Alperowitz, cofounder, Vietnam Summer.
George Christian, former presidential press secretary.
Clark M. Clifford, former Secretary of Defense.
Raymond Flynn, former Lieutenant, 173d Airborne Brigade.
Col. Gains Hawkins, former intelligence analyst, USMACV.
Paul R. Longgrear, former Lieutenant, 5th Special Forces Group.
Maj. Gen. Joseph McChristian, former Assistant Chief of Staff for Intelligence, USMACV.
Don Oberdorfer, journalist.
Carl Oglesby, former president, Students for a Democratic Society.
Walt W. Rostow, former National Security Adviser.
Frederick B. Tuttle, Jr., former Democratic party activist and colleague of Allard Lowenstein.
Gen. William C. Westmoreland, former Commander, USMACV.

We also wish to thank the following veterans who provided us with personal accounts of their experiences in Vietnam: William Avery, Stephen Banko, Robert Cahill, Richard Champion, Michael Charlton, George Costello, Leonard Demaray, Joseph DiStefano, Walter J. Dunlap, John B. Dwyer, Gregory Flynn, Philip Gioia, Bruce Gleason, A.J. Golden, Robert Houck, L. Erick Kanter, Lee Lubinsky, Anthony Monaco, Robert E. Moon, III, William Peters, Eric Read, Eugene J. Schwanebeck, Brian Sullivan, David Sutcliffe, Wayne P. Wilson.

Photography Credits

p. 7, courtesy of Department of Manuscripts and Archives, Cornell University Libraries. p. 9, Nihon Denpa News, Ltd. p. 13, Wide World. p. 14, Timothy and Mai May. p. 16, top, bottom, Wide World. p. 18, top, bottom, Wide World. p. 21, Philip Jones Griffiths–Magnum. p. 25, Don McCullin–Magnum. p. 27, Catherine Leroy. p. 28, UPI. p. 29, Don McCullin–Magnum. p. 30, John Olson–LIFE Magazine, © 1968, Time Inc. p. 31, Don McCullin–Magnum. p. 32, UPI. p. 36, Larry Burrows–LIFE Magazine, © 1969, Time Inc. pp. 38-9, Don McCullin–Magnum. p. 41, UPI. p. 43, Christian Simonpietri–Sygma. p. 45, Camera Press Ltd. p. 48, Wide World. pp. 50-1, Co Rentmeester–LIFE Magazine, © 1968, Time Inc. pp. 52-4, Larry Burrows–LIFE Magazine, © 1968, Time Inc. p. 57, Dick Swanson–LIFE Magazine, © 1968, Time Inc. pp. 58-62, Robert Ellison–Black Star. p. 63, Dick Swanson–LIFE Magazine, © 1968, Time Inc. p. 65, Wide World. p. 67, Dick Swanson–LIFE Magazine, © 1968, Time Inc. p. 71, U.S. Marine Corps. p. 72, © 1968 by the New York Times Company. Reprinted by permission. p. 73, Jim Hansen. p. 74, Frank Wolfe, courtesy LBJ Library. p. 75, David Lomax–Camera Press Ltd. p. 77, Charles Harbutt–Archive Pictures Inc. p. 78, Ron Haeberle–LIFE Magazine, © 1968, Time Inc. p. 80-1, Okamoto, courtesy of LBJ Library. p. 83, UPI. p. 85, Bernard Boston. p. 86, Henry Wilhelm–Black Star. p. 87, Fred W. McDarrah. p. 89, Jeffrey Blankfort–Jeroboam. p. 90, UPI. p. 91, top, UPI; bottom, Steve David–Sullivan Associates. p. 94, Robert LeBeck–Black Star. p. 95, Jeffrey Blankfort–Jeroboam. p. 96, © William James Warren 1968. p. 97, Burk Uzzle–Magnum. p. 98, top, bottom, Co Rentmeester–LIFE Magazine, © 1965, Time Inc. p. 99, top, Budd Lee–LIFE Magazine, © 1967, Time Inc.; bottom, Declan Haun–LIFE Magazine, © 1967, Time Inc. p. 101, Ken Regan–Camera 5. p. 103, Burt Glinn–Magnum; insert, Lynn Pelham–LIFE Magazine, © 1968, Time Inc. p. 104, Lee Balterman–LIFE Magazine, © 1968, Time Inc. p. 106, Gerry Upham–LIFE Magazine, © 1968, Time Inc. p. 107, Bill Eppridge–LIFE Magazine, © 1968, Time Inc. p. 108, right, Larry Keenan, Jr.; left, Fred W. McDarrah. p. 109, Perry C. Riddle. p. 110, Lisa Law. p. 111, top, David Gahr; bottom, Keystone Press Agency, Inc. p. 112-3, John Olson, LIFE Magazine, © 1969, Time Inc. pp. 115-7, Philip Jones Griffiths–Magnum. p. 118, Larry Burrows–LIFE Magazine, © 1968, Time Inc. p. 119, Wide World. p. 121, UPI. pp. 123-5, Philip Jones Griffiths–Magnum. p. 126, Tim Page. p. 127, Y.R. Okamoto, courtesy LBJ Library. p. 129, Carl Mydans–LIFE Magazine, © 1968, Time Inc. p. 130, Philip Jones Griffiths–Magnum. p. 132, Marc Riboud–Magnum. p. 133, Carl Mydans–LIFE Magazine, © 1968, Time Inc. p. 134, Marc Riboud–Magnum. p. 135, top, Marc Riboud–Magnum; bottom, Carl Mydans–LIFE Magazine, © 1968, Time Inc. p. 137, Philip Jones Griffiths–Magnum. p. 139, Erich Lessing–Magnum. p. 141, © 1968 Daily Mails, London–Rothco. pp. 142-3, Wide World. p. 144, Marc Riboud. p. 148, Dick Swanson–LIFE Magazine, © 1968, Time Inc. p. 149, UPI. p. 150, Co Rentmeester–LIFE Magazine, © 1968, Time Inc. p. 151, Wide World. p. 153, UPI. p. 154, Philip Jones Griffiths–Magnum. p. 156, Larry Burrows Collection. p. 157, top, bottom, U.S. Army. p. 158, top, bottom, Philip Jones Griffiths–Magnum. p. 159, Larry Burrows–LIFE Magazine, © 1968, Time Inc. p. 160, top, Tim Page; bottom, Philip Jones Griffiths–Magnum. p. 161, Philip Jones Griffiths–Magnum. p. 163, Mark Godfrey–Archive Pictures Inc. pp. 165-7, Fred W. McDarrah. p. 169, Wide World. p. 170, top, Jeffrey Blankfort–Jeroboam; bottom, Dennis Brack–Black Star. p. 172, Fred W. McDarrah. p. 173, top, bottom, UPI. p. 174, Mark Godfrey–Archive Pictures Inc. p. 175, Vernon Merritt–LIFE Magazine, © 1968, Time Inc. p. 178, courtesy LBJ Library. p. 179, Agence France-Presse, p. 181, courtesy LBJ Library. p. 185, Harold Phillips.

Map Credits

All maps prepared by Diane McCaffery. Sources are as follows:

p. 11–Department of the Army. p. 15–Department of the Army. p. 34–Department of the Army. p. 46, bottom–Map by Joseph P. Davison from *The End of the Line*, published by W.W. Norton, 1982. p. 48–Department of the Army. p. 122–United States Military Assistance Command, Vietnam and United States Department of Defense. p. 124–Department of the Army. p. 143–Department of the Army. p. 146–United States Department of Defense. p. 147–United States Department of Defense. p. 178–© 1969 by The New York Times Company. Reprinted by permission. Adapted and redrawn from *Newsweek*, November 11, 1968. All rights reserved. p. 182–Reprinted from *Vietnam Order of Battle*. Copyright 1981, U.S. News & World Report Books.

Acknowledgments

Boston Publishing wishes to acknowledge the kind assistance of the following people: Tom Brown, National Archives; Major Edgar C. Doleman, Jr., U.S. Army (retired); Charles W. Dunn, professor and chairman, Department of Celtic Languages and Literature, Harvard University; Barbara Flum; Ruth Gay, Yale University Archives; Ted Gittinger, LBJ Foundation; David Humphrey, LBJ Library, Austin, Texas; Charles Joiner, professor, Department of Political Science, Temple University, who read parts of the manuscript; Don Oberdorfer; Judith Schiff, Yale University Archives; Lt. Col. Charles R. Shrader, U.S. Army Military History Institute; Jack Shulimson, Marine Corps Historical Center; Monica Suder; and Melissa Totten.

The index was prepared by Patricia Perrier.

Index

Huong, Secretary General Nguyen Van, 122, 124

I

Inflation, in U.S., 77; in Vietnam, 116, 122
Institute for Defense Analysis (IDA), 105
Intelligence, U.S., and Tet offensive, 10–2; and battle of Hue, 26; failure of, 127; and bomber strikes, 151
"International Days of Protest," 88
Intruders, A–6A, 48

J

Johnson, Lyndon B., 35, 80, *81, 83,* 165, 176, *180;* pre-Tet remarks of, 10–1; assessment of Tet offensive, 19, 20, 71; at Honolulu conference, 1966, 24; and Khe Sanh, 44; and "high level policy review," 66; and credibility gap, 67; in public opinion surveys, 68, 69; "emergency augmentation" authorized by, 73, 74; and New Hampshire primary, 77; withdrawal from presidential politics of, 82–3, 84; and antiwar movement, 90; at Honolulu conference, 1968, *127,* 128; bombing halt proposed by, 136, 177, *179,* 180, 182; hard-line stance of, 148
Joint Chiefs of Staff, 10, 44, 45, 70, 145, 150; and national mobilization, 71, 72; and proposed bombing halt, 177
Jorden, William, 138
Junction City, Operation, 22

K

Katzenbach, Attorney General Nicholas, 100
Kennedy, Senator Edward, 165
Kennedy, President John, 71, 168
Kennedy, Senator Robert, 68, 77, 92, 93, 105; candidacy of, 106–7, *107;* death of, 107, 165
Kerner Commission, 94, 95
Kham Duc, 145
Khe Sanh, 11, 19, 20, 38, 40, 42, 51, 70, 71, 73, 149; beginning of siege, 43–4; comparisons to Dien Bien Phu, 45–6, 50, 55, 59; and enemy strategy, 54–5; and enemy casualties at, 55; evaluations of role played in history by, 40, 59; fortification of, 42–3; intelligence reports, 42–3; and Lang Vei, 47; and Operation Niagara, 42, 44, 48, 49, 51; and Operation Pegasus, 51–4; siege mentality at, 46–7, 57–63; supply airlifts into, 49; U.S. decision to hold, 44–6; withdrawal of enemy, 50
Khoa, Lieutenant Colonel Phan Van, 119
King, Martin Luther, Jr., 94, *96;* assassination of, 102
Kirk, Grayson, 105
Komer, Robert, 23, 66, 120
Kontum, 12
Ky, Vice President Nguyen Cao, 120, 122, 178–9, 181; President Thieu's purge of, 124–6; arrival at Paris negotiations, *183,* 184

L

Lai Khe, 14
Lam, Lieutenant General Hoang Xuan, 30
Lam, Pham Dang, 178, 181
Lang Vei Special Forces camp, 42; attack on, 47–50
Laos, 24, 42, 46, 70, 139, 142, 148
Lau, Colonel Ha Van, 177
LeMay, General Curtis, 177
"Liberation committees," of Communists, 183
"Liberation Radio," 10, 37
Loan, Brigadier General Nguyen Ngoc, 64, *65,* 66, 122, 124, 156
Loc, Premier Nguyen Van, 122, 124
Loc, Lieutenant General Vinh, 119
Loch Ninh, 9
Lodge, Henry Cabot, 81
Long Binh, 8, 12, 14
Longgrear, Lieutenant Paul R., 48, *49*
Low, Major James F., *148*
Lowenstein, Allard, 93, 177

Lownds, Colonel, 43, 44
Lung, Colonel Hoang Ngoc, 12

M

McCarthy, Senator Eugene, 68, *77,* 93, 102, 164, 175; at Democratic convention, 165, 168; primary campaign in New Hampshire, 77, 102
McChristian, Major General Joseph, 22
McCormack, Speaker of the House John, 89, 90
McGovern, Senator George, 93, 165, 181
McNamara, Secretary of Defense Robert, 70, 75, *91*
Manh, Major General Nguyen Van, 14, 119
Mansfield, Senator Mike, 68
Marcuse, Herbert, 111
Marshall, Brigadier General S. L. A., 55
May offensive, Communist, 145–7, 160
Medina, Captain Ernest L., 78, 79
Military Assistance Command, Vietnam (MACV), 11; Tan Son Nhut headquarters, 12, 15, 42; VC estimates of, 22–3; change of command, 149–50
Miller, David, 88
Mills, C. Wright, 111
Minh, Ho Chi, 10, 27, 82, 138, 139
Minh, Ho Thong, 122, 125
Monetary crisis, international, 77, 80
Morton, Senator Thruston, 68
Mueller, John, 89
Muskie, Senator Edmund, 168
Mydans, Carl, 132
My Lai, 78–9
My Tho, 12

N

National Assembly, of GVN, 123, 180; general mobilization bill passed by, 119; and President Thieu, 124; and NLF role in negotiations, 128
National Committee for Responsible Patriotism, 88
National Liberation Front (NLF), 124, 178, 184; in Paris negotiations, 138, 180, 181; losses of, 145 (see also Vietcong)
National Mobilization Committee To End the War in Vietnam, 89, 90, 164
National Recovery Committee (SVN), 120
National Salvation Front (SVN), 122
Negotiations, Paris, representatives at, 138; regional reaction to, 139; impasse in, 141; "fight-talk" stage, 144–5; hard-line arguments in, 147–8; and "third wave," 152; and secret talks, 177; Saigon boycott of, 180, 181, 182, 184; procedural details, 181
Newfield, Jack, 107
New Hampshire Presidential primary, 77, 102
Ngai, Nguyen Duc, 135
Nha Trang, 12, 135
Nhu, Ngo Dinh, 126
Niagara, Operation, 42, 44, 48, 50
Nitze, Deputy Secretary of Defense Paul, 75
Nixon, Richard, 106; on "atrocities" of Hue, 35; nomination of, *175,* 176; and bombing halt, 180; election of, 182
North Vietnam (Democratic Republic of Vietnam), 9, 10, 11, 80, 100, 127, 128, 147, 150, 168, 177, 182; acceptance of LBJ's offer of talks, 137–8; "fight-talk" strategy, 144–5; LBJ orders partial bombing halt over, 82; and October 31st bombing halt, 177–80; at Paris Peace Talks, 139–41, 148, 177–81; rebuilding after March 31st bombing halt, 145
North Vietnamese People's Army (NVA), 8; 95B Regiment, 13; 7th Division, 14; 4th Regiment, 26; 6th Regiment, 26; 325C Division, 38, 42, 43, 44; 304th Division, 38, 43, 44; 324th Division, 38, 43; 320th Division, 43; withdrawal from Khe Sanh, 50–1; force strength of, *122, 147;* recruitment for, 123; Soviet weapons supplied to, 123–4; and raid on A Shau, 144; 2d Division,

145; May offensive, 145–6
Nuclear weapons, and Khe Sanh, 45; discussed in 1968 presidential campaign, 177

O

Oberdorfer, Don, 36, 37
O'Donnell, Kenneth, 168
Oglesby, Carl, 92–3
I Corps, 11, 12, 19, 20, 42, 54, 55, 71, 74, 147, 150, 151
"Order of battle" (OB), 22

P

Pacification program, 150, 184; and NVA's border strategy, 10; after Tet offensive, 55–6, 116
Peace movement (see Antiwar movement, Demonstrations)
Pegasus, Operation, 50–4
Pentagon, march on, 89–91, 94
People's Alliance for Social Revolution, 120
People's Liberation Armed Forces (see Vietcong)
Phan Thiet, 12, 132
Phoenix Program, 183
Phu Bai, 11, 12, 26
Phuoc, Colonel Dao Ba, 156
Phu Tho racetrack, 20, 146
Pike, Douglas, 35–6
Pleiku, 6, 8, 12, 20, 100; battle of, 13
Polls (see Public opinion)
"Population control strategy," 76
Porter, D. Gareth, 36
Port Huron Statement, 97
Prisoners of war, release of, 148
Prosterman, Dr. Roy L., 123
Provisional Corps, Vietnam, 142
Public opinion, American, after Tet offensive, 68; changing, 69; and Saigon government, 70; and reassessment of war policy, 80–1; and dissent, 86–9; Harris polls of, 88, 180, 182
Pueblo, North Korea's seizure of, 19

Q

Quang, Thich Tri, 122, 125
Quang Ngai Province, 78, 79, 151
Quang Tri Province, 8, 19, 26, 42, 54, 145
Quan Loi, 150
Qui Nhon, 11, 12
Quy, Colonel Dan Van, 156
Quyet Thang, Operation, 141

R

Ray, James Earl, 102
Reagan, Ronald, 176
Refugees, after Tet offensive, 20, 116; in Hue, 29, *130–1, 132;* relief programs for, 120; and American aid, *122, 123;* in Nha Trang, *135;* after second battle of Saigon, 156, *160*
Republic of Vietnam (South Vietnam), 20, 119, *119,* 124–6; and Tet cease-fire, 12; and American public opinion, 70; after Tet offensive, 116, 134, 135; economy, 116, 122; national military mobilization of after Tet, 119; refugee estimates of, 132; anticorruption campaign of, 119–23; and bombing halt, 178–9; and Paris negotiations, 138, 181, 184
Republic of Vietnam Armed Forces (RVNAF), ARVN 23d Infantry Division, 11; and Tet cease-fire, 12; military academy of, 13; ARVN 5th Division, 14; ARVN in Saigon defense, 14; paratroopers, 15; ARVN 8th Airborne Battalion, 19; ARVN Black Panther Company, 26; ARVN 1st Division, 27, 152; in battle of Hue, *33,* 37, 38; ARVN 10th Political Warfare Battalion, 36; "black teams" of, 36; ARVN 3d Regiment, 37, 144; proposed modernization of, 70; force strength of, *122;* M16 rifles for, 152; Regional Forces and Popular Forces, 152; and second battle of Saigon, 156; ARVN 7th Battalion, Air-

U.S. Military Units
(see note below)

Note: Military units are listed according to the general organizational structure of the U.S. Armed Forces. The following chart summarizes that structure for the U.S. Army. The principal difference between the army and the Marine Corps structures in Vietnam lay at the regimental level. The army eliminated the regimental command structure after World War II (although battalions retained a regimental designation for purposes of historical continuity, e.g., 1st Battalion, 7th Cavalry [Regiment]). Marine Corps battalions were organized into regiments instead of brigades except under a few unusual circumstances. The marines, however, do not use the word "regiment" to designate their units; e.g., 1st Marines refers to the 1st Marine Regiment.

U.S. Army structure
(to battalion level)

Unit	Size	Commanding officer
Division	12,000–18,000 troops or 3 brigades	Major General
Brigade	3,000 troops or 2–4 battalions	Colonel
Battalion*	600–1,000 troops or 3–5 companies	Lieutenant Colonel

* Squadron equivalent to battalion.

Names, Acronyms, Terms

Accelerated Pacification Campaign—plan launched November 1, 1968, by GVN and U.S. with goal of extending at least token government control into 1,200 previously contested or VC-dominated hamlets, within three months.

ARVN—Army of the Republic of Vietnam. The army of South Vietnam.

Capital Military Zone—Saigon and the immediate surrounding area.

chinh huan—North Vietnamese indoctrination sessions for all Communist party members.

CIA—Central Intelligence Agency (U.S.).

CIDG—Civilian Irregular Defense Group. Project devised by the CIA that combined self-defense with economic and social programs designed to raise the standard of living and win the loyalty of the Vietnamese mountain people. Chiefly work of U.S. Special Forces.

CINCPAC—Commander in Chief, Pacific Command. Commander of American forces in the Pacific region, which includes Southeast Asia.

COMUSMACV—Commander, U.S. Military Assistance Command, Vietnam. Position held by General William C. Westmoreland, June 1964–July 1968, and General Creighton W. Abrams, July 1968–June 1972.

CONUS—U.S. military abbreviation for the continental United States.

CORDS—Civilian Operations and Revolutionary Development Support. Succeeded Office of Civilian Operations (OCO) in 1967 as pacification high command. Under MACV jurisdiction, CORDS organized all U.S. civilian agencies in Vietnam within the military chain of command.

COSVN—Central Office for South Vietnam. Communist party headquarters in South Vietnam, overseen by Hanoi. Changed locations throughout war; according to MACV stayed within III Corps northwest of Saigon until 1968, when it moved to Cambodia.

DMZ—demilitarized zone. Established according to the Geneva accords of 1954, provisionally dividing North Vietnam from South Vietnam along the seventeenth parallel. The accords mandated that no military operations were to take place within the zone.

DRV—Democratic Republic of Vietnam. The government of Ho Chi Minh, established on September 2, 1945. Provisionally confined to North Vietnam by the Geneva accords of 1954.

IV Corps—fourth allied military tactical zone encompassing Mekong Delta region.

gom dan—"gathering" or "herding in." Term used by Vietnamese Communists to describe resettlement of rural villagers in cities and GVN-sponsored refugee camps.

GVN—U.S. abbreviation for the government of South Vietnam. Also referred to as the Republic of Vietnam. Provisionally established by the Geneva accords of 1954.

JCS—Joint Chiefs of Staff. Consists of chairman, U.S. Army chief of staff, chief of naval operations, U.S. Air Force chief of staff, and marine commandant (member ex officio). Advises the president, the National Security Council, and the secretary of defense. Created in 1949 within the Department of Defense.

JGS—Joint General Staff. South Vietnamese counterpart of the JCS.

KIA—killed in action.

LAW—M72 light antitank weapon. Successor to the bazooka, a shoulder-fired 66MM rocket with a disposable fiber glass launcher.

LZ—landing zone.

MACV—Military Assistance Command, Vietnam. U.S. command over all U.S. military activities in Vietnam, originated in 1962.

MAF—Marine Amphibious Force. Commanded U.S. Marine units committed in I Corps Tactical Zone. Acted as corps-level headquarters over U.S. Marine and Army units in I Corps area.

MIA—missing in action.

NLF—National Liberation Front, officially the National Front for the Liberation of the South. Formed on December 20, 1960, it aimed to overthrow South Vietnam's government and reunite the North and the South. The NLF included Communists and non-Communists.

NVA—North Vietnamese Army. Also called the People's Army of Vietnam (PAVN) and Vietnam People's Army (VPA).

I Corps—"Eye" Corps. First allied tactical zone encompassing five northernmost provinces of South Vietnam.

Ontos vehicle—a lightly armored tracked vehicle equipped with six mounted 106MM recoilless rifles. Originally designed for use against tanks, but primarily used in Vietnam to support infantry.

order of battle (OB)—the arrangement and disposition of the different parts of an army for battle.

pacification—unofficial term given to various programs of the South Vietnamese and U.S. governments to destroy enemy influence in the villages and gain support of civilians for the GVN.

PF—popular forces. South Vietnamese village defense units.

Phoenix—(*Phung Hoang*) an intelligence gathering program conducted by South Vietnamese Provincial Reconnaissance Units, under the direction of CORDS, designed to neutralize the Vietcong infrastructure through identification and arrest of key party cadres.

RF—regional forces. South Vietnamese provincial defense units.

RVNAF—Republic of Vietnam Armed Forces.

SANE—Committee for a Sane Nuclear Policy. Moderate American disarmament group active in the 1960s.

sapper—originally, in European wars, a soldier who built and repaired fortifications. VC sapper was a commando raider adept at penetrating allied defenses.

SDS—Students for a Democratic Society. Founded in 1962, SDS became the largest radical student organization in the country, focusing its energies on community organization of the poor and opposition to the Vietnam War.

SNCC—Student Non-Violent Coordinating Committee. Civil rights organization that brought hundreds of northern college students to the South to help register black voters during the early 1960s.

Special Forces—U.S. soldiers, popularly known as Green Berets, trained in techniques of guerrilla warfare. In Vietnam, carried out counterinsurgency operations, many of them covert. Also trained South Vietnamese and montagnards in counterinsurgency and antiguerrilla warfare.

TAOR—tactical area of responsibility.

Tet—Lunar New Year, the most important Vietnamese holiday.

III Corps—third allied military tactical zone encompassing area from northern Mekong Delta to southern central highlands.

Tri-Thien Front—North Vietnamese military region encompassing the two northernmost provinces of South Vietnam (Quang Tri and Thua Thien). Unlike other Communist military districts in South Vietnam, controlled directly by North Vietnam rather than indirectly through COSVN.

TOC—tactical operations center.

II Corps—second allied military tactical zone encompassing central highlands and adjoining coastal lowlands.

VCI—Vietcong infrastructure. NLF local apparatus, responsible for military, political, and logistics tasks in support of main force operations.

Vietcong—originally a derogatory reference to the NLF, a contraction of Vietnam Cong San (Vietnamese Communist). In use since 1956.

WIA—wounded in action.